CLEFT HEART

CHASING NORMAL

A MEMOIR

KARL SCHONBORN

Wayman Publishing

P.O. Box 160693
Clearfield, UT
84016

CLEFT HEART: CHASING NORMAL

Copyright © 2014 Karl Schonborn

Edited by Joshua Carstens, Janie Goltz, and Elisabeth Hirsch

Cover by Candiss West

Visit: **www.facebook.com/CleftHeartChasingNormal**

ISBN 13: 978-0-9897850-3-7
ISBN-10: 0989785033

Printed in the United States of America.

CLEFT HEART

For my sibs, my kids, and my wife.

Praise for *Cleft Heart*

"Gives hope to all who contend with deformities, disabilities or depression. Additionally, *Cleft Heart* reads like a mystery book and has a love story to boot."
Ronald Iverson, MD
(Adjunct Professor of Plastic Surgery, Stanford University; former President American Society of Plastic Surgeons)

"This book is about finding one's courage and strength of will under tremendous adversity, yet there is much passion, compassion and humor. It's not only a poignant piece of writing; it's a fun, witty journey."
Sandra Woffington, MFA
(Educator & Author of the novel Unveiling*)*

"The author details how he has overcome the cards dealt him. His narrative is inspiring and most helpful, particularly as he describes his changes throughout the decades."
Luis Vasconez, MD
(Chief of Plastic Surgery, University of Alabama Medical School)

"Schonborn's courage and candor are impressive as he tells of trying to become 'normal' despite endless visits to the doctors and speech therapists who give him a fighting chance at proving naysayers wrong."
Rhoda Agin, PhD
(Internationally-known Speech Therapist & Author)

"In truth, I had a hard time putting *Cleft Heart* down. Schonborn really is an evocative and winsome storyteller."
Frank Baldwin, BD (Ordained UCC/Congregational Minster)

"*Cleft Heart* is a remarkably honest memoir of resilience by a man who can now reflect on his hard-won journey toward normalcy. "
Louise Wianecki, MA, NCSP (Nationally Certified School Psychologist)

CONTENTS

Cabin Fever 7

Normal Interrupted 12

Saving Face 18

Schoolyard Bullies 32

Palo Alto, Silicon Valley 48

Outsider 54

Chasing Normal 68

A Hole in my Heart 79

Paly High 105

Schonborn Reborn 118

Preppies, Publics & Archies 133

April is the Cruelest Month 149

On the Road 162

A Junior at Yale 170

A Washington Intern 178

The Debate Cup 192

Dead Men Talk 205

Violence Changes Everything 218

European Revelations 232

Morocco, a Wall, a Letter 246

Competing with Adonis 262

The Long Way Home 269

Keeping Up Appearances 293

Before the Storm 312

Lies That Blind 332

The Tie That Binds 347

Acknowledgments 363

Discussion Questions & Topics 365

About the Author 370

CABIN FEVER

ALL AROUND THE SIMPLE cabin, giant Redwoods stood watch, unwavering in the cool night breeze that carried the sound of crickets through open windows. I undressed so as not to disturb the other sixth graders sleeping nearby in bunks. I had delayed going to bed, worried that Ron and Danny might harass me. I slid my shoes under the lower bunk bed and hung my shirt and pants on a wall hook. Stripping to my briefs, I remembered the wedgie Ron and Danny had given me as I stepped off the bus ahead of them upon arriving at camp that morning.

I crawled into my sleeping bag and extended my legs. Immediately, I heard a muffled growl followed by an inhuman shriek.

Pain shot through my big toe. "Holy crap," I screamed as I unzipped my bag, trying to get out.

Heads rose up from beds around the perimeter of the cabin. Sleepy faces changed to astonished ones. Except for Ron and Danny's.

"What's wrong, Hare Lip?" Danny yelled.

Adrenalized, I leapt across the cabin floor and pulled him out of his sleeping bag.

"*h*You'll pay *h*for *h*this," I shouted, defaulting to the nasal speech of my childhood.

As I wrestled Danny to the floor, a rabbit emerged from my sleeping bag. It jumped to the ground and raced out the door. Mouths around the cabin's perimeter opened wide, some howling with laughter.

Humiliated, I fought harder and got on top of Danny. I considered hitting him, but Ron shot me a menacing look as he scrambled out of bed. And so I bellowed in my less-than-convincing voice, "*h*You guys *h*will be sorry."

Hulking Ron pulled me off Danny and threw me to the floor, saying, "Shut the hell up, Rabbit-face. You'll wake up the counselors next door."

Danny regained his footing and started kicking me as he said, "You piece of shit, you'd better not tell!" He looked around and growled. "That goes for everyone else here."

This dimmed the ardor of the faces in the crowd, many of whom I didn't recognize. Kids had come from other grade schools in Palo Alto to study the plants and wildlife of California…like the brown brush rabbit usually locked in its cage in the main lodge.

Ron joined Danny in slamming me with his foot, expending a grunt with every kick. I tried to protect my face from harm and groaned with each kick to my ribs.

Unblinking, wide eyes still watched from all sides.

The dust and grit on the floor triggered a cough and, then, amid all the labored breathing and dull thudding sounds, a thought—*If only I could catch a foot and upend one of them.* Just when I couldn't stand the pain anymore, I managed to grab Danny's swinging ankle. He fell backward into Ron. They both went down.

I raced for the door and once outside hid in some bushes not far away. As I waited, my heart pounding like never before, I worried the sound of my panting would betray me. Ron and Danny walked within two feet of me, but the dark of night saved me. When they stopped looking for me and returned to the cabin, things quieted down enough that I could hear crickets again.

I hung my head and walked to my friend Mike Hart's cabin, which had an empty bed. I tiptoed in, woke Mike, and borrowed a blanket. Lying on the bed below Mike's, I shook violently from the cold and from the pain in my ribs and toe.

But nothing compared to the pain in my heart. It reminded me of my *first* public humiliation years ago when my mom inadvertently left me with a group of strangers for a minute. Judgmental eyes and headshakes shamed me after I made a simple statement in front of the group. Wanting to redeem myself at once, I screwed up my face and courage and concentrated on enunciating during a second attempt.

As the words started in my throat, I contracted my lips, tensed my cheeks, and gritted my teeth to make the words more intelligible. But to no avail. By the time the words emerged, they still sounded nasal and whiny as if coming from an underwater source. Upon hearing my second try, the people staring at me needed no further proof, given my scarred, asymmetrical face. A couple called me names I didn't understand. Most turned their backs and left. I stared at the ground until Mom reclaimed me. I felt awful until I told Mom. We both cried then.

Something stirred me from my reverie. I wondered, looking at the underside of Mike's bunk, *Why can't people accept me? Inside I'm just like everyone else. I want to belong.*

Before drifting off to sleep, I reviewed the hurts bullies had caused me over the years and concluded that my tears accomplished nothing. I had a choice: give in to being an outsider by not rocking the boat or fight to be accepted and live a normal life.

The next morning I stuck close to Big Mike. Exchanged glances with a few of my former cabin mates convinced me they wouldn't violate Danny's demanded code of silence. Relieved, I headed for the camp nurse to show her what the rabbit had done.

"Strange! It nips people's hands most of the time," she said as she cleaned, disinfected, and bandaged my toe.

I fidgeted, lowered my head, and said, "I sat on the ground

with it. Guess I played too rough 'cuz it bit me and ran away. She looked skeptical and said, "He's returned. Back in his cage now."

"That's good."

"I'd worry about rabies from a bite from a squirrel, but not from one from our tame rabbit."

Later that morning I told my counselor that I needed to switch to Mike's cabin.

"I have to walk to the bathroom a lot every night. It's pretty far. Big Mike's got the only flashlight I can borrow for my trips." With my counselor's okay, I returned to my first cabin for my stuff. As I walked in, I encountered Ron and Danny talking to a kid from another school. I turned to leave, but Danny blocked the door.

"Meet T. J.," Ron said. "He goes to Mayfield School."

"H-Hi," I said, my brow furrowing. *He's even taller than they are and seems old for a sixth grader.*

"Karl looks like a rabbit. Talks like a duck," Ron explained. "But he's really a dick."

The guys grinned, and T. J. grinned and leaned toward me. I noticed he'd already started shaving. *He must've been held back a few grades.*

I glanced over my shoulder, but Danny puffed up his chest, stared daggers at me, and said, "Speaking of dicks, we were just talking about how manly T. J. is."

"Yeah," Ron said. "Why don't you unzip your pants, Karl, and put your dick on the windowsill?"

"Great idea," Danny said. "T. J. will pull his out again, to compare."

T. J. reached for his fly.

My entire body flushed. I bolted, trying to dash between Danny and the doorway.

CRASH! A skull-numbing, bone-jarring whack. I had misjudged the edge of the doorframe, hitting it with my head. Blood streamed down the right side of my face. I staggered around, but remained upright. The three guys gasped, and then smiled.

Unwilling to scream in front of them, I clenched my teeth and grimaced. Drops of blood fell to the cabin floor. I touched my eye where it hurt, and sticky warm blood and sweat covered my hand.

I pulled up my shirt tail, dabbed at the blood, and stumbled down the cabin steps. Unable to see out of my injured eye, I struggled to find the nurse's office.

"Press your temple with these," the nurse directed, putting some gauze pads in my hand. "I'll check your eye when the bleeding stops."

Soon, she examined my cut to determine the extent of the injury. "You ripped your eyebrow open," she said.

Although I had begun to worry also about a growing headache, I asked, "Did I wreck my eye?"

"No. You're lucky in that sense…but you've been unlucky of late. You're my best customer already."

"I don't mean to be. I've seen too many nurses in my life."

"You'll have to stay away from the water this week."

"No swimming? No canoeing?"

"Right. Water might infect your cut, slow the healing."

"Aw Jeez," I said, as I touched the gooey adhesive on a piece of tape she'd snipped for me to play with. She started cutting the tape into a bowtie shape.

"I'm putting a 'butterfly bandage' across your wound. It'll pull the two sides of the cut together."

After leaving the nurse, I sat on a redwood stump and contemplated a week of watching others play in the stream and swim and paddle in the lake. It didn't seem fair and saddened me a lot. So, I revisited some of the stories that always flooded into my head after I had been bullied—stories Mom had told me about my birth and the start of my troubles. *If only a butterfly bandage had been all that doctors had needed to pull my face together.*

NORMAL INTERRUPTED

MOM HAD TOLD ME that Saturday midnight came and went, as did her contractions. I would now be Sunday's child, bonnie and blithe, or maybe Monday's child, fair of face. The hospital began to go dark room by room, floor by floor. All of a sudden Mom's contractions returned, and after my muffled cry at 3:04 a.m., I took my first breath in Dr. Rodman's arms. Other doctors and nurses came running to the delivery room, clustering around Mom and me.

"What's wrong?" Mom asked.

"There's a problem," Dr. Rodman said as he cut my umbilical cord and stepped away from Mom. "Get Mr. Schonborn," he barked to the head nurse.

"What's the problem?" Mom demanded, despite being exhausted.

"Don't be upset, Mrs. Schonborn," the doctor said. "The good news: you've got a baby boy. He's jaundiced, though, with bluish extremities. And anemic and—"

"Show me my baby. Show me now!" Mom cried out, trying to rise from the delivery table.

Steeling himself, Dr. Rodman gave Mom a quick glimpse of my face.

"Oh, my God!" Mom wailed. "My God!"

Instead of a mouth, I had a large triangular opening from my lower lip to my nose. I had no functioning upper lip. The gaping cleft in my gum and upper-lip area pulled my left nostril to the side, flattening my nose. More importantly, the roof of my mouth appeared to be missing. Compared to Mom, regarded by many as a Scandinavian beauty with generous blue eyes and wavy hair, I constituted a beast.

When Dad rushed in amid the tumult, he stared at me, dumbstruck.

"He has a cleft lip and palate," Dr. Rodman said, "meaning an unjoined lip and gum, and a hole in the roof of his mouth. He can't be breastfed."

"Is he going to live?" Dad asked, grabbing Mom's hand. "He's a strange color."

"His liver isn't processing red blood cells, but we should be able to fix that," the doctor said. "As for his clefts, I'm going to call a specialist in Chicago now."

None of the medical staff knew what to say after Dr. Rodman left. One whispered that they might lose me if they couldn't feed me. Another muttered that my coloring alone meant I'd flunk any neonatal healthiness test. In an eerie way, the blue purple of my fingers and toes accented my overall yellow look. And for sure, I wasn't fair of face.

At length, the head nurse addressed Mom and Dad, asking, "You guys doing okay?"

"Things could be better," Dad said.

Mom sighed. "I'm okay, I think, but I'm scared."

"Yeah. Me, too," Dad said. "Scared about what's in store."

The head nurse patted both their arms, saying, "I'm sure you're scared, distressed, even shocked. But we're here to help you get through this." A different nurse moved to adjust Mom's pillows, and another brought Mom and Dad water in large glasses.

And so, with my fraught arrival on November 28, 1943, in Boise, Idaho, the charmed life, including dinner parties with dear friends filled with laughter and political debate, ended for my twenty-seven-year-old parents.

When Dr. Rodman returned, nurses and doctors stepped

back from the delivery table. They'd been talking to my parents, trying to make them feel better.

From his dead-of-night phone call, Dr. Rodman learned he should ignore my blue purple and anemic yellow color for now. He should stretch adhesive tape from one side of my split face to the other, pulling it together so I could close my mouth. Then I should be force-fed with a simple eyedropper. If that failed, I should be hooked up to an IV feeding tube.

After taping me, Dr. Rodman handed me to Mom and gave her an eyedropper filled with milk. Medical staff again encircled the delivery table. Mom's hand shook as she held the dropper over my new mouth.

"Give him a squirt," Dr. Rodman said.

Mom squeezed the dropper several times. I spit up, and milk came out of my taped-in-place nostrils. I cried. Mom wiped my face with care.

"Move the dropper farther back, but don't gag him," Dr. Rodman, said.

Mom gave me too much a second and a third time, but her fourth try worked: I kept the milk down, eliciting relieved smiles from everyone.

"It may take hours for each feeding," Dr. Rodman said.

"Hours?" Mom moaned.

"And feed him your own milk." Turning to the head nurse, Rodman directed, "Show Mrs. Schonborn how to use a breast pump to express her milk." Sensing some privacy might be in order, the doctor encouraged the extra nurses and doctors in the room to leave.

"Can his face be fixed?" Dad asked.

"Yes."

"Thank Heaven," Mom said.

"But, it'll take several operations over many years," Dr. Rodman said.

"His brain's all right?" Dad asked.

"Yes. In fact, he's quite alert."

"So, he'll be normal?" Mom asked.

"Let's hope so. Plenty of hurdles ahead," Dr. Rodman said.

"Did I do something wrong?" Mom blurted out.

"I don't think so."

"What causes clefts?" Dad asked.

"Some are caused by illnesses in mothers, but in general they just tend to happen. My Chicago consultant reminded me that the fetal face grows from the back. Like this." The doctor cupped his hands together and then closed his fingers to create two side-by-side fists. Keeping his fist pinkies touching, he rolled his fists together, moving his thumbs toward each other.

"Pretend my thumbnails are eyes. Around the sixth week, the eyes and face move together from the back. In much the same way, the palate and lips move to join under the nose. In cleft babies, they don't join for some reason."

After sleeping fitfully until dawn on the waiting room couch, Dad used this embryology information—plus his public relations skills from work—to soften the blow to his parents when he called them. As he dialed Mom's parents, he mumbled, "Hope Rosa doesn't answer." A moment later, he said, "Oh. Hi, Rosa. It's a boy, but there's a problem."

When Dad hung up, a guy in the waiting room volunteered, "Couldn't help overhearing… Man, do I feel for you."

"Thank you. It's been a long, hard night."

"It must be disappointing, confusing—"

"All that. Got a beautiful daughter at home, luckily. Not sure what happened to my son. It's nerve-racking."

"Sure hope *my* kid's normal."

Dad walked to the recovery room where nurses had taken Mom and me. He covered most of my face with the corner of my blanket and took a few pictures of us.

"I *wish* the docs could fix him before we take him home," Dad said.

"Rodman said it'll take a long time," Mom said. "Don't put your wishbone where your backbone should be, as Grandma Gustafson always says."

"I won't, honey. We'll make it through."

Returning to the waiting room and the same guy, still his only companion, Dad wanted to be available in case an emergency developed. He read a newspaper account, and said to the guy, "An ailing Roosevelt met with Churchill and Stalin today in Iran."

"What for?"

"To discuss Allied war strategy."

(As it turned out, they decided that day to attack Germany from the west to give Stalin relief from fighting Hitler in the east. This secret plan resulted in the D-Day attack at Normandy six months later.)

Dad lowered the paper to his lap. His eyes misted over as he thought of my problems, but he raised the paper and read on, knowing people the world over faced challenges in this time of war. Dad said, "The Big Three also agreed to create a worldwide organization."

"Oh?"

"They call it the United Nations."

After stifling more thoughts and emotions about the hard road ahead for me, Dad read a news headline outloud (he'd been a news junkie since his days as a journalist):

"Axis powers announce 'Total War' against us." Looking up from his magazine, the guy said, "I'd better pay more attention to the news. Total war?"

"A war where every adult—civilian and soldier alike—is a combatant!"

Dad drove home later to relieve the sitter watching my sister, Gayle. He and Gayle returned to visit Mom and me at the hospital the next day, as they did each day for over a week. As time went on, the nursing staff tried unsuccessfully to treat my jaundice and get me to gain weight. Mom fed me most of the time, but because of complications, the staff hooked me up now and then for intravenous tube feedings.

All along Dr. Rodman poked and prodded me and exposed me to various bright lights, managing to reverse my jaundice at last. He said, "His purple color should go away when the hole, or shunt, connecting his pulmonary and aortic arteries closes up."

"When might that be?" Mom asked.

"Can't be sure."

When Dr. Rodman sent us home, he told Dad, because Mom already knew, "You must protect Karl's face at all costs."

"Anything else?" Dad asked.

"You and Laura should never have him on his back, especially when he sleeps, to keep his tongue from getting stuck in the channel in the roof of his mouth."

"And if we forget?"

"He might suffocate."

Mom and Dad named me Karl, spelling it with a "K" in keeping with their respective Norwegian and German roots. Mom liked the name, too, because it was derivative of Charles, meaning "manly and strong." And because her Grandpa Gustafson's name was Charles.

SAVING FACE

AT HOME IN OUR cottage-sized stucco house with a steep roof, my toddler sister resented all the time and attention I got. After all, as a two-year-old, she believed the world revolved around her. Mom had to entertain her while taping the sides of my face together, bathing and changing me, and keeping me from suffocating—not to mention feeding me with the eyedropper, which often took ten hours during the day and another four at night. If I were fussy or Mom got distracted and fed me too much milk or let the eyedropper gag me, I'd regurgitate, forcing her to start the feeding process all over again.

I needed more burping than a breastfed baby because I couldn't regulate how much air I swallowed. Mom held me almost upright while squirting milk from the dropper to minimize the air I'd swallow, watching always for squirminess or pained expressions on my face as signs I needed burping.

All the while, Gayle, born the night before the Japanese bombed Pearl Harbor, tugged on Mom's dress to get attention.

"Read me a story."

"In a minute, honey. It's tricky now."

"He's a bird, and I don't like him."

"A bird?"

"You feed him like birds feed their babies."

Mom and Dad had showered Gayle with attention before I came along. But Gayle still needed what I needed—to be fed, held, comforted, and loved. This, combined with my special care, ran Mom ragged until Dad got home each night. And it didn't help that Mom had to keep expressing her own breast milk. It tired her out even more, but she knew the importance of breast milk in helping me gain much-needed weight.

Both of my grandmothers came to offer aid. Unfortunately, though, the time Mom spent teaching them the proper way to feed me—plus having extra people in our small two-bedroom house—caused her to feel the extra "help" not worth it.

Soon after her visit, Rosa Stenerson, Mom's mom, sent my parents a letter about cleft-repair surgeons she'd researched. She had visited a woman in her own town of Longview, Washington, whose son had finished three of the twelve operations he would need. The woman recommended Dr. Albert Cox of Seattle, her son's reconstructive surgeon. Rosa had also located a surgeon in nearby Portland and, because of his proximity to Longview, insisted that Mom choose him.

With Dad's input and support, Mom decided to consult Dr. Cox in Seattle, but first she had to get permission from the War Rationing Board. World War II had complicated things for civilians. After much deliberation, the Board allowed Mom extra gasoline for the trip because of my special needs.

Mom packed luggage, baby gear, Gayle, and me into our new Pontiac and drove the 400 miles to Seattle. Dr. Cox, a small, balding man in his mid-sixties, met us at his office as predictable Seattle rain battered his office windows. An antiseptic odor permeated the wood-paneled examining room. After washing his hands, Dr. Cox removed the tape holding my face together as I sat in Mom's lap.

While inspecting my gaping clefts, he muttered, "Complete fissure—from the back through the gums. Lip levator muscles, a mess. Split uvula."

He lifted his eyes to Mom's and asked, "Has he been gaining weight?"

"I feed him all the time, but he gains only a couple of ounces a week."

"Yes, but he's gaining security. All the holding and hugs you're giving him while feeding contribute to his wellbeing. He won't get that during his hospitalizations."

"When can you operate?" Mom asked.

"When he weighs ten pounds, is ten weeks old, and has a ten hemoglobin reading."

"Hemo—Huh?"

"Hemoglobin. His blood count needs to be ten grams per deciliter. It'll keep him from bleeding too much during surgery. A low count means he's anemic," he said, taking me from Mom and feeling my lower jaw and throat.

"It'll be ages before he weighs ten pounds!" Mom moaned.

"Don't despair!" the doctor said, as he played with me. "He'll get there. This 'Rule of Ten' means babies heal better with less scarring."

Dr. Cox told Mom what surgeries I'd need and in what order, noting in conclusion that I could lose considerable blood during my surgeries.

Mom buried her face in her hands.

"But, bleeding's okay," Dr.Cox said, "as long as it doesn't trigger shock. We'll give Karl plenty of blood if he needs it."

"Could he…die?"

"Surgery always comes with risks."

Mom grew pale, and Dr. Cox patted her shoulder. "He's a strong boy. I don't foresee any problems."

"Should he be baptized right away…in case he dies?" Mom asked.

"That's for you to decide."

After the appointment, Mom drove an hour south from Seattle to Puyallup where Dad's parents lived. Once we settled in, Mom wrote to Dad.

My Dear Jack,

I miss you despite the din of your sister's kids, who are visiting here, too. Your folks are fine, but they get tired from all the commotion.

I like Dr. Cox. Even though he is very, very precise, he has a marvelous way with babies. He got Karl to do everything he wanted during the exam. After examining Karl, he said he'd close Karl's lip when he's heavier and healthier. Then he'd close the soft palate on Karl's first birthday and the hard palate on his second.

Now for the bad news. Karl will need more surgeries later, plus speech therapy and orthodonture. And Dr. Cox doesn't come cheap. On top of his and the anesthesiologist's fees, we'll have to pay for nurses, lab work, oxygen, and blood. We can save money by choosing a cheaper hospital, because Karl will remain hospitalized for two to three weeks after each surgery.

It all adds up, but we have no choice. We'll pay the bill on the installment plan, like our mortgage.

Once Karl weighs ten pounds, we can schedule surgery for whenever there's a free hospital bed. I guess we were naïve to think we could see the doctor and have an operation within a few days.

It's after 11:00 p.m., honey, so I'd better feed Karl and get to bed.

Love you,

Laura

The next day, Mom said goodbye to Dad's parents, piled Gayle and me back in the Pontiac, and drove a hundred miles south to Longview to visit her parents, Rosa and Martin.

"You must consult the Portland surgeon," Rosa said.

"But I like Dr. Cox," Mom replied.

"A second opinion before surgery is always important."

"All right," Mom said, too tired to battle further.

After keeping us waiting, the Portland surgeon unnerved Mom by saying, "The sooner the operations, the better. If you wait too long, Karl's voice might never be normal, and his nostrils might never be symmetrical."

Mom winced. When she recovered her composure, she asked, "Why do clefts happen?"

"Did you get sick? Drink too much? Fall while painting the nursery?"

"No. None of those," Mom said, staring down at the floor.

That night, Rosa tried to dismiss Mom's reservations about the Portland surgeon, but Mom dug in her heels. After much arguing back and forth, Mom said in exasperation, "I just don't like him! Anyway, he'll cost twice as much as Dr. Cox."

As Rosa walked out of the room, she countered with a final salvo: "Remember, it's like everything else—you get what you pay for."

Soon after we had returned to Boise, Mom called Rosa and confronted her. "I'm sorry, Mother. I feel more comfortable with Dr. Cox."

"But, Portland's so much closer to Boise than Seattle, and we live very close to Portland," Rosa retorted. "You could stay with us during the surgeries."

"Jack and I have made up our minds. We're going with Dr. Cox," Mom insisted.

After she hung up, Mom did laundry and tidied the house to get her mind off the call. But instead, details of the evening's meal prep and worry about the cost of my surgeries added to her concerns about her relationship with her mother.

The pressure continued to mount. When Mom sat down to rest, Gayle tugged at her dress wanting to hear a story. This reminded Mom that she had to enlist Dad to read more books to Gayle in the evening—even if he did come home tired. Mom wondered, too, about her relationship with Dad. Everything seemed so rushed, now, with two kids.

After placating Gayle, Mom prepared and ate a quick lunch with her. Then she put her in her crib for an afternoon nap and began to feed me. Gayle slept briefly and then awoke and started to fuss while Mom, sitting near the crib, continued to feed me. Without warning, though, I spit up my entire feeding. Mom grimaced, rubbed the back of her neck, and exclaimed, "Not again? You'll never get to ten pounds!"

As she cleaned up the mess, Gayle began to cry in earnest, and Mom reached into her crib to check her diaper.

"Wet!" Mom shouted. And as she drew back her hand, she knocked over the container with her expressed milk.

"Damn it!" she screamed, raising a fist in the air. "I hate all this feeding, changing, pumping." She started to cry and couldn't stop.

The pressure continued. Mom worried about how she and Dad would pay for surgeries, car trips, and phone calls. And she worried that the planets would never line up: the "planets" of me reaching my target weight, me being free from infections, and hospital beds coming available. But these concerns paled next to her new fears once Dr. Cox set a surgery date—that I'd choke on all the tubes in my throat during surgery or not wake up from the anesthesia.

The day before my surgery, Dr. Cox checked my nose, throat, and chest for signs of a cold or other infection and swabbed my throat for *staphylococci, streptococci,* and *diphtheria bacilli.* To keep me germ free, he arranged to isolate me from other patients and ordered the nurses attending me to wear masks at all times.

Early the next morning, an anesthesiologist whisked me to a cold operating room and nestled my head into a small sandbag covered with sterile towels to keep my head still. He counted in a measured voice as he started anesthesia going through a tiny intra-tracheal tube inserted into my mouth and throat.

Dr. Cox entered the room, sat at the head of the operating table, and studied my upside down face. His instruments rested on a rolling table to his right where a nurse sat, keeping them in order. A surgical assistant sat on his left with suction devices to keep my mouth free of blood. The anesthesiologist concentrated on the dials of his console. Transfusion bottles of my rare Rh-negative blood and various gadgets for emergencies remained nearby. Machines emitted whirring sounds, punctuated by occasional beeps.

Surgeon Cox scooped up the tiniest of scalpels in his smallish hands: lucky for me because my mouth was none too big at three-and-a-half months of age. With final form and functionality in mind, Dr. Cox set about joining the two sides of my face. The union had to be exactly right so that, when the scars contracted, it would not notch the red vermilion of my lip or distort the area between my lip and nose. Dr. Cox had to be sure there was enough tissue to build a floor for my deformed nostrils and that resultant surface scars blended into the natural vertical groove in my upper-lip area. All this had to be figured out fast, as tissues begin to swell and discolor the moment they are cut.

Dr. Cox sutured each layer of tissue and muscle under my left-side lip and nostril to its corresponding right-side layer. For the topmost layer of my lip, he connected the slivers of flesh with the right amount of tension to create a cupid's bow.

At the end of the operation, Dr. Cox put a small metal "cage" over my upper-lip area to protect and immobilize it. He attached a one-inch-wide Logan's Bow strap to the cage and wrapped it around my head just above my ears. He cinched the belt buckle to exert enough pressure to keep the cage in place over the exposed sutures.

After the surgery, Mom, Dad, and Dr. Cox peered through a

window into the intensive care recovery room where I rested in a propped-up position.

Mom exclaimed, "My God, what's wrong with his arms?"

"They're in splints to keep his hands from his face," Dr. Cox said. "Otherwise, he'd tear off the strap and rip out his stitches."

"Oh, my God!"

"Wouldn't want him to wreck all that expensive surgery," said Dad.

"I want to hold him," said Mom.

"You can't because—"

"I know, I know. Germs," she replied as she pushed her face against the glass. "Why's he propped up?"

"So he won't choke on his tongue," Dr. Cox said.

"My poor baby," Mom said.

"He shouldn't cry or eat for six hours," said Dr. Cox. "Might rip out the hidden stitches."

"Shouldn't cry?" exclaimed Mom. "That's what babies do!"

"We'll keep him sedated."

Mom visited me at the hospital every day. When my splints were replaced by a straitjacket-kind of garment, Mom understood but hated it. Wearing a germ mask, Mom fed me her expressed milk with a spoon and left what remained so that nurses could feed me in her absence.

At the end of a week, Mom watched as Dr. Cox and a nurse removed the upper-lip strap. As it came off, Mom gasped and almost fainted when she saw my new face, which was covered with a crust of dried blood. "Don't worry, I'll clean him up," Dr. Cox said, and used a variety of antiseptic-smelling liquids to do so.

"My God!" Mom exclaimed. "He looks so different."

"Yes, he does," Dr. Cox replied as he restrained Mom from touching my lip.

"He looks so good, so normal," Mom said. "Thank you. Thank you so much."

"I just connected things up the way Mother Nature originally intended them to be."

"Can I hold him?" Mom asked. "I won't touch his lip."

"Go ahead. He's healing well."

"Oh, honey. Oh, honey," Mom whispered as she held me close.

"We're not outta the woods, yet," Dr. Cox said. "We've got to keep him another week to monitor for infections."

When I came home at last, Mom wrote "Happy baby" in my baby book, because I could smile—but not coo—once Dr. Cox had fixed my face. Things also got a little easier for Mom now that she didn't need to keep changing the adhesive tape that had held my face together before surgery. However, she did have to put socks on my hands to keep me from picking at my face.

While I was in the hospital, Gayle had gotten enough attention from grandparents that she agreed to share Mom with me after I returned home. Instead of whining, Gayle read picture books to us while Mom spooned soothing milk into my ravenous gullet. In due course, I wanted solid foods and started chewing on things. Much to Mom's relief, at eight months I wanted to feed myself.

One day late in the summer, a letter-gram came.

"There must be a mistake. They're drafting me!" Dad exclaimed.

Not only a married father of two, Dad had permanent eye damage from a construction blasting accident.

But it was no mistake. Dad became part of a massive induction of American men into the military that made possible the Allied invasions of northern and southern France in June and August of 1944. This second phase of America's war strategy followed the first phase: an effort to produce more war materiel than the Axis powers.

The Navy ordered Dad to San Diego where he sweated from

reveille at 4 a.m. until *Taps* and lights out at 10 p.m. Mom told Gayle that when Dad and his fellow camp inmates weren't running or doing close-order drill, they practiced using semaphore signals, closing watertight doors, wearing oxygen masks, and abandoning ship without lifeboats.

Mom tried her best to cope with two ever-more active kids and the absence of the man she loved. Even though she and her friends in similar situations got together now and then to support one another, Mom still struggled, especially with loneliness.

As Mom waited for my next pre-op exam in Dr. Cox's waiting room, she watched a woman feed her cleft child using a sponge soaked in milk.

The woman noticed Mom's interest and said, "I've tried the Breck feeder. You know, the eyedropper with a nipple on the end. Even other fancy gadgets. Only a sponge works."

"We use an eye dropper," Mom responded. "Though it should be a turkey baster given his appetite. He's grown so large, and he's not even a year old."

Early in the morning at Seattle's Children's Orthopedic Hospital, an anesthesiologist knocked me out again. Dr. Cox opened my mouth and inserted a "bear trap": a square, stainless-steel frame with screws that kept my mouth wide open so he could access my soft palate, the roof area that ends in the hang-down uvula. Years of surgery had taught him how to sort out the tangle of distorted muscles and tendons he confronted in his pint-sized patients.

Late in the operation, Dr. Cox explained a procedure to his assistant. "I'm trying now to stretch the repaired soft palate as far back as I can and still keep the once-rogue muscles aligned."

"The soft palate's important for clear speech," the assistant said.

"Correct. Many good surgeons fail right here." Cox worked

in my tiny mouth for some time before the surgery took a turn for the worse.

"Uh-oh. We're getting too much bleeding."

"Transfusion, doctor?" the nurse asked.

"Yes, and make it quick. It's not the palatine artery, but I *am* concerned."

The nurse, assistant, and anesthesiologist went into over-drive, and soon life-saving Type A Rh-negative blood dripped into my veins.

A couple of hours later, Mom put her hands together as she and Dr. Cox approached the window looking into the recovery room. Once again, the nurses had propped me up, but this time they'd put me in a clear plastic tent.

"I can't make out his face very well," Mom said.

"It's the steam in the tent. It assists his breathing," said Dr. Cox.

"Is he okay?"

"Yes, he weathered the storm pretty well."

"What's that mean?"

"He needed a blood transfusion."

Mom's eyes turned electric blue. "You're sure he's okay?"

"Yes, he's in good shape now. He's a fighter."

A day later, back at the Schonborn grandparents' house in Puyallup—the staging center behind the front lines for my surgeries—Mom fielded a call from the hospital.

"Karl received another transfusion," a nurse said.

"Jesus!"

"Spontaneous bleeding happens. He's stable now."

"Thank goodness."

"If you want to visit Kar—"

"I'll be there in an hour." After hanging up, Mom muttered, "All the scary stuff happens when Jack's at boot camp."

When my two weeks in "Ward 3, Main" ended, Mom finished her stay with Charlotte and Cliff Schonborn, who'd been run ragged by fireball Gayle. Mom drove us to Longview for a brief visit with Rosa and Martin before making the long drive back to Boise.

On Turkey Day, Mom and Dad gave thanks for my successful surgery and for Dad's brief visit home. They joined the rest of the country in giving thanks for Allied successes in France and Italy as well as in the Pacific theater, despite Japan's effective kamikaze dive-bombing attacks.

Mom had mixed feelings about my starting to crawl—pleased that nothing impaired my motor skills but worried I might encounter more germs. Our pediatrician advised her against being overly protective. While Gayle and I napped, Mom read articles—on clefts and handicapped children—that she'd collected in a folder labeled "Karl's Special Care."

In mid-December, Dad phoned from San Diego.

"I just got assigned, honey. They're sending me to Washington, D.C., working as a journalist for the Navy's magazine."

"That's wonderful, but what about us?"

"You're coming, too. How's Karl?"

"He's fine, gaining weight and all. It's just that, with two kids by myself—"

"We'll live in war housing near the Pentagon."

"But we can't join you until Karl's surgeries are done."

"I know, I know. By the way, the Navy will pay for Karl's hospitalizations from now on. But I gotta run. The Base Commander allows each of us two minutes on these phones."

After allowing Dad a bittersweet two days with us at Christmastime, the Navy shipped him off to D.C. and left Mom to face another surgery alone with me. But first she had to keep me in one piece for three more months. Once I'd learned to walk, she hovered near me to make sure I didn't crash face-first into something. The game plan allowed no bloody noses.

Because of a profusion of viruses that winter, our pediatrician changed his tune about germs and phoned Dr. Cox to devise a plan to raise my immunity and hemoglobin count for my next surgery. It succeeded. My count reached an impressive 88 percent, and I was almost the required two years old.

"This'll be the riskiest surgery so far," Dr. Cox told Mom the morning of the surgery. "I'm grafting bone across Karl's open palate, and a lot can go wrong. Besides the danger of his arteries, pituitary gland, or other structures getting nicked, Karl might develop hyperthermia, rapid heart rate, and—"

Mom turned pale. "I feel faint," she mumbled.

"Quick, give Karl to me," Dr. Cox directed as he snatched me off Mom's lap. "Lean over. Put your head down. Take some deep breaths."

Soon Mom said, "I'm okay now," and watched Dr. Cox take me out of the room.

Mom spent several anxious hours in the waiting room. When at last Dr. Cox returned, she leapt from her seat.

"H-How is he?" she asked.

"We closed Karl's cleft palate. He's all right."

"Thank Heaven."

"We didn't have to use bone from his leg. Instead we shaved the palate bone next to the cleft and spread it like a fan across the opening."

"Oh, my God!"

"He'll be uncomfortable for a while. We sewed his tongue down to keep it away from the graft and sutures."

"Sure he's gonna be okay?"

"He'll be fine. You can check him out tomorrow, but you can't hold him for a couple of days. I'll catch you at rounds in the morning. Get some sleep."

"I will. Thank you, Dr. Cox," Mom said, and ran to the pay phone to call Dad.

The day the hospital discharged me, Grandma Schonborn had

decorated her living room with toy USO jeeps and red-white-and-blue streamers for my triumphant arrival. I had splints on my arms and straps around my chin to immobilize my jaw. A crowd of friends and relatives cheered as I marched into the living room, swinging my arms like a nutcracker soldier.

Over the next few months, Mom toilet-trained me and taught me how to use my expensive mouth to drink from a cup. I still couldn't suck—my thumb, a nipple, a straw—and I spoke nothing but nasal, unintelligible words and phrases.

When Dr. Cox determined I needed no more surgeries for a while, Mom sold the house by herself and started the 3,000-mile drive cross-country to D.C. Gayle and I played and napped on top of piled-high belongings. My favorite spot was the shelf under the back window of our turtle-shaped Pontiac, which Mom had named Pauline after the *Perils of Pauline* films.

As we left a roadside diner on the sixth day, Mom caught a headline: "'Rain of Ruin'—First Atomic Bomb Dropped on Hiroshima." Remembering General Doolittle's air incursion into Japan in retaliation for Pearl Harbor, she dreaded a similar Japanese attack on the symbols of American power: the Pentagon and the White House. With each mile she drove closer to the Pentagon environs—where Dad worked and we would soon dwell—Mom got ever-more worried.

SCHOOLYARD BULLIES

WE ARRIVED IN D.C. wringing wet from the humidity, but over-joyed to hug and kiss Dad after months apart. Soon we moved with him into emergency war housing—cheaply-built units with clotheslines in common yards.

Dad worked for the Navy's *All Hands* magazine rewriting military reports from the field about such pivotal events as the Fall of Berlin, Germany's surrender, and the annihilation of the once-mighty Japanese fleet. We lived close to Dad's office in the Navy Annex, situated near the Tomb of the Unknown Soldier and within walking distance of the Pentagon.

When the U.S. dropped a nuclear bomb on Nagasaki, Mom told Dad, "I'm scared. It's even more likely the Japanese will attack the Pentagon now."

Dad wrapped her in his arms, trying to comfort her.

"I'm sure the airspace around here is secure," he said. "Anyway, I don't think they've got long-range bombers that can get here."

"But the Japanese showed how wily they can be."

"Remember you felt a double whammy back then—Pearl Harbor *and* Gayle's birth."

Six days after the Nagasaki bomb, Dad phoned Mom from his office.

"Honey, you won't believe this. Japan just surrendered!"

"Whew! I've been waiting for this forever. The kids can grow up in a peaceful world now."

She reached over to me, grabbed my hand, and squeezed it.

Two weeks later our family celebrated, as did all Americans, when Japan surrendered to the Allies in a formal ceremony aboard the *USS Missouri*.

The Navy put Dad on the cover of the magazine's "Christmas Dream" issue to promote the Navy's goal to ferry as many GIs as possible home before Christmas. They posed Dad—wavy dark hair, wire-rim glasses, and assorted campaign medals and ribbons on his uniform—holding me in front of a Christmas tree. The only problem: the man in charge replaced me at the last minute with a fair-haired two-year-old with a perfect nose and upper lip.

"I want Daddy to hold me, not him," I protested.

Mom had to take me out of the room.

On the drive home, Mom asked Dad, "How could you let them do that?"

"The editor of the magazine outranks me. From the get go, the whole shoot was staged, right down to the unearned ribbons. If it's any comfort, others are mad, too. My Jewish colleagues hated the decision to have 'Christmas' splashed all over the cover."

The Navy deactivated Dad in 1946, after the end of hostilities. He joined the United States Department of Agriculture at its head office in D.C. ghostwriting speeches for department bigwigs and promoting new deal programs.

Soon afterward, we left war housing and rented a small, single-story house in Arlington, Virginia. A wonderful wooden swing in the yard that resembled a simple airplane put me way up higher than I'd ever been before. On occasion, my knuckles turned white. Sometimes even Mom's eyes would widen and her lip tremble, worried that I would fall out and land face-first. She would stop the swing then and sit me down to read or tell a story to me.

My favorite story involved Peter, a mouse in a church who knocked over inkwells. I never tired of hearing it. Mom would recite *Peter Churchmouse* from memory: "Peter sometimes tracked ink across the minister's hymnal pages on the pulpit, leaving 'new' musical notes where his tiny feet landed on the five-line staves."

"And so, the minister's singing stunk," I'd say, smiling so big my face hurt.

In a deep voice, Mom said, "The church brought in a cat to get rid of Peter." Then, lightening up, she said, "Oddly enough, though, the cat and mouse developed a close friendship instead."

"I like that part the best."

Mom always ended with something like, "The story shows how a lion might lie down with a lamb, how former war enemies might become friends after a war."

I loved the flashing fireflies that lit up our backyard at night like stars in a planetarium. I thought of the fireflies as falling stars and would chase them, though I never managed to catch any. Gayle caught enough to fill jars so that they'd glow by the side of our beds at night. Because Dad had punched holes in the jar lids, the fireflies survived until morning when, at Mom's insistence, we released them.

Toward the end of the next year, Mom and Dad started to fight. Dad wanted to try his hand using the photography skills he'd picked up at an earlier job as a reporter/photographer.

"My good friend Jack Hartline and I want to start a company in Seattle to produce educational films."

"Over my dead body!" Mom said, folding her arms across her chest. "I don't want to give up our financial security to indulge your film-making fantasies."

Mom changed her tune soon, though. She got behind moving "back home" after she became pregnant and realized being closer to the relatives would help her cope with a newborn and me and my special needs.

Jammed into Pauline with our belongings, we drove west in 1947. Somewhere near Denver, Mom could no longer tolerate the confines of the car. Dad put the three of us on a night train and drove on solo to meet us later in Seattle. Mom walked up and down the train aisles to alleviate the effects of her pregnancy.

It didn't surprise any of us when we woke up the next morning lying on train seats with soldiers' jackets over us for warmth. GIs returning home filled the train.

At first we lived with our Schonborn grandparents in Puyallup. I loved being around them, but when they tired of answering my incessant "Why?" questions, they would send me to the basement. I enjoyed roller-skating on the sometimes-bumpy cement floor and daydreaming in Dad's Dark Room, bathed in an eerie glow caused by its red photographer's lightbulb.

When Dad wasn't organizing and running Totem Color Films, he and Grandpa Cliff built a concrete-block lower story on the lot next to the Schonborn property. "It's gonna be our home," Dad said, though I remained skeptical until, with an unforgettable thrill, I watched workers slide a surplus war-housing unit off a huge flatbed truck and onto large wooden runners on the ground. Hydraulic jacks raised the runners and the house to the height of the concrete-block structure Dad and Grandpa had built. A couple of winches later, the workers pulled the house into place on top of the first story.

I spent the next day exploring our new two-story home and later some new parts of our property with its cattail-lined creek and small, scary forest. As the sky darkened, I headed back to the house. Unsteady with fatigue from my daylong adventure, I started up the sixteen-foot plank that rose to the elevated front door of the housing unit where, later, steps would be built. Halfway up the plank, I slipped and fell four feet to the ground.

"Help! Help me!" I cried. "I'm bleeding,"

Mom came running, fear in her eyes.

"Oh, thank God! It's only your knees, "she exclaimed as she

pulled me up to a standing position. "You had me worried. Come to Grandma's house."

"I have to walk slow."

"I can't walk fast either," she said as she patted her bulging belly.

Mom didn't like the deep gashes in each of my knees, but she disliked even more that only the immediate family could understand my speech. As soon as my knees healed, leaving scars shaped like perfect triangles, Mom drove me to Seattle so experts at the University of Washington could evaluate my speech.

Once again, serious-looking adults poked, prodded, and pondered my mouth and throat. They decided that since my soft palate had grown larger, I should start speech therapy.

From then on, despite being several-months pregnant, Mom drove me an hour to and from Seattle every two weeks for speech therapy, sweetened by art classes afterward.

"Slow down when you talk," the therapist kept telling me.

"I'm trying, but I have a lot to say."

"We've got plenty of time…and remember, too, always 'try hard' when forming your words."

"But, I already 'try hard' all the time. My parents taught me to 'try hard' when I sit on the toilet."

I loved my art classes. Giant easels towered over me, holding gigantic pieces of paper. As I painted I'd get poster paint on my arms and face, but smocks kept most of the paint off my nice going-to-the-city clothes. All the faces I painted had irregular, blood-red lips, as if a surgeon had had his way with them.

I soon had a serious rival for Mom's attention: my baby brother Scott. In fact, everyone paid him a huge amount of attention, commenting on his perfect face and fair hair with curls. I began disliking my straight dark hair and relished even more my trips to Seattle when I had Mom all to myself.

As the excitement over Scott waned and the reality of family expenses and a mortgage hit home, Mom and Dad began to fight.

"We can't make ends meet," I overhead Mom say, thinking we kids were asleep.

"Well, we're filming as fast as we can. The rain here means fewer days for shooting."

"More sun and more shoots won't help," Mom snapped. "We can't finish the house addition. We're even behind on our bills."

"Don't worry, *Energy in Our Rivers* will sell well," declared Dad.

"You've said that about every film! You've got three children to support now, and one—"

"—isn't cheap. I know, I know. But aren't his surgeries over?"

"For now, but there's speech therapy, special dental care…"

"But—"

"Jack, listen to me. I mean no disrespect, but aren't you beginning to follow in your father's footsteps? Cliff's a wonderful man, but he had trouble supporting his family."

"For Christ's sake, millions of men were dogged by the Depression."

"You've said yourself you don't want our kids to go through what you did growing up."

So, after serious thought and discussions with his business partner, Dad folded Totem Color Films and went back to work for the federal government. Once again, he championed New Deal programs; public housing in particular, which grew out of the 1949 Housing Act.

Maplewood Elementary started its first kindergarten the year I turned five: a first for the school and a first for me. I'd fantasized about being "grown up" ever since I saw Gayle strut down Woodland Avenue a year earlier to catch the bus for first grade.

Dressed in corduroy pants held up by suspenders with Scotty dogs on them, I entered a large, well-lit room with two-dozen kids in it, all my height. Mrs. Palmer, dressed in a red smock, tried her best to placate those who cried and provide a sense of welcome for all of us. As I started playing with some one-foot-cube blocks on the hardwood floor, a kid asked, "Why is your nose so funny?"

I responded, "What do you mean?"

"What'd you say?" he shot back.

I walked away, but another kid asked, "Why're your teeth so crooked?"

I sat down at once—crossing my legs, folding my arms tight—and stared at the floor.

When Mrs. Palmer noticed me, she came over and asked, "Are you okay?" When she lifted my chin, my fluid eyes and trembling lower lip answered her question.

She said, "Class, let's not ask Karl a lot of questions. Okay?"

I began to build a tower with the blocks, but soon another kid said, "Your face is strange."

I started to cry, and before long Mrs. Palmer sat down next to me and hugged me. She then told the class, "Look, Karl's building a great tower. He's pretty good at that." A couple of kids came over to help with the tower, but couldn't understand me whenever I spoke. I stopped talking for the rest of the morning. By now I felt confused and a little frustrated as well as sad, rejected, and alone.

When Mom picked me up, I asked why so many kids had said "What?" all the time. She said they needed to be better listeners. When I asked about why others stared at my face, tears welled up in her soft eyes as she said, "They're curious about your scars."

"What should I do?" I asked.

"Tell them you had surgeries as a baby that left you with scars and a different voice."

The next day Mom came to school with me. The smell of rain, mud, and wet clothes filled the classroom and the partitioned-off area where we kept our coats and boots. I played with the large wooden blocks again, Mom at my side. A girl came over, and when I told her she could help me build a train, she looked confused.

Mom said to the girl, "Listen again and concentrate on his lips," and turning to me, she said, "Tell her once more, honey. Explain a bit."

I said, "I'm building a train. You know, a choo-choo train."

The girl smiled and said, "Oh yeah, a train."

I smiled, too.

Mom helped me talk to kids most of the morning, but left to speak to Mrs. Palmer once or twice. Mom also helped serve juice at snack time and move chairs later on so we could nap on little sleeping mats.

After the first week, Mom stopped coming to school, and Mrs. Palmer intervened whenever a kid started teasing me. She said she and Mom had become friends. Still, I didn't talk much and tried not to show my teeth because I'd caught my reflection in a mirror at home. For the first time, in fact, I saw my face the way the other kids saw me—a peg-like tooth growing out of the still-open cleft in my gum, my mustache area scars, and my smushed-in left nostril. I was horrified. Seeing this helped me understand why kids stared and called me "Scarface" and "Squish Nose." All this saddened me, and I began covering my mouth and nose with my hands when I talked to people.

Besides painful earaches, I suffered from the burning sore throats of tonsillitis. After one bout, Dr. Justs recommended a tonsillectomy.

"I even know a surgeon who'll give you a two-for-one special 'cause Gayle needs one, too."

"That sounds good," Mom said.

"In rare cases, there could be severe bleeding or the soft palate could swell, obstructing breathing."

"Oh no," I objected."Don't wanna do this."

"What if you share a room with Gayle? the doctor asked. "You'd have a buddy."

Sure enough, the night before the surgeries, Gayle and I talked and talked in our hospital room, allaying some of my fears. In the OR, three big glass saucers hovered over my head like alien flying saucers. Dark green cylinders, resembling guided missiles stood in a row nearby. My shivering intensified. I wanted Gayle in the room with me.

Suddenly, intense light from the saucers blinded me...and warmed me.

"Let's begin," the surgeon said.

"No-o-o-o," I screamed before passing out.

After I came to, Mom was telling Gayle, "When you get home, I'll spoil you with French toast, soft-boiled eggs, and soup."

"Till then, we've got to eat squares of Jell-O that shake on our plates?" Gayle moaned.

So Gayle and I ate nervous Jell-O and threw up together for the next three days.

After the surgery I still had sore throats, but they hurt less. They may've been from colds I caught from staying indoors so much during rainy weather.

Unlike kindergarten, first grade with Miss Brudie involved a lunch break and recesses where different grades intermixed. One day during the first week in school, I wandered by myself amid chestnut trees at the far end of the schoolyard, searching the ground for chestnuts to put into my shiny lunchbox. All at once, two older boys confronted me.

"Lemme see that," the scruffy boy said, eyeing my lunchbox.

"No. It's special," I said.

"What? What'd you say?" the tall boy demanded.

"Nobody understands you," Scruffy said, smashing my lunchbox to the ground, causing a tinkling sound of glass breaking in my Thermos.

"What's wrong with your face?" the tall one shouted as he pushed me into the dirt. I started to cry as I watched them run away. I sat alone for several minutes at the edge of the huge, almost-deserted playground.

My first feelings of fear and then shame over not protecting my lunchbox gave way to anger and resentment. I thought *I don't like these boys, but what can I do?*

"What happened, Karl?"

I glanced up to discover Miss Brudie, who had come looking for me. "Nothing," I said. "I tripped and fell. I guess I didn't hear the bell."

"Are you sure?" she asked, coupled with a searching look.

"I need to watch where I'm going next time," I said, dusting myself off.

Later, I cringed as I handed my dented lunchbox to Mom.

"Your Thermos is broken," she exclaimed. "Damn it! How'd that happen?"

"Two kids attacked me."

"Did you tell Miss Brudie who did it?"

"I didn't know their names."

Grimacing, she looked away for a moment before saying, "I'm sorry I got mad, Karl. It's not your fault. We'll buy a new Thermos." She crouched down to my level and cradled my face. "Next time, if you don't know their names, at least describe them to your teacher." She kissed me.

"I just want to be *normal* like everybody else."

"Oh, honey, things will improve. It'll take time, though," she said, averting her teary eyes.

That night Mom and Dad's voices kept me awake.

"Just 'cause you called the principal doesn't mean it'll stop," Dad said.

"I know, but he needs more frequent speech therapy."

"We can't afford it. Anyway, can't *we* correct his speech?"

"He needs us to accept him at home, not correct his speech," Mom insisted. "Anyway, do-it-yourself speech therapy is like building the *USS Enterprise* in our driveway."

Mom told me the next morning she'd deputized Gayle to look out for me at school and that I should never be alone during lunch, recess, or before and after school. She explained how she had watched her own brother be bullied for being precocious and for having an awkward bulge in his tummy caused by a protruding hernia.

Not long after, Mom took me to a large classroom, used for Special Ed kids, at Puyallup Middle School near the elementary school I attended. Put off at first by stale air smelling of sweat, I hesitated to enter the room. When I saw a couple of moon-faced kids, I bolted. Mom collared me halfway down the corridor outside, saying, "They may look and act a bit different, but they're friendly kids."

I took a seat on one of the couches around the perimeter of the room, and instead of looking at the kids and a cerebral palsy boy, I stared at the windows almost opaque from condensation.

Soon the speech therapist—Mr. Bargmeyer—came into the room, asked Mom some questions, and told her to return in an hour. He led me to the school's cafeteria where we walked past the din of a hundred kids eating lunch. Bargmeyer pointed to a vertical steel ladder protected by a semi-circular safety cage. My eyes drifted up and I saw at the top of the ladder, high in the rafters, a glass booth with a little door.

"Wow!" I said.

"Pretty neat, huh?" said Bargmeyer. "Go ahead. Climb up."

It felt like I climbed a hundred rungs before stepping onto a platform. I then ducked through a little door into the booth. As Bargmeyer entered, breathless and disheveled, after me, he said, "People control spotlights from here during performances on the stage down below." He closed the door, muffling the chatter of students and clatter of plates.

"We'd better get started," Bargmeyer said. "Let me hear you say 'Mummy, mummy, ninny, ninny,' a few times." I complied and then repeated other words and phrases he suggested. At the end, he said, "Great! Now, can you blow this up?"

"Oh no! I can't blow up balloons."

"Then let's try this." He gave me a ruler with a groove in it. "Put one end of the ruler on your chin and tilt your head back, like a sword swallower." After I did this, he placed a ping-pong ball in the ruler's groove against my lips. "Blow. Try to push the ball up the groove."

"I can't."

"Yes, you can."

I blew as hard as I could but couldn't move the ball an inch.

"Good." he said. "Try it some more. Bet you can get it to two inches." He made notes as I practiced blowing, but despite my efforts. I couldn't move the ball beyond an inch.

Taking a break, I looked out of the booth at the kids eating below and envisioned manipulating them like marionettes. They'd long since stopped staring at us. Bargmeyer broke my reverie. "How're you doing?"

"Not so hot."

"Next time, seal off the back of your throat so air only comes out of your mouth. Your words sound nasal now because the sounds come out of your nose, not your mouth." He leaned towards me. "Open your mouth and say, 'Ahh.'"

"Ahh, ahh."

"Feel any muscles working back there?"

"Sort of."

"That's what you should be feeling when you blow or speak." He then had me do tongue-twister and diaphragm exercises that struck me as hopelessly hard. I practiced for what seemed an eternity.

"Gosh, time's up," he said, interrupting my chant-like trance.

He handed me a bag with the ruler, balls, and a sheet covered with scribbles for Mom. "Do these exercises at home, ten times in a row, three times a day."

Though I detested the exercises, I kept at them. A few weeks later, I heard Mom and Dad once again arguing at night, using words I didn't understand.

"I don't hear any difference. Karl's still unintelligible. Maybe the therapist's expertise is lisps, stuttering, stammering."

"He knows a lot about cleft speech. I made sure."

"You baby Karl too much. He needs to grow up."

"He's just a little kid."

They continued to argue. Then Dad exclaimed, "Marriage isn't much fun anymore," and Mom got quiet. I didn't understand what all this meant, but figured it was my fault. It took me a while to fall asleep.

I hated being pulled out of class for therapy. I didn't like being singled out or hearing kids muttering "Quack, quack!" as I left. Mostly, I disliked missing out on Miss Brudie's class activities.

At the start of each session, Bargmeyer would always ask me to blow a ball up a ruler. Sometimes I'd nudge a ball along with my hand, but he caught me most of the time. He gave me other blowing gadgets to practice with, like large pinwheels. And he told me to practice all sorts of phrases.

"Slowly repeat 'The boys beat the big bad bug,'" he said at one point. "And 'Buy baby a bib.'"

I responded with, "The bug boys beat the big bad bibby."

He smiled.

"Ahh ha ha," burst from my lips as I realized what I'd said.

Bargmeyer started to laugh, too, and from their expressions, the kids down below thought we'd both cracked up.

As I started second grade, I didn't know whether to be happy or sad. I liked having the athletic Bobbie Duncan in my class. Plus Miss Showers' classroom excited me, as did an assembly early on where a quick-sketch artist, like magic, drew huge Audubon-like drawings of birds right in front of us. Nevertheless, I still feared encounters with bullies.

One blustery fall day, I missed meeting Gayle at the school bus because we'd made a small, erupting volcano out of plaster of Paris in class. I'd stayed behind to help Miss Showers clean up the mess. In exchange, she let me take the volcano home with instructions to put baking soda, vinegar, and soap in it to make it erupt as it had in class.

Following our parents' directive, Gayle skipped the bus, found me, and we started walking home. From nowhere, a boy confronted us and asked me what I was carrying.

"A volcano," I said.

"What'd you say?" he retorted, annoyed. Gayle placed herself between the boy and me.

"*My* volcano," I said.

"You talk like Donald Duck," he said, pinching his nostrils together to sound nasal.

"Stop it," Gayle said.

"Try and make me," he said, grabbing Gayle's pigtails and spinning her around.

"That hurts!" Gayle shouted, hitting him with a book. I dropped the volcano and lunged at the boy. We all scuffled— snorting, swinging, and breathing with effort.

"You idiots!" he yelled.

"I'll show you!" Gayle shouted as she curled her fingers into claws. Realizing that Gayle would fight dirty, he ran off. As he did, I gazed at the pieces of the shattered volcano on the sidewalk.

I felt the hurt and anger I'd felt with other bullies, but a new sensation, that of being "belittled," swept over me.

Mom and Dad talked to us at dinner.

"Next time," said Gayle, "I'm gonna let loose."

"The hater and the hated switch roles, eh?" Dad asked.

"You *can* walk away from fights, you guys," Mom said.

"He called me names," I said.

"Sticks and stones may break my bones...," Mom replied.

"But it makes me feel small," I said, dropping my head.

Then Mom uttered a sentence that's always stuck with me: "You know, Eleanor Roosevelt, a famous lady, says something like, 'No one can make you feel small unless you let them.'"

Mom and Dad started arguing again—this time, over whether to move once more. An opportunity had opened up in San Francisco for Dad to assist the director of the Feds' housing programs in the western regional office. Dad pointed out the pros—a hefty raise, better schools, and a healthier climate for me. Mom argued the cons—abandoning the house that Jack, and his dad, built and leaving almost three-dozen relatives behind. In the end, Mom caved.

After saying sorrowful goodbyes to most of those relatives, we packed Pauline to the gills. Her loaded tail-end almost dragged on the ground. We sang *California, Here I Come* several times during the drive south, but I mouthed the words because I wasn't thrilled with the move. Once Mom whispered to me, "Where's your enthusiasm?"

I lied and said, "If I can't talk so hot, how can I sing?"

"Just try to sing."

At a gas station, out of earshot of the others, Mom confronted me.

"I know you're not thrilled about moving."

"I'll miss my teachers and especially Mr. Bargmeyer."

"I'm going to miss all our friends and relatives. Even all your doctors."

I smiled.

To assuage my fears—and perhaps her own—she told me, "You're going to love California. I promise."

PALO ALTO, SILICON VALLEY

WE STARTED OUR NEW life in northern California in Palo Alto, a peninsula town located between San Francisco Bay and the Pacific Ocean in the heart of soon-to-be Silicon Valley. Mom and Dad chose Palo Alto in part for its schools nurtured by Stanford University, which owned countless acres beyond its campus on the west side of town. The weather couldn't have been better for a cleft kid like me—moderate, sunshiny days most of the year.

We rented a one-story house called an "Eichler Home," a flat-roofed house—stained-wood on the outside and inside—with floor-to-ceiling windows in several rooms, influenced a lot by modern Japanese architecture. I didn't much like the contemporary style of our house or its location in the middle of a new subdivision in south Palo Alto. But I did like the not-too-distant orchards that filled the air, depending on the season, with the fragrances of apple and orange blossoms as well as apricots, peaches, cherries, and almonds. I considered our house at 1084 De Anza Circle preordained for us since Gayle was 10, I was 8, and Scott was 4.

In my first serious foray into our neighborhood, I discovered something startling and raced home to tell Mom.

"We've gotta run for our lives."

"Why?" she asked, jerking backward in surprise.

"There's been an earthquake. I saw a giant crack in the ground."

Mom laughed, saying "Don't worry."

Then she hugged me, explaining the crack I'd seen came from the heavy clay-like soil in the neighborhood drying too fast in warm weather. She assured me that once the rains came in a few months, the crack in the "adobe" soil would close up.

Dad faced an earthquake of sorts at his new job. As the PR guy for the San Francisco Federal Housing office, he'd kept busy writing press releases and doing staff work for top-tier administrators. Then all hell broke loose when New Deal objectives of providing low-income rentals and boosting home ownership got broadened to a mandate to improve the quality of life in American cities. Dad became insanely busy, and I missed not having him around the way he was as a self-employed filmmaker.

We had arrived in Palo Alto after school had started at Van Auken Elementary School. I had some catching up to do in my third grade class, but I didn't mind spending extra time with books and "purple" worksheets. Part of it had to have been the smell of new textbooks and Ditto-machine solvents.

Talking out loud in class terrified me because I still didn't speak intelligibly, so I rarely raised my hand. I paid a price for this because I had always done my homework and wanted to show off.

"When can I start speech therapy again?" I often asked Mom.

"You've badgered enough. I'll look into it."

A week later, she said, "Unfortunately, the slots at school and everywhere else have filled up."

"Aw Jeez," I groaned.

"We arrived here too late. We'll just have to wait our turn."

I slumped my shoulders, stuck my hands in my pockets, and shuffled off to my room.

Gayle continued to act as my bodyguard. Though kids still teased me about my face and strange speech, few were aggressive. I wanted to make a new start in California, but I couldn't smile to win kids over because I'd reveal my horribly crooked teeth. Since friendships and play groups had already solidified in school and my neighborhood, I spent most of my free time with Gayle and Scott playing hide-and-seek, chasing one another, and the like.

When they got tired of playing or I couldn't find them to begin with, I felt at a loss. Generally, I sat, head in my hands, or moped around the house wishing for a nifty radio show to start. I soon began to withdraw into my imagination though. Superheroes attracted me: champions from movie shorts like Superman and comic-book heroes such as Batman, the Phantom, Captain Marvel, and Flash Gordon.

Wanting to be like the Space Patrollers I saw on a neighbor's TV, I drew dials and levers on the inside of the box our new water heater came in and cut holes in its sides to view the moon at night.

And later wanting to be a submarine hero like Captain Don Winslow, also on TV, I ordered a baking-powder sub from a Kellogg's cereal requiring a box top and a quarter. When I finally got the tiny sub after weeks of waiting, I filled the bathtub to the brim to allow for an impressive dive.

Barging in on my fun, Mom shrieked, "Do you know how much water you're wasting?"

"I only wanted to see how deep it would go."

"And look at the water all over the floor."

"I'll clean it up."

"Darn right you will."

Not only did that mail-order sub teach me patience, it taught me about water conservation in California.

I soon resorted to exploring the wider world around me by bike. California became my own three-ring circus, including not only De Anza Circle and nearby Van Auken Circle and Metro Circle, but also the Louis Road and Moreno Avenue neighborhoods. My bike became my little clown car, moving me from ring to ring, 'hood to 'hood, adventure to adventure.

As I gained Mom's trust, I rode my bike farther and farther until I got all the way to the frontage road that paralleled "Bloody" Bayshore Highway—a two-laner notorious for head-on collisions—that would soon become Interstate 101. There, on a vacant expanse of land, I watched workmen grading parking spots to slope downward toward a yet-to-be-installed drive-in movie screen. After the men left each day, I climbed onto immense road-graders and bulldozers—fantasizing myself driving them. My imagination sought the power I lacked in real life. One day I pushed the start button on a road-grader. The roar of the engine struggling to start scared the bejesus out of me, and I never tried it again.

Once I broke Mom's "not after dark" rule and rode to the new drive-in, knowing I might get spanked for it. A few blocks from the theater, I watched young drivers cram their friends into their car trunks to sneak them in for free. At the drive-in fence, I gawked at lovers who paid little attention to the movie. Just when things got exciting, for them and me, their windows would steam up. I'd turn my attention to the huge screen and marvel at cinematic lovers with faces three-stories high, touching each other's lips before kissing. It seemed so natural. I went home, sneaked in a back door, and touched my scarred lip, wondering if any girl would ever touch it.

When Mom discovered the next day I'd been out after dark, she said, "Dad will deal with you when he gets home."

Dad didn't want to talk about the infraction. He got a thick ruler and spanked me.

After tears and sobs, I sulked and later overheard Mom ask Dad, "Weren't you a little harsh?"

"He gets into a lot of trouble."

In July, we traveled up to Washington for our vacation. Stenerson relatives from Mom's side, including six cousins, met us at Spirit Lake in the shadow of Mt. St. Helens. After being intrigued by the rainbows created by gasoline spills on the water surface near the dock, I drove an outboard motor boat, caught a trout that Aunt Irene cooked, and accompanied Uncle Frank on his fireboat to check out a fire along the shoreline. Uncle Frank let me help guide the boat's fire-hose to spray water on the fire. I decided I wanted to be a forest ranger just like him.

After all this fun, Mom took me to see Dr. Cox in Seattle. I hated visiting him this time. Couldn't I just laugh and play like my cousins did?

Mom asked, "Is there anything surgical that can be done for his speech?"

"Because Karl's mouth still needs to grow," Dr. Cox responded, "fixing soft palate irregularities now would not improve his speech for long."

"How about skipping yearly checkups for hearing loss?"

"I hate them," I said.

Dr. Cox smiled at me. "Not a good idea. If you can't hear right, you can't speak right."

The next day, we drove to Whidbey Island, north of Seattle, and met Schonborn relatives—a bunch of adults and sixteen kids—for several days of camping in the rain. My uncles caught salmon. I swam in the chilly water of Puget Sound, which made me shiver and my heart flutter. Then, while visiting friends who lived on Lake Washington in Seattle, we watched in horror as a hydroplane racer flipped his boat end-over-end and died amid the wreckage.

Later, during a visit to Grandma Schonborn's en route home, I had to pee so bad, I let go on Gayle, who had taunted me by refusing to get off the upstairs toilet. Afterward, Gayle got even by claiming I had spit on the last piece of sugar cream pie so that no one but me could have it. I denied this but admitted I loved sugar pie. I also loved Grandma's butterscotch pudding, which I mispronounced "Boy Scout" pudding.

In Palo Alto, Mom had often talked about "When we move

back home to Washington…" Now, on the final leg of our trip back to California, she said, "It will be good to be home again."

Nonetheless, while Mom had made peace with California, my peace in the Golden State was soon to be shattered.

OUTSIDER

DAD LIKED THE EICHLER-STYLE house we had rented so much that he bought a brand-new one across town after our vacation. He said he lucked out because war veterans got great financial breaks when buying houses.

"You kids will like having two bathrooms and enough land for us to add a recreation room in the future."

Dad got right to work building storage space, as Eichlers had neither basements nor attics. This would be the sixth house I would live in, and I hoped we wouldn't have to move again.

Mom liked the comforting effect of being on a quasi-traditional street. She looked out on landscaped bungalows and ranch houses across the street, quite different from the tree-less new Eichlers on our side of the street. I wondered if the people who lived across the street hated looking at flat-roofed houses with stained wood siding.

"I think the street has a split personality, like 'Skits' our cat," Gayle often said.

"I don't get it," I'd usually say. "You mean 'split' 'cuz all Skits does is eat and sleep?"

I rode my bike around other neighborhoods in north Palo Alto exploring some of the older areas of town. I loved the leafy, beautiful neighborhoods that clustered about University Avenue, featuring stately homes that were generations old, often English Tudor, Mediterranean, or Spanish in style, as I learned later.

One thing I didn't like about our new living situation: the black rotary phone in the hallway. It intimidated me because people, even relatives of mine, interacted with me by the trait I hated most in myself: my voice. Also, our "party line" meant eavesdroppers could listen to my horrid nasal voice without my knowing it.

My new elementary school, Green Gables, stood just a few houses away from ours. It consisted of two flat-roofed, rectangular structures containing six classrooms each, joined at right angles with the principal and secretary's office at the merge point. A huge overhang held up by 5-inch diameter steel support poles allowed us to walk outdoors from classroom to classroom without getting rained on. A paved expanse of playground cradled two sides of a football-sized grassy field.

The first day of school, as Gayle and I entered the school grounds, buzz-cut narrow-faced Danny Gemelli and his sister Gina confronted us. Both were our respective ages, but much taller than either of us.

"You new here?" Gina asked.

"Yes," I said.

"What?" said Danny. "I can't understand you." He moved in a menacing manner to get closer to me. "Say that again."

"He said, 'Yes,'" Gayle growled.

"I want *him* to say it," Danny said.

Glaring at Danny, Gayle said. "Don't get any closer."

Moving toward Gayle, Gina asked, "Can't he defend himself?"

Gayle's eyes narrowed, "Get away from us. Now!" she barked. "I don't want to fight, but I will, new school clothes and all!"

Danny and his sister backed off.

"We could beat you up easy," said Danny.

"'Cuz you're so short," Gina said.

Suddenly the school bell rang, and we all ran to our respective classrooms across the school grounds, which seemed sullied with venom and hate until a surprise September rain washed them away. Fortunately, Danny and I had different fourth grade teachers, and so did Gina and Gayle.

Old feelings of fear, inadequacy and resentment returned and prevented me from concentrating in class.

When Mom and Dad found out about the verbal dustup, they chewed Gayle and me out for threatening the Gemellis during the encounter. At the end of the dressing down, Dad hinted at the consequences if we used our fists instead of words the next time.

"No fighting, or else."

I remembered Dad's thick ruler and shuddered.

The real outcome of the dustup: Mom got a speech therapist for me right away.

I hated getting up in front of my new fourth-grade classmates and talking, which "show and tell" required. I wanted in the worst way to describe a precious bottle cap, trading card, or comic book from my various collections, but I knew kids would snicker, finding my speech hard to understand.

Mom encouraged me to confront my hesitation and shyness by putting on puppet shows. She showed me how to make hand puppets and a cardboard box "theater." I kept asking Gayle to join me.

"I've told you many times, I'm 'beyond puppets.'" she said. "I don't even play with dolls."

"I'll help do puppets," Scott said.

"You've tried. You can't keep them on your hands," I replied.

So, I became a one-man-show, often using puppet heads of Snap, Crackle and Pop of *Rice Krispies* fame.

I also put on magic shows, rounding up everyone, including Skits the cat, to witness absolutely incredible, stupendous feats in darkened rooms. While I may have been developing public speaking skills and overcoming stage fright, I failed to master even the simplest magic trick. Scarves fell out of my sleeves and tiny, foam rabbits popped prematurely from between my fingers before I could wave my wand. And "invisible" black threads, holding things supposedly flying unaided through the air, would invariably appear, glinting, no matter how dark I made the room, so that Scott would laugh hysterically and Gayle "bust" me for fraud.

I saw nothing but freckles and glasses when I first met Belinda Kelly, who Mom said had just graduated from college with the latest speech pathology techniques in her arsenal.

"Will I ever speak right, Miss Kelly?"

She answered my question with one of her own, "Have you heard of Winston Churchill?"

"Yes."

"Well, Churchill spoke nasally and mispronounced his S's. But he worked hard to overcome his problems, becoming a great debater and statesman."

"I want to be a great debater, too."

"Okay, then, let's get down to work," she said. "Try speaking more slowly, so you can remember which muscles you're trying to use."

"Yeah, Mom makes me eat slow, too, so food and milk won't come out of my nose."

"Good," Miss Kelly said. "Now repeat after me: 'He thrusts his fist against the posts and still insists he sees the ghosts.'"

I did so with mixed success.

"How about 'Copper-bottoming, um, my Man? No, aluminu-ming, um, Mum,'" she said.

"Copper-bottoming, um, my Mum. No, aluishishing 'em…C'mon, this is hard." We laughed.

"The snow sufficeth. It sufficeth us," she said.

"That's easy. The snow's sufficient. It sufficeth us."

"Not bad! Remember, too, you need to speak louder."

"Okay."

"I've heard you've done some blowing exercises in the past. I want you to continue with them." She gave me some straws and told me to use them to drink milk at home. "They'll strengthen your speech muscles," she said.

As I started to leave, I turned and said, "That session raced by. I think I like you."

Miss Kelly smiled. "I like you, too."

At the next speech session, Miss Kelly said, "Let's try using this modified stethoscope that lets you hear and sense speech coming out of your nose."

I gazed at the stethoscope, which, instead of the usual bell or flat cylinder, had something at the end resembling the nose clip some swimmers use to keep water out of their noses.

"Neat," I said.

Miss Kelly put the stethoscope buds in my ears and attached the nose thingy to my nostrils, saying, "Now, do you hear air escaping from your nose as you say 'Number, Numbness, Numbskull?'"

"Yes," I said, smiling.

"English has only three nasal sounds, 'M,' 'N,' and the 'NG' sound that occurs at the end of words such as King. Now say 'Help,' 'Horse,' and 'Apple,' listening for escaping air again."

"I still hear some," I said.

"Repeat the words, and try hard to seal off your nose with your soft palate."

I repeated the words, noticing less air coming out of my nose.

"Again," she said.

Even less came out this time, and I said, "Amazing."

Jumping up, she exclaimed, "You've gotten rid of some of the nasality! Repeat once more."

I tried even harder this time.

"That's it! You're working the soft palate better," she said.

"Now I get it."

She grinned and hugged me. The time flew by as we practiced exercises for some time until she looked up at the clock.

"Oh gee, Karl, it's time to stop. Here's an at-home exercise for nasality. Hum an 'M' forward in your head. Then merge the 'M' into an 'Ah' in the same breath. Pinch your nose as you do this and vary the quality of the 'Ah.' Once the pinch makes no difference, you've got the quality of 'Ah' you want."

"Okay."

"You've done a great job today."

Mom sat in on speech sessions from time to time, and one day Miss Kelly gave her advice to share with the family. That evening I overheard Mom tell Gayle, "Try not to correct Karl's grammar."

And Mom told Dad, "Be patient. Don't finish Karl's sentences."

Dad objected, saying "I've been trying to be patient, even when I don't understand Karl."

"Well, try harder. The speech pathologist wants him to slow down. And…you've got to let him express his emotions, too."

"Okay, okay."

Over the months, Miss Kelly had me working on word and sound rhymes in addition to tongue twisters and M's and N's. Unlike Bargmeyer, she concluded I'd compensated for my soft palate's irregularity. She announced I wouldn't need soft-palate surgery to prevent nasality. When my parents and I heard this, we cheered.

But my improved speech didn't keep Danny from calling me Hare Lip and mimicking Donald Duck's speech in my presence. I always wondered *Do I sound that bad?* And it always made me remember the first time someone called me Hare Lip. Mom had to explain that the derogatory term referred not to *hair* on a lip like a mustache, but to the vertical slit that runs from the mouth to the nose in hares and rabbits.

My schoolteacher, Miss Hill, had a limp, and when kids joked about it, I always cringed. While I understood she had a handicap, as I did, I hungered to fit in so much that I laughed along with the rest of the kids at their Miss Hill jokes. Though she never spoke about the cause of her limp, I assumed the dreaded polio virus had caused it.

One day, while teaching about Thomas Jefferson, Miss Hill said, "Interestingly, besides being a genius Jefferson stuttered."

She looked right at me and smiled. I took comfort in the fact that another famous person besides Churchill had a speech problem. Even more comforting: that I had an ally in Miss Hill.

Our special relationship extended only so far, though. Unable to read my handwriting, Miss Hill orchestrated a campaign in and out of school to fix it. Mom, a co-conspirator, nudged me to improve my penmanship by having me write letters to every living relative I had.

Moreover, Miss Hill concluded, as the school year wore on, that I needed to learn more "self-control" despite being a "most capable child." On my report cards, I had gone from being "A fine boy" and "A joy" to "Lacks consideration for others," "Has difficulty in conforming to situations," and "Walks around class when should be in seat." In response, Dad reminded me now and then of his thick ruler if I didn't "shape up."

Mom began to volunteer in classrooms at Green Gables and got involved in the PTA. This may've been to keep an eye on me, but more likely to keep tabs on all three of her kids at the school. (I had mixed feelings about Scott starting school: it meant he'd learn games like kickball which he could play with me, but it also meant he'd no longer worship me for going to school.)

Still, Mom couldn't control everything. One warm afternoon recess, I strayed to the far end of the school where workers would soon erect a multipurpose building in an open lot. Out of the blue someone grabbed me from behind, squeezing my arms against my body.

"Quack, quack, quack, Hare Lip!" said a voice I recognized.

"Leave me alone," I yelled.

"Talk right!" Danny taunted, tightening his grip.

Mustering all my strength, I threw my elbows back and up to break free. One elbow bloodied Danny's lip, enraging him. I started to run, but he caught me and threw me to the dirt where we wrestled until a teacher's shout brought us up short.

"Stop fighting, NOW!"

"He busted my lip," Danny whined. "Now I'm a hare lip."

"You started it," I shouted. "You grabbed me!"

"Off to the principal, you two," the teacher said.

As I walked to the principal's office, I picked small pieces of gravel and debris out of my bloody hands, seething with anger at Danny getting me in trouble.

The principal had always struck fear in my heart because his tanned, leathery face reminded me of my only gruff uncle and because he had paddled me early in the year for running through the school sprinklers. Today, he calmly heard my side before getting Danny's.

"Luckily, you're in different fourth grades," Mr. Parsons explained. "You're in greatest danger of meeting on the playground. Therefore, I'm going to have you stay in your respective classrooms at lunchtime for a week."

"Sheesh," Danny said.

"And you'll go without morning or afternoon recess as well."

Then, he let us both have it with his long flat paddle. I could barely sit when I returned to class. I was mad as hell at Danny and a little mad at Mr. Parsons.

Later that day, Mom met with Mr. Parsons, who told her Danny had other issues besides being a bully. Mom heaved a sigh of relief that the violence wasn't all my fault. She did persuade Mr. Parsons to alert the school's teachers to my susceptibility to being bullied and the fragility of my mouth and face.

That night, when Dad got home, I didn't know what to expect.

After Mom told him what had happened, Dad sat me down and, after giving me a long serious look, said, "The world's full of bullies, son. Given the money we've spent on your face, you can't fight every bully you meet."

"All I need to hear is 'Hare Lip,' and I'm swingin' my fists."

"That's not good. Did you know Lincoln's son had a cleft lip and palate?"

"No, but I bet having a president for a dad kept the bullies away."

"You're right, but only because Lincoln had Tad schooled at the White House."

"What should *I* do about bullies?"

"Call for help or run. If that doesn't work, protect your face and curl up on the ground."

"That's cowardly."

"You're smart and strong. You can afford to lose a fight."

"But didn't you fight Hitler?"

"At first I signed a pledge in college not to fight…then Pearl Harbor happened."

"Didn't you box?"

"Boxing's different. It's a sport, and…"

"So, you're not gonna spank me?"

"Correct." He smiled. "I've chosen to lose this fight."

"Whew."

"You know, bullies have made my life hard, lately."

"Huh?"

"Bullies are really anyone who treats others disrespectfully. I've had to fight sleazy contractors at work who take advantage of government programs designed to help people upgrade their homes."

"What do you mean?"

"'Tin men,' aluminum-siding scammers, have cheated my

office, the U.S. Government, and homeowners out of a lot of money."

I didn't quite understand Dad's example, but I got his idea that bullies operated in places besides schools. I also realized Dad's refusal to spank me grew out of strength, not weakness.

Oddly enough, the mix of "or else" threats and teaching moments caused a dramatic turn-around for me at school: I regained "self-control," at least in Miss Hill's eyes, as evidenced by improved grade-report comments at the end of the year.

When we first arrived in California, we attended the traditional-looking Presbyterian Church in Palo Alto. Gayle and I attended Sunday school, where we learned about Psalms, the Virgin Mary, and the Ten Commandments. I loved most when we got to stick felt-backed cut-out figures onto a felt display board.

"Karl, put Jesus where he belongs," our Sunday school teacher directed at one point after putting a triangle shape on the board.

"That's easy," I said, "He goes on top of the mountain. But why don't we ever get to put him on the cross?"

"That's a bit grim," said the teacher. "Anyway, Good Friday is many months away."

Mom had to explain to me later why Good Friday was really Bad Friday.

Dad didn't like some of the Presbyterians' notions, especially "predestination" and "resurrection." He also found the Palo Alto pastor's sermons uninspiring. After he started taking us kids to Unitarian gatherings, Mom dragged her feet for six months before coming along, perhaps wary of a church without a creed or, at the time, even a building.

Taking a cue from Jesus' resilience, I resolved to do something about the hard knocks and rejection I'd endured. At the start of the summer I had no playmates except my sibs. If Gayle had Girl Scouts and Mom took Scott on an errand, I wanted to cry because the loneliness hurt so much. I could busy myself only so long with comic books, my stamp collection, and other diversions.

So I biked to the house of Miles Schachter, whose father's research had helped make the atomic bomb possible. Miles' wrinkled forehead, drooping eyelids, and downward-looking eyes made people say he carried around some of his father's post-Hiroshima sadness.

"I'm glad you rang my doorbell," Miles said.

"Well, I'm happy you're home and can play."

"Ya wanna bolt some metal girders together to make a bridge?"

"Sure!"

I returned the next day with my own Erector set, and together we had enough pieces, pulleys and wheels to assemble a mobile, foot-high crane. We built and played, pretty much without talking.

A few weeks later Miles' family took me to the amusement park at the Santa Cruz Boardwalk. The funhouse mirror distortions made my face worse than ever. After seeing the freak show, I told Miles, "I feel sorry for, but curious, too, about the freaks we saw."

"I know what you mean."

"Maybe people feel the same way about me." I said.

"Naw…Well, maybe a few do."

I gulped. My cheeks burned as we walked to the Wild Mouse ride.

Miles and I couldn't get enough of the ride. I loved the two-story high Wild Mouse with its tiny cars jerking back just as we seemed about to go off the track into space. I also loved the spinning disk on the ground that threw everyone off until one triumphant person remained; it tapped into my competitiveness…though Miles usually won.

Speech therapy didn't take a break for the summer. In fact, Miss Kelly worried enough about my slow progress that she recommended I build models with Dad to force me to practice interacting more in everyday settings. At first, Dad and I built simple balsa-wood planes and cars, layering them with coats of paint to make them shine.

"Be sure to paint each coat smooth without any brush strokes showing," Dad said.

"That's hard."

"Well, if you're gonna do something, do it right."

Dad made me read the instructions out loud, which was the reason we were building models together. I cherished our model-making sessions. Long after I'd achieved my speech goals, Dad and I tackled wood and metal HO-gauge railroad cars and even 24-inch-long hand gliders made of wooden sticks that we covered with orange and red tissue paper. I hung the planes from my bedroom ceiling because they were too fragile to fly.

We were among the last on our block to get a TV. One day, Dad brought home a big, round, glass funnel mounted on a silver base with lots of exposed electronic parts. Having studied electronics in the Navy, he hooked the funnel up to a radio, which acted as a tuner, and, voila, we had our first television set. Not being inside a cabinet, it looked like some gizmo the family's mad scientist had created. Dad left it up to Mom to keep inquisitive five-year-old Scott from electrocuting himself by sticking his fingers into the Rube Goldberg contraption.

We had the TV for one reason only: Dad wanted to watch the Democratic Convention of 1952 live. After a week filled with debates and red-white-and-blue speeches, which mesmerized me, Dad's hero Adlai Stevenson won the nomination on the third ballot.

As summer wore on, Danny started hanging out with Ron Allen, a new kid in the neighborhood with curly dark hair and a kind of looseness about his body. One day, the two of them materialized from behind a wall of bushes. Danny angled his leg in front of me, just below my shins, and down I went, face first.

"God damn you," I cried.

Before I could rise up, Ron said, "Stay down" and pushed me down with his foot.

Bending over me, Danny slammed his fists repeatedly into my back and shoulders. As I turned my head up to see him, a fist connected with my face, bloodying my nose and flipping me on my back.

"I don't believe this," I sputtered as I raised my torso up and supported myself on my elbow, knowing that I should've followed Dad's advice to curl into a ball.

"You'll pay for this," I shouted. "You'll get it." But my high-pitched voice betrayed the thinness of my threat.

"So?" Danny said, glaring at me with his steel-blue, beady eyes, his hate cold and unflinching. Ron then pushed my chest with his foot, knocking me flat on my back again. I rose up again on my elbow. With a swift kick at my elbow, Ron flattened me onto my back yet again. Danny put his hands on his hips, and Ron quickly copied him.

"Let's leave this deformed piece of shit right here," Danny said.

"But—" Ron said.

"That's enough!" Danny barked.

In a flash, Danny whirled around and started walking away with a quick determined stride. Ron followed, but turned to look at me a couple of times either to be sure I wasn't coming after him or out of a yearning to finish me off. He clenched and unclenched his fists and muttered, "You're right. He really is strange looking."

I lay there staring into the sky. *Why does God let this happen to me?* I thought. My nose and back hurt, but mostly my spirit hurt. I felt weak and worthless. Helpless and humiliated.

Eventually I got up, wiped the blood from my face, and tried to think of an excuse for why I looked like I'd encountered a wrecking ball.

"Mom, someone opened a Dutch-door in my face. Bloodied my nose."

"Oh, no. Let me look." After she satisfied herself my nose was okay, she asked, "Where?"

"The top half of the door at school where they sign out balls to you."

"That one opens inward, not outward. So…you got into another fight? Your father will deal with you tonight, young man."

That night, Dad said, "You'll have to try even harder to stay away from bullies, now that they travel in pairs."

"They ambushed me."

"Then try hard to have an older kid, like Gayle, always in sight."

"That's impossible.

"I don't know what else to suggest."

Clearly, the two of us came up short.

After stewing for days over what to do about Ron and Danny, I ruled out building up my muscles because I'd need to take a course or buy expensive exercise equipment. Instead, I decided I'd become fast enough to outrun them. I liked track and practiced sprinting whenever I could for the next month. At the end-of-the-summer track competition at Green Gables, I ran the 50- and 100-yard dashes as if my life depended on it. And it did, as it turned out.

CHASING NORMAL

UNDER THE STERN GUIDANCE of my fifth-grade teacher, Mrs. Kiehle, who kept Mom posted on my progress during PTA Council, I had to learn history, decimals, long division, and creative writing—or face the music at home. I paid attention and studied dutifully, but Mrs. Kiehle expected wonders from me because Gayle had excelled in her class. During class I couldn't wait to play Capture the Flag where I pushed myself to run fast in order to liberate captured teammates from "prison" on the opponents' side of the field. And when basketball season started in November, I played daily to increase my running prowess. I even talked Mom into driving me to basketball clinics around town.

When midyear report cards came out, I overheard Mrs. Kiehle telling Mom, "Karl has a good mind. I love his written stories, except for the grammar."

"That's nice to hear," Mom said.

"But I'm afraid Karl's garnered a lot of 'Needs to improve' check marks on his report card."

That afternoon, Mom solemnly showed me the marks next to "Sitting still," "Talking to seat-mates," "Listening to directions," "Conforming to situations," and "Consideration for others."

"It's not like I've committed crimes," I said.

"No, but your misbehavior seems to annoy others, just like your fence walking."

"Huh?" I said, playing dumb.

New Eichler houses had begun to displace the orchard be-hind our backyard fence, and the construction aroused my cu-riosity. So I had started walking along the four-inch-wide tops of the redwood fences separating the old Eichlers from the new. I had thought my life as Karl Fencewalker, superhero, remained a secret.

"Our neighbors probably dislike your fence walking," Mom continued.

I knew I shouldn't add "lying" to my repertoire, so I said, "The construction workers wave at me."

Mom knew she had me where she wanted me. "But I bet *residents* don't wave 'cause you're not being considerate, not re-specting their privacy."

"Well, I've never seen any bare bosoms or bottoms."

"Even if just one surprised sunbather scampers out of sight, that's one too many. No more fence walking, Karl. Understand?"

"Yes."

One afternoon in February, when I might have run along-side older neighborhood kids gunning for the junior high track team, Mom took me to the dentist to see if something could be done about my crooked teeth. I had told her that I wished I could wear a Halloween mask all year round so no one could see my face. She worried that I rarely smiled. One of my two front teeth had come in almost sideways and the other one angled back in my mouth toward my split uvula.

"You're too young for orthodontia," the dentist explained. He picked up the tongue depressor that gagged me whenever he used it. "See this?"

I nodded. He handed it to me.

"Put the top end of it behind the tooth that juts back. The middle of the tongue depressor should rest against your chin."

"Like this?" I said.

"Yes. Now apply gentle pressure to the other end of the depressor."

"You mean use my chin as a pivot point to push the tooth forward?"

"Yes," he said.

"How often and for how long?" Mom asked.

"Every day, as long as possible," he said.

I almost rolled my eyes. *Great. Brilliant.* I thought. *Now I'll have a small, stunted chin on top of everything else.*

Still, every time I watched TV or movies, I dutifully complied...with drool running down the tongue depressor. I thanked God—or whoever ran the show, since the Unitarians had me asking some tough questions—that my schoolmates didn't see me: dorky wasn't the word.

Dad often rescued visiting office dignitaries from their San Francisco hotels, treating them to dinner at our house and a touch of suburbia. He'd bring office colleagues home, too. These visits forced Mom to drop everything and cook fancy dinners. Not so great for her, but the visits allowed me to try my new-found speech skills on adults other than relatives and teachers. The animated dinner-table discussions we had with guests also inspired us to debate during our everyday dinners.

We'd debate almost any topic, but the upcoming presidential election frequently dominated our discussions. I'd bait Gayle and Dad by saying, "I like Ike because he'll get rid of Communist spies in the government."

"You can't support that fear-monger Joe McCarthy," Gayle would snort.

"He's trampling on the rights of us government workers, what with loyalty oaths and all," Dad would say.

And off we'd go.

Despite the emotion Dad displayed during our dinner-table debates, he was an emotional minimalist, as were so many other males of his generation. Nevertheless, he did display plenty of feelings during an incident while his parents lived with us so Grandpa could help add on that recreation room to our house.

Grandpa knew carpentry, having built his house and much of ours in Puyallup. But did he know childrearing? After noting my irreverence, my lateness to dinner, and risky play around the add-on construction area, he confronted Dad in the living room one evening. I cowered in a corner as the evening sun turned the floor-to-ceiling windows in the room into blazing mirrors.

"What Karl needs is a good spanking!" Grandpa said, leaning backwards a tad with his hands on his hips.

"He's too old for that," Dad replied. "Besides, he's a good boy. Just gets carried away. Doesn't use his head."

"You're spoiling him, Jack," Grandpa said. Then he pivoted and looked directly at me.

"No, I just have a different approach than you."

"Different? You're right. You're indulging him."

Slamming his fist on the bookcase, Dad growled, "Believe it or not, we're strict with him. We send him to his room. Take away his privileges—"

"Those new-fangled child-rearing theories don't work," Grandpa snapped. "It's easier to build a boy than mend a man."

Both enthralled and scared by this battle of the Titans, I slunk away after it ended like another of the evening shadows. Dad's defense of me brought a smile to my face.

Still, that battle resonated. By the end of the school year, I had "turned it around"…at least in class. Mrs. Kiehle didn't give me any more "Needs to improve" check marks. In fact, she wrote, "Karl is developing very fast. I have enjoyed him very much this year."

Because I'd beaten Ron and Danny in 50- and 100-yard foot-races organized by teachers and also by after-school program directors, they left me alone for a while. This allowed me to befriend some kids in Cub Scouts who hadn't been in classes with me and didn't know how bad my speech used to be.

In order to get more arrowhead-shaped badges for our Scout uniforms, we tied knots, built wooden birdhouses, and learned Morse code. Any time this got tiresome, my new friends and I would head off on our bikes for hours on end. Using balloon tires, narrow tires, girl's bikes—it didn't matter—we'd jump over ditches, get airborne off dirt mounds, and race until we panted like dogs. Our parents trusted Palo Alto residents to rescue us when necessary, and they did, offering solace and the occasional Band-Aid after a spill.

Some of us later carried our need for speed into constructing all sizes and shapes of wooden go-carts. A gas engine soon entered the picture when I helped well-off Pat Flaherty tinker with his metal go-cart complete with a steering wheel. Like a modern-day Tom Sawyer, Pat made getting grimy seem like so much fun I'd have probably paid him to get greasy trying to fire up his always balky go-cart engine.

I had been looking forward to sixth grade until I learned both Ron and Danny would be in my class. Just as Danny had made fun of Miss Hill's limp, he savaged our new teacher, a Japanese-American named Mr. Ida who insisted we call him 'Pete.'

"His hair is cut too short," Danny said the first day of school. "And he hides his slanty eyes behind thick glasses."

"Look at my drawing of him," Ron crowed as he pointed to a war time caricature of Mr. Ida on his orange-brown Pee Wee notebook.

Ron, Danny, and some others—accustomed to seeing Japanese-Americans doing yard work and other low-level jobs in the community—thought of Mr. Ida as a foreigner. Later, we all learned Mr. Ida had been forced to live in an internment center as a kid despite being born in America.

I had no time to formulate a strategy to deal with Ron and Danny before the whole class bused off to a weeklong camp in the Santa Cruz Mountains to study biology and ecology. The first night of camp, Ron and Danny put a rabbit in my sleeping bag. Then they beat me and kicked me in the ribs until I managed to escape. The next day, I ran smack into a cabin doorframe, trying to avoid being humiliated by them again. The camp nurse provided no stitches for my brow laceration, and I never told a soul about the real circumstances of the wound or the bite on my toe.

"You're gonna have another scar on your face, Karl," Mom lamented as she peeled the bandage off my brow.

"Don't worry," I said. "The nurse says the scar will shrink."

After waiting months to see if it would, Mom took me to a plastic surgeon, Dr. Berner, who cut out the scar tissue and re-closed the wound with proper stitches.

As cold weather began to arrive, Mom had a harder time dealing with a different medical issue. Her good friend and former college roommate, Dorene Archer, was dying of colon cancer in nearby Cupertino. Mom ran errands and sewed for Dorene and her family. Mom had to pretend to be merry during Christmas because Dorene had died December 23rd, leaving two kids and a husband. (He later remarried someone named Mary, and several years later, Mary also died young; her death, as it turned out, would have an even greater impact on Mom than Dorene's.)

My music career, such as it was, had got off to a rocky start. While my hearing may have been marginally okay, my ability to carry a tune wasn't. And even if I had learned to hear sharps and flats and discern pitch, I still had that sometimes "nasal" voice. Musical instruments became my only option.

I couldn't seal off the back of my throat enough to blow on a wind instrument. Stringed instruments were a possibility, but they lacked "machismo" in my mind. That left keyboards and percussion, and so the school music teacher taught me the accordion. But when I progressed to a large accordion, it weighed me down so much I had to abandon it.

"Since the accordion is out, the piano makes sense," Dad said.

"I really don't want to learn piano, but I will if you also get me drum lessons," I responded.

"Okay, son. You've got a deal."

I took piano at Mrs. Reingold's house, distracted by drumming day dreams all the while. One Thursday, I declared myself on strike and refused to ride my bike to her house. Mom reminded me of our deal, and her blue eyes began to get fierce. When I capitulated at the last minute, I raced down the street with my head down—angry, focused, and pedaling hard—only to smack into a parked car. This time no blood, no injuries, and no scars. Just embarrassment.

Meantime, I was learning to play drum cadences and march in a drum corps. Mr. Olmstead taught groups of us the basic strokes by having us stand around tables mimicking his mama-daddy rolls, paradiddles, and flams.

After some basic drills and combining of strokes into cadences, he'd say, "Time to march."

We quickly fell into rows and columns in the huge hall where we met.

"The usual contest, Guys, except this time the winner gets a free pair of drumsticks."

I'd easily keep up with my dozen or so peers as we marched forward in formation a few steps, turned, and marched in the opposite direction a few steps.

Then the fun began as Mr. Olmstead barked out more complex orders: "To the left, turn, march," "Reverse step, march," and the like. Invariably, after each order, one kid would be going off in a direction opposite the group and would be sidelined. Mr. Olmstead increased the tempo of his orders until everyone was sidelined except the winner. Even though I'd try to concentrate and listen carefully, I rarely won. Guess I marched to the beat of a different drum master.

Of course, the real fun entailed marching and drumming in parades celebrating, for example, Palo Alto's May Day, Menlo Park's Fourth, and San Bruno's Festival of Flowers.

In addition to bullying me physically, Ron and Danny tried to get me in trouble at school by disobeying my orders as a street-crossing guard and signing my name to filthy limericks in bathroom stalls. They did this often enough that I had to set other kids straight who'd begun to believe some of the accusations.

"My friend Russ asked me," Scott said one day, "'Is your brother a delinquent? Why is his face messed up and why doesn't he talk right?'"

"What did you say to Russ?" I asked.

"I said you're a great guy. That you run fast, collect stamps, and build model planes and trains."

"Thanks."

"But I also say, 'He can't do magic tricks.'"

I laughed, and then I threatened to saw Scott in half. He knew I'd botch that trick, too, so he ran. I caught him and tried to tickle him to death.

Under Mr. Ida's direction, our sixth-grade class wrote a script for our own radio-show parody and scheduled auditions for various roles. Thanks to my speech therapy, most people now seemed to understand what I said, so, after much inner turmoil, I decided to compete for the sportscaster role, knowing that, if I won it, I'd have to speak in front of parents and the whole school. Unfortunately, I had to beat out Danny during the audition to be held one day immediately after recess.

Toward the end of recess that day, I confronted Danny, standing arms akimbo in front of the boys' restroom.

"Let me in," I demanded. "I need to pee."

"Sorry, you'll have to fight me!" Danny snarled.

I looked across the playground and saw Ron standing in front of the other bathroom, grinning at me. He was even bigger than Danny. Just as the bell rang, I felt pee run down my leg. But I refused to let tears run down my face as well.

Throughout the audition, I hoped no one would notice my wet trouser leg. But, of course, they did…with guffaws. Still, I beat out Danny for the role partly because I brought humor to the situation, working my wet trousers into the script at the very end by saying I got so excited in the closing seconds of the game that I peed in my pants.

On performance night, I had butterflies in my stomach—until showtime. When my turn came, I narrated a game played between Jail (Yale) and Harved inmates at the Jail Bowl. The game ended with a Jailbird going so long for a pass he broke free of the prison, only to be "tackled" by the rat-a-tat-tat of a prison turret gun.

"What a wonderful job, Karl," Ed Doll's mom gushed.

"Great work! You kept us in stitches," Mike Hart's dad said.

Mom and Dad stood next to me, beaming, as several other parents congratulated me, especially those who hadn't heard me speak for some time. The long hours of speech therapy and home exercises had finally paid off.

After most of the families had left, Mr. Ida approached me.

"Karl, I'd like you to present a roving Ma Bell telephone exhibit to our school next month."

I quickly looked at Mom's moist, approving eyes and said, "Wow, I'd be happy to."

"The exhibit's designed to let people hear how their voices sound over the phone," Mr. Ida said.

I gulped, knowing that few people, including me, had ever heard tape recordings of their voices.

"The exhibit has eight tape-recorders connected to dummy phones to give eight people feedback at once," he said.

When the exhibit arrived, the sound of my voice startled me, but I had to soldier on because I'd given my word. At a school-wide assembly, I talked into one of the phones and my taped voice played back so that everyone in the audience could hear. I cringed and a few kids laughed, but once my presentation end-ed, I smiled broadly.

The summer of 1955 brought with it interesting developments besides Palo Alto's unending, temperate, sunny days. I had reached the age for orthodontia at last. The orthodontist blithely said at my first appointment,
    "Your years with tongue depressors have done absolutely no good."
    I winced and glared at Mom, who always supported our chat-ty Bible-quoting dentist when I voiced skepticism about tongue depressors.
    "A few years of treatment, followed by the use of a retainer, will vastly improve your 'dental profile,'" the orthodontist con-tinued. "Your cleft makes your case difficult, but, luckily, you have no under-bite or over-bite to complicate things."
    Mom's shoulders relaxed…until the office manager showed her the estimated cost for the treatment. Mom received a little payment passbook just like the one she had had for Dr. Cox's cleft repair surgeries.
    My new braces hurt a lot, but I kept reminding myself that someday my teeth would be straight.
    Mom's parents visited us at the start of the summer and gave us a multi-volume encyclopedia, intended in part to help me do as well in junior high as Gayle seemed to be doing. I loved opening various volumes to random pages and devouring their information. Dad's parents also visited, and Grandma Charlotte spent extended periods of time resting in Gayle's bed since she had heart trouble brought on by diabetes. She had become pale and fragile.

Green Gables continued its tradition of offering summer rec-reation and crafts programs. Lots of us came to play a variety of team sports with skins versus shirts on asphalt as well as on turf. Whatever the sport, I tried to win, especially if I competed against Ron and Danny. But Danny, a natural athlete, excelled at sports. Tall and muscular, Danny almost always beat me now when the recreation leader timed us in the 50- and 100-yard dashes. My plan to outrun him when he hassled me had van-ished into thin air.

Late in the summer, though, Danny's family abruptly moved away for some reason. I asked different kids, but no one knew why the Gemellis had left. In any case, I celebrated that now I only had Ron to deal with—or so I hoped.

It had been a high-flying summer of playing sports, biking all over town, and marching in a couple of parades with my drum corps. However, days before starting junior high, it all unex-pectedly crashed to earth.

A HOLE IN MY HEART

MOM TOOK ME TO Dr. Robertson, our family doctor, for a routine checkup before school. As I waited in the exam room, I looked at the tall glass jar of antiseptic-smelling liquid containing odd medical instruments. I'd stared at scores of such jars for hours over the years while waiting for doctors. Not that jars with silvery instruments in bright pink fluid are intrinsically interesting, but in an all-white, sterile room, the bright color grabs your eye.

I also looked at the blood-pressure cuffs with dangling cords and squeeze bulbs hanging on the wall. One cuff let Mr. Hyde—I mean, Dr. Robertson—keep inflating until the pressure on my arm made me cry "uncle." The other, the larger one, allowed him to check the pressure in my legs.

Dr. Robertson entered the room, putting my thick file on the seat of a low, roll-around stool. He applied the cuffs to my arm and leg while I lay down, then used his stethoscope on my chest, back and lower legs, frowning all the while. He had me stand up, and he listened to my heart again—and then pressed on my fingernails, checking them.

"Do you get breathless when you run?" he asked.

"I dunno. I guess I get tired after a couple of races or half an hour of basketball."

"I've looked at your file with some care because you're almost a teenager," he said. "You're about to go through a major period of growth. We need to make sure nothing will complicate that."

"Okay," I said.

"So, I'm restricting you from sports."

"No sports?!" I wailed.

"You must refrain from strenuous activity. Starting now. And no PE at school."

"But, but—"

While I began imploding emotionally, Dr. Robertson turned to Mom. "Mrs. Schonborn, I'm restricting Karl because I'm worried he might have a serious heart defect."

"Wh…what do you mean?" she asked.

"I mean that developmental heart defects are common among cleft kids. Karl shouldn't do anything competitive or anything involving a stopwatch."

"Are you sure? Isn't there a test you can do?" Mom asked.

"Yes, I'm sure. And there are no tests and no fixes for the murmur I'm hearing. Our only recourse is to wait. As I explained to Karl, he's about to grow a lot, and his body will need all available energy for that."

Dr. Robertson told me to get dressed and motioned to Mom to follow him to his office. As they walked down the hall, I caught snippets of words and phrases—murmur, aorta, tetralogy, rheumatic fever as a kid. When I buttoned the last button on my shirt, I heard the doctor say to Mom as they re-entered the room, "Surgery would be too risky." As I went through the motions of saying goodbye to Dr. Robertson. I just kept muttering to myself, "No sports!" "No sports!" "No sports."

On the drive home, I asked Mom, "Am I going to die? If so, will it be fast like those heart attacks I've heard about? Or a slow decline, like Grandma Charlotte?"

After hearing Mom repeatedly say "I don't know" to my questions, I just stared out the car window, lost in sadness.

That night as I lay in bed, I heard through the wall from Mom and Dad's bedroom.

"Dr. Robertson said defects can occur throughout the body in cleft kids," said Mom. "He called it a 'syndrome.'"

"Jesus Christ, Karl's problems never end."

"He has a serious heart murmur—organic, functional, something—I can't keep the terms straight," Mom said. "The whooshing sound could be from a twisted or swollen aorta, from a tetralogy."

"A what?"

"A tetralogy is a combination of four defects. Many blue babies have a tetralogy."

"Oh."

"Or the sound could come from a hole in Karl's heart or a valve damaged by rheumatic fever."

"Has he ever had rheumatic fever?" Dad asked.

"Not that I ever knew. The bottom line is that Dr. Robertson doesn't know what's wrong."

"Is there nothing we can do?"

"Nothing," Mom said. "Dr. Robertson said we can only wait."

I couldn't sleep. My mind raced. Just a week ago, I'd strutted around the community pool in my slick, nylon suit with a Red Cross "swimmer" patch Mom had sewn on. I'd also just won the third-place City Award in basketball. I'd come to see myself as an athlete, and athleticism would be my ticket to friends and acceptance. Then again, I sometimes gasped for breath, exhausted, as I biked home from an "away" game. After a while, I fell into a troubled sleep.

For the next few days, losing my chance to compete caused me to lose my mind. Every heart skip, every dizzy feeling, or every momentary pain made me think death had me by the throat. For some reason, though, I didn't go to Mom with my fear and trembling. I worried about my heart in silence.

There had to be something I could do. I didn't want a hole in my soul even if I had holes in my heart and the roof of my mouth. I came up with a plan.

The next chance I had, I rode my bike—slowly—to Palo Alto's main library and pulled as many medical books off the shelves as I could carry. I took the heavy books to a remote table, gasping for air a bit as I walked. This worried me, spurring me to dive forthwith into articles about hearts and their defects. Feeling ashamed for some reason, I covered the books with a *Boy's Life* magazine when people walked by.

I learned, among other things, that my weak heart had to pump four-thousand gallons of blood—as much blood as could fill a Doughboy plastic swimming pool—day after day, nonstop, for the rest of my life. Despite struggling with Latin terms and medical jargon like tetralogy and morbidity, I drove myself to find out what caused the "murmur" or "whooshing sound" Dr. Robertson said he heard through his stethoscope. I found that murmur sounds come from blood flowing through holes in the heart caused by birth defects: that is, through narrow, leaky, or odd shaped arteries or valves. A really loud murmur can vibrate or "thrill" the chest, and can be detected by a hand on the chest. Luckily, I couldn't feel mine.

I learned that blue babies might have a few or many congenital holes or defects of the heart. These cause the unusual color, texture, and swelling of the skin of these babies—all indicators of poor circulation. Had I been a blue baby or more likely a "pink tet," a tetralogy sufferer without blueness? I looked at my fingernails, as Dr. Robertson had; they were a confounding purplish pink with a little lateral widening called "clubbing" by tetralogy experts. I pressed on my nails, as Dr. Robertson had, to see how fast blood returned to them, and the blood didn't return that fast. I had to pursue this.

Standing in front of the mirror in the library restroom, I determined my lips and the inside of my mouth to be purplish-pink, confirming to me that I was a "pink tet." My skin became clammy and hot at the same time. I wanted to cry. Instead, I bolted from the library, giving up my "research."

I walked my bike home, rather than ride it, hoping a miracle would heal me, even though I knew Unitarians didn't believe in miracles. I dreaded the start of school the next day.

At Jordan Junior High, my homeroom teacher, Mrs. Penley, taught us English, Social Studies, and Science. It comforted me to have several kids from my elementary school in my homeroom class, along with Lee Sims from the Unitarian Church. Freckled, with red hair and a wide smile, Lee also knew me from my "glory days" when I'd given his touch football team fits during games between our respective elementary schools.

A kid seated next to me, Matt Collins, started whispering, "You know, Mrs. Penley wears a mask."

"What?" I asked.

"She's got so much makeup, if she smiled her face would crack."

"You're mean," I said, but I couldn't stop myself from smiling.

Matt's sarcastic comments about our next teacher also conflicted me, but waiting for my upcoming PE class rattled me most. Since the school required every student to take PE, Mom had to work hard to get me excused from the physical activities. Because PE provided important time for students to socialize with one another, Mom arranged for me to stay in class and help around the gym.

At our first PE class Coach Gil, a tall thin man with a pronounced Adam's apple, lined the boys up alphabetically on the asphalt and then shouted over the wind, "Get your mothers to buy one of these along with your gym suit."

He held up an elastic kind of belt and waved it around.

"What do you call this?" he asked.

No one responded.

"An Egyptian slingshot," he said.

Everyone laughed quick, nervous laughs.

"Naaw! It's a jock strap. Most of you have family jewels to protect now, and an athletic supporter does just that."

I looked quizzically at the kid next to me. "Supports your balls," he whispered.

"Now, for some reason Schonborn, over there in the 'S' section, doesn't see fit to participate in PE," Mr. Gil said, looking straight at me.

A hundred heads turned toward me.

"He can hand out towels!" Ron Allen yelled.

Peals of laughter rang out. I cringed and looked down. I hated Ron with a passion.

The next day I checked out balls and equipment to classmates. And, yes, I handed towels to them after their showers at the end of class, never making eye contact. I almost threw in the towel because guys treated me like a girl, and not just any girl, but one with a permanent "bye" in PE because of an endless menstrual period or something.

Dark-haired, swarthy-complexioned Matt confronted me. "You're a sissy.

"Go to hell," I said.

"But, hey, maybe you're pregnant!" he added with mock concern.

Ron and Matt started hanging out together. I avoided them.

Something I couldn't avoid was the fallout from the fact that President Dwight Eisenhower had suffered a heart attack while golfing in Denver. Heart specialist Paul Dudley White, concluding Ike's heart attack hit 3 on a scale of 1 to 5, kept him in a hospital for seven weeks until he could climb the gangway unassisted onto Air Force One.

The media swung into high gear, publicizing the steady increase in the incidence of heart attacks in America since 1910. What I learned terrified me: an epidemic of sudden death now stalked the country, with Ike almost its latest victim. Healthy appearing people dropped dead every day. Would I be next?

The publicity surrounding Ike's heart attack turned me into a full-blown "cardiac invalid."

"I'm worried I'll be next," I said to Mom, for the umpteenth time one day.

"Huh? Well, okay," she mumbled and continued preparing dinner.

I interpreted Mom's nonchalance about my condition as meaning she, too, was worried the Grim Reaper had me in his sights. All this worry hit me at the worst possible time. According to Dad,

"Junior High's an exciting time in life, a time when boys became 'men.'"

I felt incapacitated. I gave up more and more physical activity and withdrew from even my elementary school friends to inhabit my own little world of worry. Anything about hearts unnerved me: Valentine hearts, songs about broken hearts, phrases using the word "heart." It didn't matter whether I really had a hole in my heart; I had a psychological hole you could drive a truck through. I was a mess. Whenever Dad traveled, I worried about his plane crashing because I'd seen a movie about singer Jane Froman's near-fatal plane crash. And when Mom left me alone in the house, I'd worry that no adult would be around should I collapse.

I reckoned I'd received a death sentence, only the time and place were uncertain. Physical death truly had a sting for me because it reminded me of the social death I experienced when people rejected me. Neither Mom nor Dad seemed comfortable discussing death, so I never confronted them with my fears.

Religion gave me no solace, either. Recollection of the Presbyterians' "Yea, though I walk through the valley of the shadow of death" conjured up images of great peril: snakes, craggy rocks, chasms on the way to a premature Hereafter. And the

Unitarian emphasis on social justice, with little apparent concern for everyday fears, meant I would receive little support for my situation. And so I continued to worry.

In due course, though, I decided to confront my fears head on. I befriended a certified blue baby at school, Terrence Crano, whose visage and skin exuded blue as opposed to my purplish blue. I reasoned my darker complexion kept me from looking bluer, like Terrence. I figured since I couldn't participate in sports anymore, I'd hang out with boys who couldn't either. I also befriended Blake Johnson, a boy who walked with crutches, shoulders askew, due to polio.

Polio petrified me, as it did many people. I feared the iron lung most, the coffin-like cylindrical contraption that helped paralyzed people breathe. I'd seen a photo of a room filled with these. They had windows on the sides of the cylinders for viewing the patients' limbs and mirrors at the ends—outside the iron lungs—to allow patients to see activity around them.

Then Jimmy Thomson, the eldest and tallest of the twelve Schonborn cousins, found himself in an iron lung. He played trumpet and had just started restoring a Model A coupe with his dad. Jimmy died just before Christmas. At first, doctors thought he was the first person ever to die of polio after getting all three vaccine shots, but later they discovered he had died of a rare disease that mimics polio.

Through my tears, I told Mom, "The Grim Reaper had no right to take Jimmy."

"Yes, honey, Jimmy died way too soon," Mom said, folding me in an embrace.

For a good week, Mom and I spoke in a flat, affectless way about Jimmy. I wondered if our voices would ever be animated again.

And as if Jimmy's sudden death wasn't enough for me to deal with, more cleft issues knocked at my door. My cleft messed up the bony turbinates that filtered air in my nose, and this made it difficult to breathe through my nose. So, as a mouth breather, I always woke up with a dry mouth. When I caught even the mildest cold, my entire nose clogged up, and I ended up with congested, adenoidal speech.

Also, when I got tired and forgot my speech therapy techniques, my voice became nasal again. And if I became excited while drinking, liquid came spilling out of my nose, to the guffaws of onlookers. To add to my oral-facial distress, my braces still made my teeth hurt much of the time. Just when the throbbing subsided, the orthodontist tightened my braces for another round of hurt.

I sought refuge from my cleft and cardiac worries by crossing the street from our house to my old elementary school playground to hit tetherballs hanging from their poles. I'd wrap and unwrap the balls around the poles, again and again.

One day I noticed a tall, athletic man kicking footballs from a tee. After a while, he asked me if I'd hold some balls because the wind kept blowing them off the tee. I was thrilled, but a little scared, until he showed me how to pull my hand away at the right moment. From then on, I upped my playground visits because I'd figured out he was Gordy Soltau, a San Francisco 49er wide receiver and placekicker; he lived in our neighborhood. After I got to know him, he signed my football. It became a prized possession.

My only true school friend, Lee Sims, got excited about the football, too, and as a result we played many miniature football games using his 1'-by-2' electric, vibrating football field and a tiny felt football.

Lee and I began to collaborate on various class projects for Mrs. Penley. One day, Ron confronted me in class and said, "Lemme copy that paragraph, Karl."

"Hell no," I said.

"Buzz off," Lee said, his fair cheeks turning red.

"Shut up, Shorty," Ron shot back.

Mrs. Penley noticed the commotion, walked to the back of the room, and asked, "What's the matter, boys?"

"Nothing," we said.

She handed us all science papers she'd just graded and returned to her desk.

As we prepared to leave class, I took Lee aside, "Ignore Ron, he's a jerk."

"I wish I wasn't so short," Lee said.

"I wouldn't mind a few inches myself."

"When people ask what I wanna be when I grow up, I say, 'Taller.'"

"Good answer," I laughed.

Ron and his buddy Matt cornered me outside Mrs. Penley's room. "You're a real kiss-up," Matt said.

"Penley loves your ass," Ron snickered.

"Wha d'ya mean?" I asked.

"Who else gets A's on their papers?" Ron said.

"If you did your own work, you'd do well, too," I sneered.

"You dipshit," Ron said.

"Kiss, kiss, Sissy," Matt said.

As they walked away, Ron said, "You're lucky you hand out towels in PE. Otherwise, I'd finish you off."

I dropped my head at first: the Grim Reaper's Charon could ferry me across the River Styx to death, and Ron threatened to push me into Charon's boat. I began to feel threatened and unworthy. Then I remembered Eleanor Roosevelt's admonition and lifted my head up high.

"You're not going to rob me of the satisfaction of getting an 'A,'" I shouted at them.

Later that day I sought out Terrence to ask him a question about purplish-blue skin color. But, a chill ran down my spine when I learned he'd stopped attending school and no one knew why. Had he died? If he had, would I be next?

I decided to revisit the medical section of the local library. I learned that a person's skin might appear purplish or blue if the blood supply is inadequate, if anemia is present, or if veins don't drain well. People with insufficient heart capacity suffer from swelling in the legs, ankles, and feet.

"Negative for me on that count," I said to myself, for reassurance.

Inadequate blood supply can also make parts of the body feel numb.

"Negative, too."

Nevertheless, people with septal defects, holes between the heart's two upper chambers, have few, if any, symptoms.

"Uh-oh. That could be me," I mumbled.

If strep throat turns into rheumatic fever, it can damage valves, causing back-flow and murmurs.

"That could be me, too."

Whatever my issue, I read that heart surgery is always risky and often doesn't solve problems. I blanched and almost cut my research short. Luckily, though, I didn't.

I tracked down information about cardiac problems causing sudden death and learned that heart disease—not defects present at birth or due to rheumatic fever—is responsible for people dying unexpectedly. And heart disease takes years to develop.

"Whew," I uttered.

I—weirdly, no doubt—celebrated by flipping through a history of surgery that included pre- and post-operative pictures of people with clefts. It didn't surprise me to learn that the ostracism clefts often experienced motivated them to get surgery. What *did* startle me was that in some countries, people banished clefts to back rooms due to beliefs, like those espoused in the Old Testament, that clefts had been touched by Satan and made imperfect and impure.

Even in more recent times, great writers promulgated backward beliefs regarding deformities. Gayle quoted her ninth-grade English teacher just a week ago:

"Shakespeare perpetrated archaic beliefs, my English teacher says, which could've got *you* in hot water back then."

Gayle put her hand over my mouth, but I burbled out, "What do you mean? " as I squirmed to get free.

"Shakespeare's ruthless protagonist in *Richard III*, for example, convinced audiences for centuries that Satan had touched deformed people."

I didn't feel impure or sullied by Satan, but I realized some of my classmates might be uninformed about clefts and, therefore, have a low opinion of me. I decided to reverse any negative opinions I encountered and work at being accepted. And if I wanted acceptance, I knew that I'd better be accepting and nice to others. I already asked people about themselves a lot, making them feel special, but now I vowed also to be less judgmental, to give people the benefit of the doubt.

I recognized that this constituted a "friendliness campaign" and, as such, might allow me to do well in student government. That might give me a shot at appearing normal—maybe even provide a way to get girls to like me, since now I couldn't use sports. Paradoxically, student government would involve talking and public speaking. But I thought, *I can improve my speech through exercises even if I can't do anything about my heart. I have some control over my problems.*

So, after practicing diplomatic friendliness for a few months—by copying my dad's gregariousness—I told Lee, "I'll help you in your campaign for a student government position."

"Great! And if I win, I'll help *you* run for office."

Lee won. And in the next election, with Lee's help and campaign advice from Gayle, I prevailed and won a position, too. I reveled in my victory. I stood tall when Lee said, "I guess some kids think you're okay."

Over time, as I got better at winning votes, I avoided the top spot of any school organization, since presidents had to give speeches, often at assemblies. Vice-presidents could keep quiet in public, so I only ran for V.P. slots.

Lee often remarked, "I guess you want to be a bridesmaid, Karl, never a bride."

In the process of creating a new persona, I decided to listen to another internal sign: my "art murmur." I took an art class in school where I sketched and painted. In earlier years I had drawn a lot, mostly cartoons of superheroes and of my own creation: a caped Captain Cleft, who took vengeance on bullies and always won girls' hearts. My drawings and artwork had evolved now, but I still had to haul Dad into my room to see my latest stuff.

Dad *did* praise me readily for successful writing assignments.

"Congrats on the bang up job on your Johnny Tremain essay!" he said when I'd barely let anyone know the grade, let alone flashed the paper around the house.

I'd rewritten a paper on a novel set in colonial Boston about Tremain, a silversmith who had to give up his craft after spilling melted pewter on his fingers, leaving him with a deformed hand. He later helped the colonists rebel against England.

Over the summer, I helped Lee insert advertising supplements into newspapers and then fold his papers into "tomahawks."

"I'm amazed you're able to get those tomahawks to land on even the smallest porches as you ride by."

"You could learn to do it."

"I don't have the stamina to ride my bike *and* carry the heavy newspaper bags."

I did have the strength, though, to ride Lee on the handlebars of my bike from time to time. One day—passing some Jeffery pine trees with a lavender, almost vanilla cookie, fragrance —I said, "I dare you to put your foot in the front-wheel."

"You're a crazy mother," Lee responded.

I repeated the dare, God knows why, on other carefree days in the summer.

School began on a high note with a field trip to California's Gold Rush Country. The first night, Lee and I teased a precocious, well-developed classmate in our hotel room.

"Let's play strip poker," I said at one point.

"You gotta be kidding," she said, though with an alluring laugh.

"Come on, we've heard you love to play," Lee urged.

The three of us continued to banter and joke around for an hour or two. Once or twice, Lee and I each brushed against her breasts while feigning clumsiness. He and I walked on the wild side that night, and, luckily, our teacher and chaperones never heard about it.

While hormones drove my attraction to the girl, my artist's eye and sensitivity to "looks" drove my interest in female faces. If beauty was in the eye of the beholder, I saw beauty every-where. I liked copper-brunette Carol-Jean Thompson—with wide-set, pretty eyes—who grew up around circuses as a little kid. She and her hesitant smile hung out at a roller rink where she'd hold hands with me while skating to *Earth Angel*. I loved the feeling of her soft delicate hands in mine and the solid sound of our roller-skate wheels on the hardwood floor. Yet outside the rink, Carol-Jean remained standoffish with me.

And so, I joined the marching band as a drummer in order to be around Carolyn Moore, whose short hair and warm smile also cast a spell over me. She flirted with me, but may have been too busy as a cheerleader to bother having a boyfriend.

Carolyn played flute. Lee played oboe in the school orchestra and clarinet in the band. Gayle truly had a knack for the clari-net and performed Mozart's Concerto in A at the all-girl talent show, known as the Girls' Jinx, at Palo Alto High School, Musicians capable of breath control surrounded me, but I couldn't blow up a balloon or even pop bubblegum.

Moreover, the wool uniform and heavy drum I had to march with in the band made me feel faint on warm days. So I quit the band and joined the orchestra.

Miss Welch said, "Don't play the snare drum. I can teach you the tympani."

"But I can't distinguish notes. My clefts affected my hearing."

"There aren't many tympani notes to master. I'll help you."

I did like playing the tympani but always worried about making loud mistakes. A black kid, Billy White, in the percussion section kidded, "When you mess-up, Schonborn, you stand out, just like I do."

"There you go again, being sensitive to being black, White."

"I can't help it."

"I know. I'm sensitive to 'facial' discrimination the way you are to racial discrimination."

As the timpanist for the All-City Orchestra, I got to know David Packard, the son of one of the founders of the newly created Hewlett-Packard company. Though David attended a different junior high than I did, the Hewlett kids went to Jordan. I knew Eleanor from music classes and her brother, Walter, from math classes. And I also knew, very slightly, a girl with a haunting voice who sang *Scarlet Ribbons* at the Girls Jinx. Her name was Joan Baez. My sister had introduced us. At the time, we were all just Palo Alto kids.

In due course, I found hammering the tympani in a symphony didn't impress Carolyn, and I said to Dad, "If you buy me a drum set, in return I'll stick with the tympani."

"There you go again, bargaining around drums," Dad said.

"I'll even pay for my own trap-drum lessons and for accessories like a hi-hat."

"Okay, if you mean the thing with two cymbals that goes 'ker-chunk.'"

Several kids, including Pat Flaherty from my neighborhood, helped me form a band, and we played a number of gigs, including one at a Unitarian Youth party. I concluded after a while, though, that band guys had trouble keeping girls. You could get them to go with you to a party, but you couldn't dance with them while you played your hot music. Someone else did.

Backed up by Matt's cutting words, Ron Allen still used his size to intimidate me and his muscle to shove me out of his way when it suited him. This troubled me less than it used to because I'd met enough other "outsiders,"—outcasts, minorities, and handicapped kids—that I didn't feel so alone anymore. Also, I had caught up to other boys in height and weight and my voice had deepened, giving me some "heft" vis-à-vis Ron. Oddly, my changing voice undercut my newfound confidence now and then, when it would break into a squeaky falsetto.

I freaked out, therefore, when my Social Studies teacher, Mr. Burns—who'd assigned us topics to debate in class—asked me to join Lee and two other students in a debate in front of the Palo Alto School Board. The topic: "Should the filibuster rule be dropped by the United States Senate?"

People packed a large room, a mass of mothers in swirling dresses and fathers in intimidating suits and ties. Lee and I had prepared like crazy, but I shook from head to toe. My questionable heart thumped fast and loud. I didn't hear the applause as Superintendent Dr. Henry Gunn introduced us.

I heard myself begin an opening salvo at the podium:

"The Filibuster Rule guarantees the minority will always have a say. Take it away, and the Senate is reduced to a tyranny of the majority."

When I finished, Dan Jacobson from the opposition stood up and fired away.

"But Senator Wayne Morse from Oregon just wasted everybody's time last week by talking for twenty-two hours to oppose the Tidelands Oil legislation!"

A few minutes into the debate, I sensed this might be fun after all and whispered a rebuttal idea to Lee, who was up next. When my turn rolled around again, I asserted, "The judgment of filibustering minorities is usually well-founded—filibustering has only killed bad bills. No important legislation defeated by filibustering has ever been subsequently enacted in a later session of Congress."

The opposition's Verity Cook let loose again.

"The House doesn't allow filibustering, and it's more representative of the people than the Senate."

Lee shot back, "The House needs the filibuster as much as the Senate because without filibustering, there's no freedom of speech!"

And on it went until Superintendent Gunn ended the debate and said, "You all did so well, I can't decide which side won."

Among the school board members who applauded us was Dave Packard. He, along with Bill Hewlett, had just taken Hewlett-Packard public after moving the company to a new set of buildings in a 200-acre expanse Stanford had set aside from its land holdings for light-industry. Mr. Packard sought me out and clasped his giant hands around my right hand. "Atta boy! Your side hit the nail on the head. This country is all about freedom and freedom of speech."

"Thank you," I said, beaming and feeling on top of the world.

Mom and Dad seemed to be relishing the moment as well.

During the summer of 1957, Mom kidded that our house—with friends, relatives, and dinner guests passing through—had become Grand Central Station. One important visitor was Grandma Schonborn. Grandpa had just died, and Grandma missed him. By then she had already had two heart attacks, so she rested in bed most of the time with a tall, green oxygen tank standing ready nearby. Her steady decline plunged me back into worry about my own heart. When she died in August, I convinced myself my heart would be the next to fail.

I cried for both Grandparents and the loss of their love which I'd felt all the years I'd lived with them or next door to them. The tears fell for me, too, for I disliked the sorrowful, downcast, pessimistic side of myself that had reemerged.

At the start of ninth grade, Miss Dingman, in Ancient History, talked about the Greek orator and statesman Demosthenes.

"He stammered and mumbled as a boy," she told our class.

"But statesmen back then had to speak in a loud, clear manner," I said, remembering that they spoke outdoors and before microphones had been invented.

"Yes, he built strength by reciting verse while running along the seashore and shouting to be heard over the roar of the waves. His determination to overcome his speech impediment even led him to practice talking with pebbles in his mouth."

That night I practiced my speech drills with gusto for the first time in a long while.

The next day, Miss Dingman showed us a picture of a rugged part of Greece, which she said comprised the city-state of Sparta. She continued, "While creating an army that defeated the Persians, and later the nearby Athenians, Sparta examined every newborn for deformities."

"Just like Hitler did," Lee piped up.

"Correct you are," she replied. "They threw deformed and weak babies—who might not handle the rigorous, mandatory military training—into a gorge."

This frightened me, but Lee's mention of Hitler's eugenics bothered me even more because the Nazi purge of the handicapped had occurred in the recent past. Luckily, that sort of thing didn't happen in the U.S., though I'd heard of nasty things happening to minorities and those with mental illness.

I later got some insight into congenitally caused handicaps in Biology class from Mr. Sperry.

"Heart defects form in prenatal stages—at five or six weeks, or even at nine weeks when arms and legs, fingers and toes form," Mr. Sperry said during an embryology discussion.

"That's when cleft lips and palates happen," I said, remembering Mom telling me about them.

"And do you know why clefts happen?" Mr. Sperry asked.

"No," I admitted.

"Well, no one knows. It's a real mystery. Researchers are looking into folic acid. They think that a lack of it—or Vitamin B9, as it's also called—in pregnant women might be a causal factor for clefts."

I couldn't wait to get home to tell Mom. She looked in her nutrition books and found that leafy vegetables, citrus fruits, beans, and whole grains contained folic acid.

"I think I ate enough of those back then."

"Did you do anything different before you had me, compared with Gayle or Scott?"

"Not that I know of. Why?"

"Just curious, that's all. Not trying to blame you or anything. By the way, Mr. Sperry also told us about the 'golden ratio' of symmetry—1.618. It's expressed in many of nature's creatures and shows up in measurements of Mona Lisa's face and those of other 'beautiful' people."

"Well, you know symmetry isn't everything, hon."

But symmetry may've been why I loved staring at Mom's face, beyond her light blue eyes and delicate skin. Her well-proportioned face, perfect nostrils, and full Cupid's-bow upper lip left my visage in the dust.

On a brisk, sunny November afternoon, while walking home carrying my autographed football which I'd just shown to a new kid in the neighborhood, Ron and Matt ambushed me again.

"Gimme that!" Ron demanded, grabbing hold of the football.

"No! Leave it alone!"

"C'mon, let go," Matt said.

"It's mine!" I shouted.

"Not anymore," Ron said, brandishing it in the air.

Robbed of my only claim to fame, I shrieked, "It's special. Gordy Soltau signed it."

"Bullshit! You don't know Gordy Soltau from Shinola," Matt said.

"His name's right here!" I yelled as I lunged for the ball.

"You wrote it yourself!"

"No, I didn't!"

I pulled on the football to get it back, but Matt pushed me hard, and I fell to the sidewalk.

"You don't need it, you're a benchwarmer for life," Matt scoffed.

I got up, but Ron's well-placed punch between my shoulder blades knocked the breath out of me. Bent-over, I stared at them as they ran off, shouting, "Squish nose! Duck face!"

As I slowly straightened up, I fought off tears and the temptation to give into feelings of inadequacy and misery. I resolved not to be Ron and Matt's fool or doormat ever again. I tucked in my shirt and carried on with my day, not even telling Mom, though she sensed something had happened. I fantasized about taking up Dad's sport of boxing to get even, but of course, my cardiac condition nixed that. Those bullies just weren't worth dying over.

I refused to let a couple of bullies define me or my attitude toward the world. Resorting to violence would only drop me to their level. But Ron had my autographed football, and I had to do something. I wracked my brain for just the right tactic and after some time came up with a plan, but I'd need Lee to make it work.

"I gotta stand up to them," I told him. "Otherwise I'm gutless, half a man."

"They're pecker-heads," Lee said.

"I've come up with a Hail Mary plan, but I need your help."

Lee grinned in anticipation. "Count me in."

The next day, I met Lee at a spot where I knew Ron and Matt would be walking home after junior varsity football practice. We hid behind some bushes, and I opened the shoebox I'd brought.

"Fantastic," Lee said as he looked inside at the contents.

"Shhh…not too loud."

"Hey, here they come," said Lee. "Get ready."

I jumped out in front of Ron and Matt and said, "You like footballs so much—catch these." I grabbed two "water" balloons from the box and let 'em fly. They each hit their targets and popped.

"What the—?" Ron bellowed. "It's paint!"

"God damn it!" Matt yelled, as he wiped red paint off his face and shoulders.

I took out the remaining two balloons and heaved them, scoring direct hits again.

"You—" Ron shouted as he lunged forward, but slipped.

"You mother-fucker!" Matt screamed as he raced toward me.

By then, I was gaining on Lee who'd started the getaway bike a moment before. I jumped rear first onto his longhorn handlebars as I'd done many times before. Matt almost caught us, but we got away unscathed. I couldn't believe how and elated I felt. Deep down, I sensed I'd finally lost the fear I had of Ron and Matt. I also realized I'd gained a friend for life, the best buddy a guy could ever have.

Carolyn Moore liked me enough to let me walk her home once in a while. Her sparkly blue eyes, crescent-moon arcs highlighted with eyeliner, seemed to squint and smile at the same time.

"Tell me about her," Mom said one day.

"Her perfect mouth rivals yours," I said.

Mom smiled.

"She has a younger brother named 'Bo,' and her parents' new Plymouth with sleek tail fins puts our Plymouth station wagon to shame."

I took Carolyn to the school's Valentine's Dance. Her skin glowed. Her light brown hair glistened. She smelled like a bouquet of flowers. It was the first time I'd gotten close enough to a young woman to notice such things.

I loved holding her hand during the pauses between dances.

Carolyn's father drove us home after the dance, and when my brief visit with Carolyn ended, I gathered my courage and tried to kiss her goodnight on her porch. She let me kiss her, and I marveled at the perfectness of my first kiss. I "floated" home that night as I walked the three blocks between her house and mine. I looked at myself in the mirror and ran my finger over the irregularity of the red flesh of my upper lip. And despite the scar that extended upward to my pushed-in left nostril, I smiled.

I dreamed of driving Carolyn to and from dates. I wanted to drive so bad that one day, with no one home, I decided to practice rolling Grandpa Schonborn's '52 clutch Plymouth sedan—which Dad had inherited—out of the carport and driving it back in. Piece of cake. After releasing the emergency brake, I rolled the car out a car-length and serenely braked it to a halt. Putting the key in the ignition, I smiled smugly and turned the key.

The car lurched forward, crashed into a carport support post and snapped it in two, leaving jagged ends looking like the two ends of a broken lance.

"Holy shit," I yelled.

I felt stupid…scared that the roof might fall or Mom might drive up. Mostly, I felt like an inept knight who'd botched carrying off a fair maiden. Soon, fear kicked my brain into high gear. I had to work fast or the carport might collapse.

I grabbed the car jack from the trunk and, placing a long two-by-four on the jack shoe, wedged it under the carport roof. I jacked up the corner of the roof six inches, which allowed me to match up the two jagged ends of the support post. Next, I lowered the roof with the jack, guiding the ends of the post until they reunited. The brown stain on the posts was undamaged, and no one could tell the post had ever been hit. In fact, I didn't tell anyone what had happened until I reached the safety of young adulthood.

Carolyn invited me to a Rainbow Girls dance at the local Masonic Lodge. We slow-danced to *Somewhere Over the Rainbow*, she in a formal dress and I in a new suit. I experienced "ecstasy," a term Dad had had engraved inside Mom's wedding ring. I even fantasized Carolyn might be willing to date only me.

After all this, though, I failed to get a goodnight kiss.

I complained to Lee, "I don't get why I've lost ground since the Valentine's Dance."

"She's holding back?" Lee asked.

"Yes. Maybe 'cuz of my face. Or my voice. I think it gets nasal, snuffly when I'm nervous around her."

"You don't want to hear this, but someone told me a tall football player has won the other half of her heart."

"Damn!" And after an uncomfortable silence, I said, "I'm gonna fight for her."

I resolved to win over her whole heart. I knew charm and coaxing on my part would make Carolyn mine. That would be my summer project.

"Dare me to put my foot in your front wheel," I challenged, as Lee rode me home on his handlebars one afternoon.

"Someday I'm going to," he said.

"Can't decide," I joked, "if I'm a spokes-man or a stunt-man."

"For that brilliance, go ahead and do it," Lee countered.

Inhaling a quick breath and tensing up, I replied with bravado, "Okay, I will. Just remember, this is for science. Nothing more, nothing less."

"Hurry up, dammit!"

"I'm getting ready. Give me a second."

I then jammed my left foot into the spinning wheel. In an instant, a sickening, end-over-end crash accompanied the twanging of breaking spokes. Then silence.

Lee got up off the asphalt and raced over to me.

"How's your foot?"

I flexed it. "It's not broken."

"Check out this busted wheel. It's hopeless."

"Your dad's gonna kill us," I said, hobbling around clutching my foot.

"I just need a new wheel, not a new bike."

"Let's not tell anyone about this," I said, "even though science experiments are supposed to be published."

We never again spoke about the "broke spokes" episode, though we did debate which of us went haywire first that day.

At an end-of-school Unitarian Youth party, Lee fast-danced to *All Shook Up*, but I held out for a slow dance because I'd gasped for breath during *Whole Lotta Shakin' Goin' On*. Lee and I enjoyed meeting a visitor to the youth group from the other junior high in Palo Alto: dark-haired Sharon Belton, who resembled Audrey Hepburn. Like me, Sharon had a blond-haired younger brother.

"Genetics can play some weird tricks," she said.

"My brother and my clefts can attest to that," I responded, laughing.

Sharon attended the Episcopal Church in town but confessed that Unitarians threw better youth group parties; that's why she had crashed our party. She danced with me several times, and during a lull late in the evening, I asked, "What do you think about girls who flirt?"

"I don't like them," she said. "I don't have a big enough bust to flirt."

Dad won a helicopter ride at a school fundraiser, and despite misgivings about my heart, I agreed to ride in his place. The chopper lifted me straight up one afternoon in a noisy but thrilling ascent. Sitting in a plastic bubble looking straight down scared me at first, but the pilot calmed me by his confident manner. As we sped along at 120 miles per hour, I saw how the electronic industry's tentacles had spread everywhere.

"Hewlett-Packard's buildings stand out amid others. See them there, in Stanford's light-industry park?" the pilot said, pointing.

"Yes!"

We then flew north over Redwood City to see the Ampex buildings.

"Ampex created the first videotape recorder," the pilot noted. "In fact, rumor has it that employee Nolan Bushnell is inventing a video arcade game, and Ray Dolby, a new sound system."

"Wow," I gasped, barely soaking everything in.

The pilot turned on a dime and flew south to show me the immense hangars for blimps in Sunnyvale and a huge blue cube being built to house the Air Force's satellite test center. As we wound-down our trip, I saw more "crop circles"—the hallmarks of Eichler tract-home developments—which had gobbled up more and more wide-open fields and orchards.

One early-summer night, for some hare-brained reason, Lee and I decided to sleep on the flat roof of my old elementary school. We each told our parents we would be sleeping at the other's house. Up on the roof, we talked, watched the stars, and finally fell asleep—until swift kicks woke us before dawn.

Officer Michenski drove us to our respective houses in the darkness. As he dropped me off, he said "I'll be calling your parents in a few hours."

A mix of guilt and shame swept overwhelmed me

"You guys will probably spend time at Juvenile Hall." Lee and I looked at each other, fear in our eyes.

I jumped every time the phone rang that day, but Officer Michenski didn't call. A few days later, I thought of confessing to Mom and Dad, figuring they'd been contacted in my absence. I even thought of running away, becoming a fugitive for the rest of my life. I waited a week and then a month for the police or my parents to confront me. No one ever did.

Nonetheless, toward the end of the summer, I knocked on Lee's door one Saturday.

"Lee's not here," his sister said. "He got on a plane yesterday for Boston."

"I can't believe it," I said.

She explained that her parents had shipped him off to attend Phillips Academy in Andover, Massachusetts. I wondered what triggered their decision. Had they figured out some of our escapades? Had I been a bad influence?

Sitting down on the curb in front of Lee's house, I cradled my head in my hands and fixated on the pavement, trying to stifle tears. When I got home, I looked up Andover in the encyclopedia and learned it ranked among the fanciest of boarding schools. I'd have to wait until Christmas to see Lee again.

To make matters worse, just as my campaign to win over Carolyn reached a crescendo, she told me her family had to move to Los Angeles. I cursed my fierce fate and found myself over the next week going through the motions of wishing her luck, saying goodbye, and promising to write.

I'd experienced a double whammy, with Lee and Carolyn gone. As a result I felt upset, cheerless, and depressed, but I didn't share my feelings with anyone. My two confidantes had departed, and I didn't think anyone else would understand. Alone and abandoned, I felt vulnerable with high school starting in a few days.

PALY HIGH

THE MERE LOCATION OF Palo Alto High School—across the street from Stanford—terrified me. Situated on the western, older side of town, "Paly" (the school's nickname pronounced pal-lee) boasted dramatic Spanish-style buildings with red tile roofs and an auditorium and bell-tower campanile dating back to 1919. Enrollment strained campus resources, with tenth-, eleventh-, and twelfth-grade classes each numbering around 400.

During the first several weeks of school, social groups and cliques formed around me. Some like the Gents Club formed by chance. Others formed by design, such as the school social clubs that tended toward obscure initials (G.I.G., R.I.F.) and names like Bonzer Coves and Carae Amicae.

"Why does the school paper feature the exploits of the 'in' crowd?" I asked Gayle, knowing she'd worked on the paper once.

"It's like gossip," she said, "people want to know about the attractive and the well-off."

"I feel left out...scarred face, no money."

"It's hard! I know about money woes myself."

I missed Lee Sims. For some reason, I didn't think to write him, and phoning cost too much. I also didn't want to ask anyone why he'd been "shipped off" to Massachusetts, thinking I might've been the reason.

It was 1958. Palo Alto, and much of America, pressured people to conform, especially regarding physical appearance. At Paly, girls had to wear matching fuzzy socks and sweaters. Guys had to wear belt-in-the-back Ivy League khaki pants—not the mail-order Sears Roebuck ones I'd grown up wearing. Guys also wore button-down Oxford cloth shirts. (In reality, I loved my white, narrow-striped Oxford shirts.)

However, styles kept changing. Once-mandatory saddle shoes gave way to suede white bucks, then to tan desert boots. By the time I got my desert boots, everyone else's showed the dirt and scuff marks of age. Craving acceptance, I asked a neighbor,

"Can I throw my new shoes on your roof?"

"Why would you want to do that?" he asked.

"I need to make 'em look old. Rolling down your steep roof and banging on the ground a coupla times will do the trick."

Even more than acceptance, I longed to have a girlfriend. Whenever an attractive girl gusted by, I acted like a downed electrical wire, sparking and jumping all over the place.

Despite presenting a happy façade to the world, my soul blubbered and snuffled as much as my speech once had. Forlorn, I retreated to television and sitcoms like *The Life of Riley*, *The Ann Sothern Show*, and *The Danny Thomas Show* (I loved Marjorie Lord). And then, an epiphany one day while watching *Leave it to Beaver*…

Rather than yearn to be the All-American Wally who always "gets the girl," I resolved to "get a life." I'd stop using TV to distract me from my loneliness. I'd become an independent operator and a universal citizen. I would cope with the cliques by floating among them, belonging to none. And I'd do what I'd been successful at in junior high: student government and debate.

"I can help you with your political campaign," Gayle offered,

"That would be great."

"Since my boyfriend's president of the Legislative Council, he can endorse you."

Not surprisingly, this help allowed me to win a seat on the

Council representing my class. Alas, my arch nemesis, Matt, also won a seat.

But so did John Hand. A student government star in junior high with whom I got along well, John helped me counter Matt's attacks and obstructionism on the Council. We often had help in this regard from several girls on the council, including breathtaking Leilani from Hawaii.

Stanford University and the leaders of an embryonic Silicon Valley pressured Paly to respond to the Sputnik gauntlet the Soviets had thrown down the year before. Their pressure to "hothouse" Paly's curriculum with more math and science coincided with initiatives by Harvard University to get high schools across the country to offer advanced placement college courses.

Besides this academic pressure, many high schoolers endured psychological pressure as part of the first generation born in the shadow of nuclear weapons and the doomsday scenarios they engendered. And so it was no surprise that Joan Baez's pacifist mentor, Ira Sandperl, came to Paly to talk about nonviolence. Joan had just graduated from Paly where she developed a reputation for always having a new song *and* a new dress. Of late, she also had a new singing venue—the coffee houses of Harvard Square.

Ira, as Sandperl liked to be called, had been invited by my English teacher, Mr. Leon, to teach our class about nonviolence and its relevance to our fear of nuclear war.

Ira began by saying, "A couple years ago, Joan invited me to speak to *her* English class. Because I wasn't authorized by a faculty member, your vice principal immediately threw me off campus. Said I was too radical."

After our class stopped laughing, Ira went on to say, "Tolstoy and Thoreau, along with Gandhi, not only wrote brilliantly, but also helped develop the modern ethical philosophy of nonviolence."

Ira's humorous, anecdotal style—and above all his stories about Gandhi—entranced our class. His final pitch for nonviolence appealed to me as a way kids might defend themselves from bullies.

Yet, soon after Ira's visit, skepticism about nonviolence crept into my brain like fog: I'd already learned in history classes how Hitler executed not only Jews and political enemies during the Holocaust, but also people born with birth defects. My Germanic surname wouldn't have saved me either. Could nonviolence have saved me and others, such as my handicapped Electronics teacher Mr. "Hank" Martin? He had a high voice, crippled fingers, and a limp that forced him to walk with a cane.

John Hand told me Matt always called Mr. Martin "Hopalong Hank." While I smiled, I thought of Kathy Philbrick in my English class and Miss Hill, my fourth-grade schoolteacher, both crippled from polio. I told John,

"Mr. Martin's got arthritis of some sort. Matt's a mean bastard."

"But he's got a pretty girlfriend," John replied.

"Poor girl. What's her name?"

"Sharon Belton."

"Sharon? Jeez, I met a Sharon last summer during a church party. From another junior high. Looks like Audrey Hepburn with blue eyes."

"Yeah. That's her. She's here at Paly now, even though you'd expect she'd go to Cubberley High. I guess school-district boundary lines shift between junior and senior high."

"We've got a big tenth-grade class, but I'll keep an eye out for her."

Some days later I ran into Matt, who'd been somewhat restrained during our encounters after "seeing red" with Lee and me.

"Hey man, people are saying you talked to my girlfriend," Matt challenged.

"Yeah, I met her last summer. Hardly said two sentences to her."

"Well, stay away from her!"

"Look, any girl who likes you is of no interest to me."

Still restricted from PE, I continued to hand out towels. A cluster of coaches surrounded me now. They pushed Paly kids to excel in sports, just as Paly administrators pushed them to get results across a wide range of sports. Coaches Wiser, Jamieson, and Mercer doubtless considered me a slacker, while more generosity flickered across the faces of coaches Fisher and McWilliams.

I couldn't avoid seeing Ron, who had PE the same hour I worked in the gym. One day he confronted me.

"Hey, pencil dick, why don't you hand out towels to the swim team in the afternoon?"

"Get lost," I said.

"Matt and I have made the varsity swim team already."

"I should care?"

"Whatever happened to Lee Sims, anyway? A flunk out? A frickin' loser."

"He's back East…far away from assholes like you."

Later that day, I complained to John during a student government meeting that I didn't like swimmers.

"Well, Milton Saier is a swimmer, and he's a great guy," John said.

"You're right, I guess. It's just certain swimmers—Ron and Matt."

"You know Matt's from an old, wealthy San Francisco family."

"Yeah, I heard. You'd think he'd be a decent guy, instead of a bully."

Although I'd decided to be an "indie" rather than join cliques and clubs, I did join one as part of my campaign to be accepted: the school-sponsored Forum Club. The club debated various national and international issues, sometimes against students from other high schools. Mr. Leon led the club, much to the delight of girls like my friend Jean Herz who said, "He looks like Yul Brynner, only more handsome."

As "s"-sound nasality still plagued me, before I'd debate a topic or "perform" in some way, I'd practice a speech-therapy phrase to decrease it. "The snow sufficeth, it sufficeth us," I said.

"You're odd," fellow debater Jean said.

I repeated, "The snow sufficeth, it—"

"Well, you can be odd as long as you give the opposition hell today."

"I will."

And I did, helping Jean and the rest of our team beat our opponents, who argued that funding for schools should be dependent on teachers swearing loyalty to the U.S. Words—in debate, in particular—came with less difficulty now because in Latin class, we learned about prefixes, suffixes, and word roots besides learning about the Roman Empire. For a dead language, Latin could be pretty lively.

I continued to like skate-girl, Carol-Jean Thompson. But she ran with the performing arts crowd, and I rarely bumped into her. So I pretty much admired girls from afar. At one noontime sock-hop, I stood around awkwardly in the gym with my hands in my pockets to keep them warm. Amazingly, a twelfth-grade friend of my sister asked me to dance. Trying to look suave and together as we danced, I couldn't believe this curvaceous beauty had asked me to dance. I held her hand when the music stopped and peppered her with enough questions that when the music started once more, she had no choice but to slow dance with me. She did seem compliant when I pulled her close. I began to think this could be something real.

Then, when the music stopped, she said, "I really must get over to the gym entrance and sell tickets to latecomers."

"W-What?" I mumbled.

"Your sister's counting on me to make this sock-hop a success."

My shoulders slumped, and I jammed my hands deep in my pockets again. Conway Twitty's *It's Only Make Believe* started playing as I shuffled to the edge of the gym, thinking, *I know why she asked me to dance. I wish I were boyfriend material.*

That night, as my head hit my pillow, I thought of my sister's friend's breasts against my body as we slow-danced. I felt my body heave, my groin ache. Since Scott and the family hadn't come home from a church function, I considered yielding to the strong urgings of my body, which washed upon me regularly like tides these days. After mentally wrangling with the contradictory Unitarian and Presbyterian messages about masturbation, I gave in to my nocturnal urges. Even though lustful urges brought with them the possibility of "eternal damnation," I found them to be awesome new emotions.

Still, I wanted a girlfriend in the worst way. I put a photograph I'd found of a pretty girl in my wallet. She was my pretend girlfriend. Unlike a child's imaginary playmate, though, I didn't talk or play with her. I just showed off her picture now and then to impress complete strangers, usually males my age.

I talked to John Hand a lot about my difficulties with girls… and sometimes I talked to Mom.

"I just want to look normal, Mom."

"What do you mean 'normal'?" she asked. "A boring, perfectly regular face?"

"Yes."

"I think you have more important things to worry about."

And so I did. I still worried about not having a normal heart. My cold hands seemed to be a sign that I had poor circulation. If I knew I'd have to shake hands with someone, I'd rub my hands or sit on them, to warm them. But when they did get warm, they'd feel clammy. I couldn't win.

In due course, though I grew tired of worrying and sitting on my hands on the sidelines. I resolved to "get some backbone," as Great-Grandma Lydia often counseled her husband, Grandma, Mom, or anyone else caught in a moment of weakness. I threw out the imposter in my wallet and, despite my cold hands, decided to take ballroom dance lessons at Beaudoin's Studio, where more girls than guys had signed up. Mom and Dad considered the lessons an expensive frill, and so I had to do chores around the house to pay for them.

Whenever I talked to girls now, I cradled my chin with a hand, looking thoughtful when in fact I was covering my scars with my fingers. When someone photographed me, I'd turn my head a tad, favoring my right profile over my left with its smashed in nostril. I'd even choose seats on the far side of classrooms so kids could only see my right profile.

I asked Mom to write Dr. Cox to see if my nostril could be fixed. She agreed to write, but mostly because she needed the dental X-rays she had lent him. Dr. Cox responded saying I needed to give my face more time to mature before I'd be ready for reconstructive surgery. He did say the ugly peg tooth growing out of my cleft had enough bone that my dentist could cap it when my braces came off.

The time had come to see if my self-improvement program was paying off. I literally had to put myself on the line, the phone line.

"I hate the phone…I hate calling girls," I told Mom, who'd noticed me staring at our phone on a desk in the main hallway.

"Then don't," she said. "But remember, you wowed 'em at the Ma Bell phone exhibit."

I picked up the phone receiver and dialed all but the last digit, paused, then slammed it down. Mom slipped away.

"Courage," I muttered to myself and dialed the complete number this time.

"Hi. This is Karl, the guy...er...you met with Kathleen...er... at the Youth party."

"Oh. Hi," she said. And then, after hesitating, "How'd you get my number?"

"I asked information for it. Kathleen gave me your last name."

"I didn't think I'd given it to you,"

"The reason I'm calling...I was wondering if you could go to a dance at Paly with me next Friday."

"Gee, I can't..."

"Some other time then?" I asked.

"Well, I don't know...Say, Karl, I've really got to go now. I'm expecting a call," she said.

"Oh, sorry...Bye," I said.

I suffered the same fate with two more girls.

I pounded my fist on the desk, shouting, "I'll never get a date!"

Mom came into the hall and put her hand on mine.

"Yes, you will."

"When I finally master the phone, the good ones will all be taken," I said, wallowing in self-pity.

"Not true. Many of the good ones take their sweet time to date. You're sixteen. Be patient. You've got lots of time."

That Friday, dateless and still concerned about my hearing and my heart, I turned to a library for solace and some answers. Stanford had just moved its medical school from San Francisco to Palo Alto, and, as a PR move, locals were invited to visit its library. At one point I trembled when I read that clefts often experience "conductive hearing loss due to Eustachian tube dysfunction." The book's print blurred for a long moment.

Then, later, reading that "recurrent infections can lead to middle ear tumors" rattled me even more, given that I got earaches every time I caught a cold.

But I soldiered on and checked the *Index Medicus* for further information.

Handing the reference librarian a note with years and volume numbers, I said "I need *Pediatric Cardiology* and *The American Heart Journal* for these issues."

"Keep your voice down. Whisper. This is a library."

"I'm sorry," I whimpered, turning red as I noticed others staring at me.

I'd been scolded plenty in libraries for not whispering. Whispering had always been difficult for my messed up vocal apparatus: either I spoke too loud or too soft. I knew I had to develop a "decent" whisper someday or suffer the continued wrath of librarians and people sitting around me in movie theaters.

I plowed through an armful of journals about heart defects, thanking Miss Schmit's Latin class for helping me understand many of the medical terms. One article spelled out how German measles and advanced strep throat could cause dreaded valve defects and their backflow murmur noises. Although I may have had red-colored skin rashes typical of these afflictions, in all probability I'd never had either disease.

Then a real bombshell: an article stated that clefts are prone to having swollen abdominal arteries that can rupture, causing instant death. Cold sweat beaded my forehead.

"Jesus Christ," I said aloud. I clasped my mouth, realizing I didn't whisper.

I carried on to avoid fainting. An article described clefts with Marfan syndrome, which includes holes between heart chambers and something called patent ductus arteriosus, PDA. I should have stopped there, but no dice. I unearthed more about the mysterious PDA. Left untreated, PDA results in excess blood in the heart, causing it to fail sooner or later. I had several of its nefarious symptoms: breathlessness, fatigue, heart-rate fluctuations, and bluish dusky skin. I stumbled out of the library in a daze, hoping I might have at least one girlfriend before my heart gave out.

I agonized about my situation for days. Then, a simple, blinding insight: I had no time to waste, and I'd been wasting plenty of it. Whatever time I had left in my life, I'd better get to living it. I decided to run for elective office again and cast a wider net for romance.

At the start of the eleventh grade, my classmates elected me to Legislative Council, but re-elected Matt, too. However, I had enough allies on the council that he couldn't intimidate me during meetings.

I told fellow council member John Hand, "Leilani continues to distract me, but a pretty newcomer is draining off some of her electrical charge."

"Do you stare at both of them during council meetings?"

"Afraid so. Guess I'm guilty of 'looksism' or maybe worse."

Early in the school year, our council debated changing the school dress code and reforming student government, which involved, among other things, abolishing our own council. Changing the dress code passed, but, when it came time to vote on abolishing the council, none of us voted to give up our positions. I learned something about "power" that day.

While I managed to get dates with girls I considered friends, almost sisters, I gave up "cold calling" girls I didn't know well. I did try to meet girls at dances out of the area. A classmate and his older brother took me to a few dances near Santa Cruz. Held outdoors on a huge wooden floor illuminated by colored lights, the dances turned menacing when brawlers started fighting over girls.

I found something more my speed when I attended a Quaker retreat led by Ira Sandperl and bookstore owner Roy Kepler, a pacifist, in November in Marin County, just north of the Golden Gate Bridge.

Ira started the retreat off by asking, "What can just one person do about war and peace?"

Most of us attendees just looked at one another.

"A lot, it turns out." Ira said. "We'll explore many possibilities this weekend."

During the retreat, I explored romantic possibilities, too. I met many wonderful girls and decided to attend future retreats, including a weeklong one held at Lake Tahoe on the topic of non-violence and national defense. Still, despite all the kind-hearted, do-good pacifist girls I met at various retreats, I never got anywhere romantically.

Over the Christmas holidays, wanting some winter warmth, Mom and Dad drove the family to northwest Mexico to camp outside the Sea of Cortez village of Puerto Penasco, and for a time I stopped obsessing about girls. The family enjoyed Mom's *huevos rancheros* for breakfast, her tacos for lunch, and her enchiladas for dinner. When not eating spicy food, we hung out in our tent on the beach enjoying a respite from work and school routines. We played among the sand dunes and one day visited nearby lava fields. Immense moon-like craters fascinated all of us and Scott in particular, as he had been studying geology in school.

Despite being a temperate time of year in the Sonoran high desert state, our fishing and shrimping village suffered record-high heat and humidity late in our visit. The sun kicked into overdrive, leaving me enervated if no palm tree, palapa, or cabana on the beach gave me shade. The day before departing, we explored the village of Puerto Penasco under a brutally hot midday sun. As we trudged through the village, beads of perspiration drenched my shirt and shorts. I slowed my pace. My heart-defect research raced through my brain. But as the intense sun continued to bear down on me, thoughts of death and being cremated soon gripped me.

"Dad, I gotta stop," I pleaded.

"C'mon, son," he said, "it's not that hot."

"But I can't go on," I mumbled.

"We're not far from the car."

"I'm going to sit down."

"No, you're not," Dad said.

"I'm feeling faint."

"You're not gonna faint," Dad said. "Tough it out."

I sank to the ground and sat.

Everyone stopped, and Scott said, "He's turning red."

Mom confronted Dad. "It *is* hot, honey. He's not used to it."

"You're spoiling him," Dad fired back. Looking straight at me, he said, "Get up. Be a man."

I got up and started walking. My sandaled feet scraped alongside one another. My heart pounded, so I imagined it exploding, and telling Dad, "I told you so." I kept looking straight ahead. One foot. Then another. Then, the dirt road became blurry. It began to swim.

"I'm dizzy."

"You're too much into yourself, son," Dad said.

I couldn't breathe. I descended into my own personal hell, thinking of the valley of the shadow of death. My knees buckled and I lost consciousness.

SCHONBORN REBORN

I COLLAPSED ONTO THE dirt road. Dad quickly moved me into some shade, where Mom poured carbonated water into my mouth and over my face. I slowly came to.

"You must drink the rest of this water, Karl," Dad said, handing me the glass container of bottled water. "Scott and I will go get the car."

Mom and Gayle kept reassuring me I'd be okay.

Back at the campsite, I rested under the shade of a tarp Dad and Scott had hastily tied between the car and the hot tent. While feeling better physically, I felt worse emotionally. My cardiac limbo frustrated Dad, and though he meant well, his stinging words hurt big time. I felt misunderstood, dismissed, beaten down.

That night, despite feeling listless, I managed to sleep on and off in the sultry heat, which didn't break until after midnight. In the morning, Mom declared, "I think your color is much better. Keep drinking water, though."

"I bought more bottled water at the store last night," Dad said.

My energy slowly returned. On the trip home, Mom made sure I kept drinking bottled water until we got to the U.S. border where I filled my canteen with safe water again.

Mom took me to see our family physician and explained what had happened. Dr. Robertson asked her about nausea, muscle cramps, and my fluid intake; and then he turned to me and said,

"Your reaction to the heat came from dehydration and your heart problem."

Mom pounced, "Can you explain 'heart problem' better?"

He replied, "I've told you all I know. But, luckily, a new X-ray machine has just been perfected—a kind of fluoroscope with an image intensifier. Cardiologists can watch hearts in motion now."

"Can they watch Karl's?"

"Well, the nearest machine is in San Francisco."

That day, Mom scheduled a fluoroscopic exam for me, and a week later we made the long drive to the city. On the way, Mom said, "You should have no problem with the chalky-tasting milkshake you'll have to swallow."

"That's easy for you to say," I responded. Then after a long pause, I scowled, "This better be worth it."

"Hold your arms up like a giant 'V,'" Dr. Collert ordered.

"Do as he says, Karl," Mom said.

"Hmmm," Dr. Collert purred as he studied my heart beating in black and white on the large X-ray box between him and me. "Interesting."

"What's that mean?" I asked.

"Don't talk. Hold still."

After a long silence, when the tension grew unbearable, Mom asked, "What do you see, Doctor?"

"Well…"

"Well?"

"Hold on, let me check another angle," he replied. "Turn to your left a bit, Karl."

"My arms are getting tired," I said.

"Just a bit longer," Dr. Collert exhorted. When he finished, he told us he had to do some calculations and left the room.

As I dressed, I fumbled with a thousand buttons and buttonholes, none of which I could find or match up. When I settled down at last, all the defects and diseases I'd read about sped through my mind. Then Mom and I walked down the hall to Dr. Collert's office.

"So?" Mom asked, almost pleading with the doctor.

"I didn't see anything irregular. Really, he—"

"Yes!" I yelled. A spasm of pure joy forced my four limbs outward like a Russian kick dancer's. I almost fell off my chair.

Dr.Collert, with a quick chuckle, turned to me and said, "You don't have a tetralogy, PDA, or any other serious anomaly. And if you have a hole between your heart chambers, it'll close up over time."

"My God. That's wonderful!" Mom said…then broke into tears.

"Hal-le-*lu*-jah!" I said, embarrassing my inner-Unitarian. My heart pounded with joy and almost sprang from my chest. I'd never been so pleased to hear it pound. "I did hear a murmur, but it's functional."

"Functional?" Mom asked, struggling to regain her composure.

"I mean 'innocuous.' Probably, the murmur is a naturally occurring sound of blood whooshing through his vessels, valves. Nothing to worry about." Then, addressing me again: "Go out and play all the recreational sports you want to. Just stay away from competitive, varsity sports."

"Why?" Mom asked, causing my ears to perk up.

"Because we cardiologists and our gadgets aren't infallible. Like Dr. Robertson, I'd rather err on the side of caution."

Mom glanced at me.

She then asked why I'd suffered from the heat in Mexico when no one else in the family had.

Turning to me, the doctor said, "Likely as not, you had heat exhaustion as well as an anxiety attack."

"Anxiety attack?" Mom asked, puzzled.

"Yes. A number of my restricted youngsters—and certainly many of my heart attack oldsters—become anxious about their hearts. It's understandable, given all the unknowns, and especially if there's also a birth defect like a cleft. They, and perhaps you, Karl, perceive themselves as more frail and incapacitated than they really are."

"But Karl *is* frail now," Mom said.

"Yes, but he can become strong. We know that the less active people are, the more out-of-breath they get upon exertion. So a self-fulfilling prophecy's at work."

"I get it," I said. "I need to get back in shape. Though not too fast."

"Correct."

Dr. Collert had it right. Anxiety had turned me into a cardiac invalid; a heart patient who, afraid he'll drop dead at any moment, needlessly limits his exertion. My years on the sidelines had, if anything, worsened my condition by preventing me from staying in shape. No wonder I didn't have the stamina needed in Mexico.

On the way home, I said, "I consider myself reborn."

"Unitarians don't believe in that."

"Well, my old self has died."

"You mean your old self-perception has died."

"Yes, and I'm still living, and so I'm reborn."

Dad had trouble accepting I'd been a cardiac invalid: that is, psychologically incapacitated. He didn't understand the way Mom did that the mind can, in effect, steal the body. A person can become neurotic about health; and anxiety, all by itself, can make a person sick.

On my part, I decided if my mind could deceive me, it could also rehabilitate and heal me. I'd just have to adjust my attitude. I vowed, therefore, to do as much as I could to rebuild confidence in my body. The time had come for a full-scale heart offensive.

First, I needed to get off "restricted" PE status. Mom and I met with PE coordinator Mr. Jamieson.

"He's pretty much been given a clean bill of health," Mom said.

"What? An invalid one day, an athlete the next?" Mr. Jamieson bellowed.

"It's not that simple," Mom replied. She told him about Dr. Robertson's pessimism and then the new X-ray machine that allowed Dr. Collert to be more sanguine. She concluded, "The teen growth spurt stresses the heart, and so some restrictions may've been good for Karl. Dr. Robertson just went overboard."

Mr. Jamieson frowned at me and asked, "So what *can* you do?"

"I…uh…can take part in most sports," I answered, "Only I should start out with care."

"Okay, okay," Mr. Jamieson said. "We'll try to manage PE-Lite for the Turnaround Kid."

Before actually being allowed to play basketball or touch football, I had to jog the perimeter of the athletic field several times over a number of days with a coach watching in case something happened. And I had to deal with classmates confused by my move from "inactive" to "active" duty." Only humor would help the reinstatement of this "pup," as the National Football League termed players "physically unable to perform."

On my first jog, I alternated running and walking and clowned around whenever kids looked my way. In fact, my first lap around the field was no laughing matter. The panting, sweating, and gasping for breath reminded me of collapsing in Mexico. But, day-by-day, bit-by-bit I grew stronger. Before long I wished I could open up and push myself as I had in elementary school. I longed to run full throttle, to pump my arms and legs—run like a cheetah—but in my head, I kept hearing Dr. Collert's call for caution.

Soon though, I started playing right field in baseball, lineman in touch football, and guard in half-court basketball. But I realized I had to practice to get up to speed again, so Scott and I shot hoops, fielded softballs, and tossed footballs at nearby Green Gables.

When kids questioned my new circumstances, I'd say, "My old religion used to forbid exercise. Now, my new one requires it...plus sex, drugs, and rock 'n' roll."

Turnaround Kid, for sure.

A downside to my new bill of health: my parents required me to do more challenging family chores. Besides mowing the lawn, I had to help Dad work under the family cars. I did not like the greasiness, the confinement, and the cramps I got holding tools just so. Still, I did like the togetherness of working with Dad, especially when we built stuff.

Some days I had to hold lumber in place for him so he could nail it. Other days I held large pieces of plywood while he cut them on his table saw. One day, he tried to flick a little piece away from the furiously spinning blade and ripped his hand and thumb so badly he had to have surgery and countless stitches. He lost movement and feeling in part of his hand. As a result, though he gained feeling, at least so I sensed, for some of the medical challenges I'd faced.

As the school year progressed, I fretted over doing well, since colleges focused on marks earned in the eleventh grade. Latin, Chemistry, Algebra II-Trigonometry, and Advanced English had killed off better students than me. I ended up working nonstop, firing up my academic after-burners. The only effortless moments in my day came in my art class, which I took, in part, to lighten my load.

I liked sketching better than painting: I thought of it as "drive-by" painting—fast and satisfying to the artist if not to the art model (the "victim?"). At the end of my class, I'd bump into Sharon Belton every so often since she took an art class after mine.

I asked her at one point, "Why does your boyfriend object to every suggestion I make in Leg Council?"

"Matt's not the most positive guy. Even puts me down."

"He still calls me 'Lip' and 'Smush Nose.'"

"Yeah, he got that from Ron."

"Well, tell Matt he can't hassle me in Council next year. I'm running for vice-president of our class."

"I'll vote for you. I'm sure you'll win."

Since success had eluded me on the dating front, I decided to cast my net beyond Paly and pursued an intriguing girl from Cubberley High, whom I knew from Unitarian Youth. We had flirted after Youth meetings for months and found ourselves alone in her house one evening. We kidded around on her couch and began to make out. I summoned all the courage I had and moved a hand to her blouse and breasts.

"Stop! My mother will kill me," she said.

"Uh? What?"

"She'll be home any minute…but kiss me again."

As I went to kiss her, she pushed me away. I fell back on the couch, placing a pillow over my lap. My mind wasn't the only thing aroused. When she noticed, she asked me to leave. She avoided me at Youth meetings after that.

Then one day, out of the blue, I got lucky…in the guise of sexy "Red" Halpern. More mature and less conventional than most girls, twelfth-grader Red debated alongside me in the Forum Club and fired guns as a member of the rifle team.

I kidded with her a lot, saying, for example, "This is my rifle. This is my gun. One's for killing. The other's for fun."

She remained matter-of-fact until one day she invited me to her house by a dry creek. After introducing me to her parents, she took me down into the creek and to a point well hidden by bushes and trees.

Red knew how to kiss with her lush lips. After a while, she led my hands to her breasts which I felt through her brown sweater. I soon slipped a hand under her sweater, feeling her warm skin and silky bra. She kissed me even more fervently. My hands travelled under her bra, and I reveled in getting to second base at long last. I couldn't stop smiling when I left her that night.

This became a repeated activity. Every so often I'd visit Red, say hello to her parents, and go to the creek to fool around. She never let me unsnap her bra or go any further. Nonetheless, I finally felt like a man, delighting in the pleasures of the flesh. Red and I didn't date in the usual sense. She insisted we keep our trysts a secret from everyone.

Sharon yelled at me in the hall one day as I whisked past her. "Don't bother saying 'Hi.'"

I stopped and turned towards her, saying, "Sorry. In a hurry, I guess."

"You like older women?"

"What do you mean?"

"Red."

"Bye," I said, turning and walking away. "I'm late for Forum Club."

How Sharon had found out about Red baffled me. I didn't know whether to be embarrassed or proud.

The many college admission tests I had to take during 1960 almost returned my anxiety level to that of my cardiac invalid years. Stories of older Paly students getting perfect SAT scores freaked me out. I missed the deadline for taking the Preliminary SAT on Paly premises, and had to go to the sprawling Stanford campus and ferret out an obscure building for the test. I appreciated knowing I wouldn't faint, since the timed, pressure-laden test triggered heart-pounding, panicky moments.

I thanked my lucky stars, though, that I'd kept up with world affairs which the PSAT test covered. Paly Forum Club debates on politics and international issues dovetailed well with Unitarian Youth meetings, where we argued politics more than religion. A big difference between the two enterprises stood out: at Youth meetings we also sang songs from a certain local singer's first album.

After Paly, Joan Baez had moved to Boston with her family and enrolled in Boston University. But her voice yearned to sing. She dropped out of school and sang in Cambridge coffeehouses and on the streets around Harvard Square. This led, with astonishing speed, to a recording contract and her first album, issued a mere two years after she graduated from Paly. I played that thrilling album over and over.

Just as the school year ended, Mom's mother, Rosa, died of cancer at seventy-three, and Mom went to Longview, Washington, for the funeral. When Mom returned, she didn't cry or show a lot of emotion around us. I wondered: *Was Mom "keeping it in" for our sakes? Did she cry when she was alone or at Grandma's service?*

One rare evening after Grandma's death, when Mom and Dad had to be out for dinner, Mom said to me, "You and Scott should fix yourselves some spaghetti."

She had left a large, stainless-steel stock pot on the stove with an inch of clear liquid in it. Untutored in the culinary arts, and with Gayle away at college, I added more water to the pot and boiled some spaghetti. After adding tomato sauce and a few pinches of Italian Seasoning, I summoned Scott to the table and we inhaled the spaghetti.

When Mom got home and discovered I'd cooked pasta in the pot with Rit dye remover, she freaked out. She phoned Dr. Robertson in an instant. He asked her to read him the warning on the side of the Rit box.

"DANGER: Harmful or fatal if swallowed," she read. She

looked at Scott and me, fear-stricken, as she continued. "Avoid contact with skin or eyes. Contains basic zinc sulfoxylate formaldehyde."

For a few moments that stretched out forever, we all waited for the doctor's reaction.

"Did they add water to the dye remover?" he asked.

"Yes," said Mom.

"Does anyone feel nauseous?"

"No."

"Then I wouldn't worry. If anyone feels nauseous tonight, induce vomiting and come to the hospital."

It was a long night for the family, but no one needed hospitalizing.

During a summer job, I found myself running a "death camp" at the Palo Alto Medical Research Foundation, ironic for someone who'd feared death for so long. I fed bright-orange azo dye to rats to give them cancer so research doctors could study them. At one point, I met Blair Chapman, the lively daughter of one of the researchers—a kind of Dr.-Death-meets-perky-Doris-Day moment. Whenever Blair visited the lab, she kept me in stitches. Ever so often, we went to the nearby Peninsula Creamery for milkshakes. I looked forward to her visits.

Late summer found me transfixed in front of the TV as John Kennedy wrestled the Democratic nomination from Adlai Stevenson, who had twice lost to Ike. Even more fascinating were the Kennedy-Nixon debates, where Nixon found himself too intense for the new, casual medium of TV. I watched Nixon use more forceful debating skills and yet lose to calm, smooth Kennedy. I wondered, *Will I ever have the confidence to debate in front of an auditorium of people, let alone an audience of millions of TV viewers.*

One of the topics in the TV debates, the education-and-missile gap between the U.S. and the U.S.S.R., hit home in a big way since I struggled in my AP, advanced placement, courses. Mr. Martin taught my AP Physics class, which national experts had created in a hurry to help America win the space race.

Just as ornery in Physics as in Electronics, Mr. Martin loved to rail at our lab group in his New York accent.

"I want youse guys to stop and think about relativity," he'd say as he pointed an arthritic index finger at us.

"But we don't get it," I'd proclaim, speaking for my hapless group.

"Youse guys!" he'd respond in a high-pitched voice, waving both hands in the air. "You never get it. I can't believe you're in AP Physics."

Kids belittled him behind his back. The harder the physics got and the lower kids' grades became, the more the name calling and mockery, an early lesson for me in scapegoating.

My twelfth-grade AP English teacher, Mr. Vittetoe—an egghead, Adlai look-alike—didn't want to prepare us just for writing-skills exams, but for a life where words and precision with them mattered. A stern taskmaster, Mr. Vittetoe flunked me on my first essay and gave me middling grades on my next few attempts. Finally, after an essay on *The Scarlet Letter*, in which I wrote about strategies Hester Prynne might use to reduce her stigmatization, he proclaimed "This is very encouraging, Karl."

"Thank you," I mumbled.

"Decided to get down to work at last, huh?"

In another essay on *The Scarlet Letter*, I wrote that the killing of cleft kids in poor countries amounted not only to a peculiarly vicious form of eugenics, but also to "cosmetic murder." I had been inspired to explore the treatment of people with stigmas and disabilities by scriptwriter Dave Lewis, wheelchair-bound due to a baffling disease contracted on Okinawa during World War II. I knew Lewis as a fellow Unitarian where he moved with ease among church buildings saying witty things in a deep, deliberate voice.

While I enjoyed writing essays and getting passing grades from Mr. Vittetoe now, I did not enjoy battling Matt. As class vice president, I had to come up with enough funds to pay for the "Senior Ball," which unfortunately involved going to the Legislative Council for money. I had to fight Matt tooth and nail, but prevailed after several council sessions. After one of these sessions, I bumped into Sharon, who was waiting for Matt outside the council room.

"Did you know Matt calls you 'Stick?'" I asked, having overheard Matt use that term for her.

"Better than 'Skinny,' I guess."

"Try being called 'Smush Nose,'" I said.

She paused. "What if I call you 'Special K,' after the cereal?"

"Fine by me." I tried to sound casual, but Sharon surprised me.

Suddenly, Matt walked up, startling us both. He glared at me and said to Sharon, "Call him 'Smushed' during the week…and 'Smashed' during the weekend."

"Shut up!" Sharon retorted. "You're the drunk, not Karl."

I started thinking about colleges. Mom believed I would apply to Stanford and Cal Berkeley, but I saw Stanford as too familiar and Berkeley as too big. Mom then encouraged me to "think East Coast," and this encouragement, plus Gayle's success in getting into a good college, propelled me to "reach for the moon" just as President Kennedy was urging the country to do literally. *East Coast*, I thought. *How about Ivy League?*

Since I couldn't afford to visit far-away colleges, I looked carefully at their promotional materials and their course catalogs, which sometimes had pictures. Yale appealed to me for many reasons, among them the fact that forensic icons like John C.

Calhoun, Daniel Webster, and William F. Buckley, Jr., debated within its hallowed walls. Regular debates against Oxford's celebrated debate teams set the standard for Yale's teams. I wrote application essays for Yale and other schools on debate-like topics, such as "How should our society deal with its dissenters?"

Mr. Vittetoe wrote one of my recommendation letters. He touted his good students as energetically as a coach might promote his or her star athletes. Mr. Bunton, who taught me Chemistry, wrote another.

"Karl dreamed up a chromatography experiment where he separated out the various colors in black ink," he wrote. "His sophisticated experiment impressed me."

The prospect of admission interviews dredged up old worries about my nasal speech so I practiced some of my old exercises. Venture capitalist William Draper, III, interviewed me for Yale at his Sand Hill Road office. Known later as the "Godfather of Silicon Valley," Mr. Draper listened with interest to my reasons for wanting to attend his alma mater. I left the interview feeling good about Yale and my chances for acceptance. By contrast, I didn't like Harvard's *group* interview, where an idea was thrown out and candidates had to fight over airtime. It reminded me of coaches tossing a ball into the midst of their players, and rewarding the one who got possession of it. *Was Harvard looking for someone aggressive or someone thoughtful?*

Even though I now qualified as a BMOC and was tall, suave, and moneyed enough to date fellow twelfth graders, I found that Stanford freshmen monopolized the time of many Paly girls my age. So I chased the younger ones, and after being turned down by several for the Senior Ball, got an enthusiastic "yes" from Blair Chapman, whose side-splitting humor kept me laughing over banana splits the summer before.

With a date secured, I hunkered down to help organize the ball, managing to rent the posh Menlo Circus Club. This would be Paly's first off-campus dance in twenty-five years. It would feature an eight-piece band. For PR purposes, I had to appear in a dreaded photo shoot with our tall class president and pretty class secretary. As always, I presented my best—my only—profile when the flashbulbs went off. I let myself smile, since I'd just gotten my braces off and my cleft-tooth had been capped.

Blair and I had a great time at the ball, but, surprisingly, dancing a time or two with Sharon excited me the most. And Matt's vehement objections didn't cause the excitement. He no longer intimidated me.

For the remainder of the school year, I flirted with Sharon and she flirted back, mostly via eye contact. I found it perplexing, this end-of-school mutual attraction with Sharon, a girl I once intensely disliked for being Matt's girl.

At one point she asked me, "Who're you taking to grad night?"

"You," I said.

"Too late. Matt already asked me."

"Well, I guess I'll have to ask McMurray," I said in jest.

"McMurray? My best friend? Don't you dare!"

As college responses rolled in, Dad seemed as thrilled about the scholarship I'd won to Yale as the acceptance itself. I knew, though, that I'd measured up to his high standards at last.

On graduation day, Grandpa Stenerson phoned me: "I'm so proud of you, Karl. High school graduation's great, but getting into Yale's really special."

"Thank you, Grandpa."

"You know, my brother's son went to Harvard. Smart boy, but not smart enough to choose Yale."

Mom said the gold and silver seals on my diploma—recognition for academic and extracurricular achievements—impressed her. I told her I relished being voted friendliest kid in the class.

I attended grad night with Liz Kuhn, a good friend, and

danced a couple of times with Sharon despite Matt's "I've-been-betrayed again" looks. Later I wondered, *Am I attracted to Sharon to spite Matt or do I really like her?*

Bill Hewlett came up with an idea of hiring a bunch of local kids for the summer to groom them to become future electrical engineers at HP. Sixteen of us from eleven different area high schools got a rare chance to work while we learned about the burgeoning electronics industry. We worked the first half of the summer in engineering labs (fascinating) and the second doing assembly-line tasks (not so fascinating).

Bill and partner Dave could be seen from time to time around the Stanford Research Park building, usually in white shirts and ties, sleeves rolled up. The "HP way" of doing business had started, and suit coats remained on coat racks. Bill reminded me of myself: earnest and warm, but restive and always worried that things could go wrong "in a heartbeat." His physician father had died when Bill was twelve. Like me, Bill lacked imposing stature.

Dave Packard, on the other hand, was born with it all and had a quiet confidence as a result. He'd lean against a desk or slouch against a wall while talking to people, perhaps to downplay his six-foot-five frame. Just as bright as Bill, Dave always joined Bill at company picnics at Adobe Creek Lodge, cooking and serving burgers to us employees.

Late in the summer, I went to a party for students from the San Francisco Bay Area going to Yale. I met a sophomore named Bill Fink, who rowed crew at Yale and who talked me into driving east with him in September. I also met a fellow freshman admittee, Steve Clark, a tall, blond-haired kid. Relatively quiet, Steve differed from the rest of us "talkers" at the party. A naturally gifted "doer," shattering records in every pool in which he swam, he was arguably the fastest swimmer in the world. He'd just set a new world record for the 100 meter freestyle.

PREPPIES, PUBLICS & ARCHIES

IN THE PRE-DAWN MIST, Dad shook my hand and wished me well. Scott did the same.

"I love you," Mom whispered.

As she hugged me, I sensed her beginning to cry.

"I love you, too." I said. "And I'll be back soon at Christmas."

Everyone waved goodbye as I rode off with my companions—Bill Fink from Atherton who wanted help driving his car to Yale, and Lee Sims who had to get back to New England for his last year of prep school. Much to Mom's relief, our heavily laden car couldn't go faster than 60 mph.

The three of us rolled into Chicago several days later and headed for the *Chicago Sun-Times* building. We toured the newspaper's offices and then parts of Chicago with the paper's editor whom the Sims family knew. We spent the night with the editor's family.

Early the next day we continued east and approached New York City as its lights slowly came on in a dazzling display. The noise and energy of the city both thrilled and intimidated me as we passed through it. Eventually we reached the Connecticut Turnpike, and the warm, muggy air of a New England September night rushed through the car. As we sped toward New Haven, Connecticut, my excitement grew.

"See you back home in three months, buddy," I said to Lee as we dropped him off at the bus station for his trip north to Massachusetts.

"Give 'em Hell, Karl."

Bill and I parked at Yale's Phelps Gate and schlepped my stuff a short distance to red-bricked Lawrance Hall. Sweating from the nighttime humidity, I appreciated having my room on the first floor and close to the campus cops at Phelps Gate, should I have a medical emergency. Mom had requested such a set-up in a moment of "over protectiveness." Alone for only a moment in 173 Lawrance after saying goodbye to Bill, I heard a ruckus outside the door as my two roommates arrived. They'd grabbed a bite to eat at the Yankee Doodle Café.

A tall, fair-haired guy with well-chiseled features extended his hand and said, "I'm Bryce McGregor, from Darien."

"I'm Karl Schonborn. Where's Darien?"

"It's between here and New York City," Bryce said, his voice exuding money and something else. I couldn't tell.

The other fellow—a taller, more symmetrical version of myself—reached out his hand. "I'm Ned Hooper. Nice meeting you."

"Where'd you prep?" asked Bryce, as he looked me over.

"Huh?" I said.

"He means 'Where'd you go to school,'" said Ned.

"Oh, Palo Alto High. Near San Francisco."

"Public school, eh?" Bryce mumbled, turning to stare out the window.

"How about you guys?" I asked.

"Hotchkiss," Bryce said, still turned away.

"Horace Mann…in the Bronx."

"Oh," I said, not having heard of either.

"What d'ya think of the 'turd turret'?" Bryce asked.

"Turd turret?"

"Our bathroom, outside the door, is in one of our building's turrets," Bryce said.

"We share it with the guys across the landing," Ned said.

Even though I had arrived a day early, Ned and Bryce had

beat me by a few hours and staked out their turf: Bryce had talked Ned into letting him have the single room—something about never having had privacy at boarding school. So Ned and I were relegated to the double, off the living room. I brushed my teeth in the bathroom—a round, tiled room—and, too tired to stay up late, said "Goodnight" to the others while they hung a Yale banner in the living room. Exhausted, I lay down on my mattress without bedding and, pondering the prep school mystique, fell asleep.

The next morning, after looking out my back window at the amazing New Haven Green—a sixteen-acre town commons, home to three churches—I walked into the living room where Bryce was putting empty beer bottles on the fireplace mantle.

"Wow!" I said as I looked out the front window at the red brick buildings arrayed around a quadrangle called the Old Campus. "I can't believe this place…now that it's daylight." "Never been here?" Bryce asked.

"Only seen photographs."

"I feel like I grew up in this place. My father, grandfather, lots of uncles went here."

The Old Campus and its tree-rich lawn surrounded by mostly colonial-style buildings housed nearly a thousand eighteen-year-old males in one place. The buildings served as halfway houses, easing us into Yale's rigors and sophistication.

Nothing could have prepared a Californian like me for what I saw as I walked across the campus to breakfast at the dining hall several blocks away. Yale was a time-warped world of the past—mostly Gothic—unlike anything I'd ever seen before. I wandered among large, gorgeous neo-Gothic buildings, many with small grotesque gargoyles and gnomes tucked away in the strangest places.

After breakfast in the huge, white-columned Freshman Commons, I continued walking around the campus. Some of the buildings I passed were residential colleges for non-frosh undergraduates: Gothic-style—and in a few cases, colonial-style—edifices enclosing large lawn quadrangles and surrounded by shallow moats filled with plantings. A few modern buildings under construction struggled into existence amid the Gothic splendor of the undergraduate buildings, the Law School, the Hall of Graduate Studies, and the Payne Whitney Gym—dubbed the House of Payne.

Soon I encountered the people that came with the buildings. Freshman orientation week meant meetings with advisors, reading-comprehension assessors, proctors of impossibly hard placement exams, and tour guides showing off Yale's impressive library. I often hung my head, feeling overwhelmed and intimidated. I thought, *Will I flunk out before even starting? And will I flunk the complicated physical exam at the Gym?*

I had barely passed the pushups, sit-ups, and swimming parts of the exam when technicians drew my blood, had me fill a test tube with saliva, and "checked my posture" by taking front, back, and side nude pictures of me. The last dubious exercise was based on an achievement-physique hypothesis later proven bogus; protests and lawsuits eventually ended the taking of "posture pictures" at male and female Ivies.

After all the testing, I found myself sitting with Ned and Bryce in ornate Woolsey Hall listening to President A. Whitney Griswold say,

"A third of you freshmen have been number one or two in your schools academically and nearly all the rest of you, honor students. Over half of you hail from private prep schools."

Bryce nudged me with his elbow.

The President continued, "Your class has stalwarts from twenty-four foreign countries and every state in the U.S. except Montana. Yale's a serious place and will pour on the work. Indicative of this, faculty will call you 'men' and address you as "Mr." from now on."

In the course of a few minutes, I'd gone from being Karl, a

lowly high school student, to Mr. Schonborn, an adult with all the privileges and responsibilities thereof. I experienced my first pangs of homesickness and wondered, *Do I belong here?*

My roommates and I walked together back to Lawrance Hall after the President's convocation. Ned wore his dark hair slightly longer than most of us crew-cut West Coasters did and had attentive, slightly bulging eyes. I learned he hoped to qualify for the Freshman Glee Club, having a tenor voice from God himself, the same god who'd gypped me out of a decent voice and nose. Bryce, in full prep wear, seemed straight out of a clothing catalogue for golfers, especially one that sold garments with lots of small animal icons. He said he hoped someday to have the largest beer bottle collection in the U.S.

Back at Lawrance Hall, Bryce pounced on me: "See, you public school guys are outnumbered. The President said so! And tell me, how many Californians are there in our class?"

"Maybe 40," I said.

"Pathetic. There are 70 here just from the Phillips Academies—Andover and Exeter."

"Well, *some* of us Californians do come from Cate, Thacher, and other west coast prep schools," I said, having just boned up on prep schools in the Columbia Encyclopedia.

"They don't count. Gotta be one of the Eastern Fifteen—I just read it somewhere. Yeah, here in the *Atlantic Monthly*." He threw the magazine at me. I found the article and the list included the Phillips Academies as well as Middlesex, St. Paul's, Lawrenceville, Groton, Kent, St. Mark's, St. George's, Taft, Brooks, Choate, Deerfield, Milton, and Hotchkiss.

"That's it," said Bryce. "Just fifteen. Read 'em and weep."

"So, you're an upper-class Preppie, and the rest of us are under-class Drones?" I retorted.

"Exactly," he said.

"Welcome to class warfare in America," Ned declared. "I sense a crumbling of Jefferson's notion of democracy here."

So that was the other thing Bryce's voice exuded: Entitlement. Not to say arrogance.

Bryce and Ned represented two of the more interesting challenges I'd face at Yale—old-money Preppies and exceedingly bright big-city kids, often called "Archies." Both pushed me out of my comfort zone at the time, so I excused myself to scour my course catalogue for classes to take.

To indulge my growing interest in medicine—and at least keep open the option of going to med school, I resigned myself to taking a pre-med science course each of my four years. But I still had a chance to take many courses from Yale's sprawling elm tree of knowledge. After consulting with my advisor, I selected my classes. I ended up with Chemistry, Calculus, Political Science, Sophomore English, and beginning French every day at 8 a.m., comprised solely of freshmen dumb enough to choose so early an hour for such a class.

Actually, the first week of classes I tried another introductory French class, but the lightning-fast pace drove me into the more relaxed class of Nancy Regalado, a comely recent Wellesley grad. At the time, female instructors, let alone female professors, could be counted on one hand at all-male Yale.

To be able to eat breakfast and get to class on time, I depended on my new Zenith clock radio. Every few mornings, Bryce would scream through the walls: "Kill that goddamn alarm!"

"Sorry," I'd say as I struggled to silence it.

"Why're you going to that *French* class, anyway?" he'd growl.

"Don't want to miss a thing…besides, Camus excites me."

"Christ, how'd I end up with a Weenie for a roommate?" Bryce would yell.

Bryce and other Preppies derisively called kids like me from the public school system, "Publics." Fair enough. But I disliked being called a "Weenie," Yale students' pejorative term for the socially awkward and overly studious. I considered myself neither, but Bryce had caught me studying in the basement of Connecticut Hall where known Weenies studied.

Connecticut Hall—the oldest building on campus with a statue out front of Yalie Nathan Hale regretting he had "but one life to give to his country"—seemed an unlikely place for "unmanly" Weenies to congregate. I often fled to Conn Hall's basement if I couldn't concentrate in Lawrance, usually when Bryce got louder and louder after he'd emptied more beer bottles for his collection. Upon going to bed, I'd sometimes grin while flicking my alarm clock on, knowing payback—in the form of a loud alarm—loomed just a few hours away for Bryce.

Bryce and others also called Science and Engineering majors Weenies, so we pre-meds tried to distance ourselves from those majors, who often wore pen protectors in their shirt pockets and slide rule calculators on their belts. Maybe I shouldn't have been so smug, because Chem and Calculus threw me for a loop. Those classes added academic shock to the weather shock (humidity) and culture shock (assertiveness) that I experienced in the East. To keep up, I put in 18-hour days of relentless studying. Ultimately, I narrowly escaped getting a "first warning," where the Dean asks students with grades below 70 to see him "at one's earliest convenience."

Mother Yale required us to wear coats and ties. I didn't mind because it meant I'd be able to fit in, at least sartorially. A tie, blue blazer, and khakis became my uniform. On hot, humid days, some Preppies, tired of dress codes throughout their schooling, just wore a coat, a tie, shorts, and shoes. No shirt. No socks.

I wore a different uniform, a white busboy's coat, when I worked inside the Freshman Commons dining hall for my scholarship, bursary job. As I chowed down one day before slinging hash, a fellow "bursary boy" exclaimed, "Damn! You eat a lot."

"Big appetite, I guess."

"Chairman Mao's got a big appetite, too."

"But he also devours women, alcohol, and adulation," I said.

"Look, I'm 'Stark.' Jerry Starkweather to be exact."

"Great name, 'Stark.' I'm Karl Schonborn."

"Schoenberg…Schorn…Hell, can I call you 'Schorny'?"

"Why not? I've been called worse."

Since my cardiac invalid days had involved little or no stair climbing, I often dreaded flights of stairs, even after being freed from my invalidism. Yale's classroom buildings, with their numerous flights, challenged me on a daily basis, and I took my pulse surreptitiously on the landings amid students rushing by. Likewise, I'd check it when biking up Science Hill on the rickety bike I bought. If my pulse was high or my heart seemed stressed, I'd walk the bike for a time.

After a while, I realized that my shortness of breath stemmed from being out of shape. I grabbed some funky gym clothes and headed for the "Cathedral of Sweat"—the other nickname for the Gym because benefactress Mrs. Payne Whitney had wanted her donation to help build yet another campus church. A none-too-alert octogenarian, she never figured out her money went to build a cathedral-like gym instead, featuring pools, rowing tanks, and a basketball amphitheater stacked on top of each other.

I ran a few tentative laps around the rooftop track. Track team guys in snazzy shorts and tops whizzed past, as did profs, grad students, and faded track stars from the community. I alternately ran and walked for fifteen minutes before exploring the rest of the immense Gym, amazed by a bunch of rooms with high ceilings and low doors and by half a century of "manliness" captured in photos lining the walls of the enormous, fifteen-story structure.

As Bryce rushed out the door to attend an open house for potential recruits to the Fence Club (a.k.a. Psi Upsilon fraternity), he scoffed at my vow to return to the Gym every week to reclaim *my* manliness, which I'd lost during my invalidism. I looked at Ned, lounging on our ragged sofa.

"What's with those rooms with pint-sized doors at the Gym?" I asked.

"You mean the squash and racquetball courts?"

"I've never seen them before."

"We use 'em when we can't play tennis outdoors in the winter like you Californians."

"And you use little, hard balls?"

"Yes. Did you know—the smaller the ball here, the more status-y the sport?" Ned asked.

"What?" I exclaimed.

"Preppies aren't too wild about playing with big balls, like footballs and basketballs, even softballs. Too ordinary."

"But you're a Preppie."

"Horace Mann's not your typical prep school. A day school. No boarding. Lotsa New Yorkers. Lotsa big city kids," Ned said.

"So you're also not going out for those other Preppie sports: fencing, polo, sailing?"

"No way," he said.

Despite the tension between Preppies and the rest of us Publics (snobby blue "Bloods" vs. scrappy "Crips?") and despite us hailing from forty-nine states, freshman unity soon emerged from a deeper bond—our maleness and frontal-lobe immaturity. Rowdiness, water balloon fights, and shoving a giant eight-foot bladder ball back and forth across the Old Campus brought us together. We waved away our differences with our handkerchiefs while singing, "For God, for Country, and for Yale." And quick and dirty bonding resulted the day we chased off campus a marching band from another Ivy school that audaciously paraded across campus after thumping our football team.

Feeling a bit homesick, I went to hear Joan Baez sing in Woolsey Hall, next to Freshman Commons. I went backstage after the concert and awkwardly introduced myself as Gayle's brother; she folded me in a big hug. This gave me bragging rights for quite some time, even among Preppies.

Baez inspired me to try winning a Preppie to the cause of social justice. As I listened to Yale's Battell Chapel bells ring the following Sunday, I turned to Bryce.

"You're a certified White Anglo Saxon Protestant. Let's go to Battell."

"You kiddin' me?" Bryce said.

"C'mon, Battell's beautiful."

"Look, I did mandatory chapel at Hotchkiss."

"The organ's amazing. Over 3,000 pipes. They're exposed. You can count 'em!"

"Okay, okay. I'll come. Believe it or not, I like organ music."

During our walk to Battell, I breathed in deep the crisp autumn New England air. I surprised myself by feeling downright comfortable in the traditional, stain-glassed church, and Bryce loved the sacred music swelling thunderously from the organ pipes. We paid close attention as the associate chaplain described the church's civil rights activities, including those inspired by Reverend Martin Luther King, Jr., who employed Gandhi's tactics of nonviolent protest.

"You know," I whispered in Bryce's ear, "Battell's chaplain, William Coffin, and my Unitarian minister in Palo Alto, Dan Lion, will soon join the Freedom Riders in nonviolent direct action."

After the service, I tried to get Bryce to commit to being a tutor with me, the only social justice activity I could manage at the time, in Battell's program for kids from New Haven's black community.

"Not for me," he said.

Enjoying the campus debate fostered by the unfolding civil rights movement, I joined the Yale Political Union, the oldest debating society in the U.S. (Yale's president, Whit Griswold, had found-ed the Union as an undergraduate in the '30s, modeling it after debating societies at Oxford and Cambridge.) I chose the Liberal Party from a handful of possibilities ranging from far left to far right in their political philosophies, and met with fellow Liberals to determine our positions on various debate topics before Union meetings. A speaker represented each party's stance on the floor, and after fierce debate, students belonging to all parties voted to determine the Union's stance on a given topic.

The Union often invited prominent politicos such as California's Governor Ronald Reagan to join its debates, where we'd challenge these superstars, whose presence often drew big audiences. I enjoyed seeing the big shots in action and up close, since they almost always passed by my serving station in the cafeteria line at Freshman Commons.

Of all the speakers I heard at Yale, I most enjoyed William F. Buckley, Jr.—author of *God and Man at Yale* and Yale's patron saint of all things forensic—despite his in-your-face conservatism. Buckley's politics did not appeal to most Yalies. At the time, as Buckley's book pointed out, Yale and many elite campuses across the country embraced liberalism.

But Buckley's style often carried the day even when his arguments didn't, as in debates with Yale Chaplain William S. Coffin, Jr. and others over civil rights. The relationship between Buckley and Reverend Coffin—both steeped in Christianity and both members of Yale's Skull and Bones society—intrigued me. Despite losing battles to Buckley, Coffin began winning the war. Coffin hosted Martin Luther King, Jr., in January at Battell Chapel, where King preached about "the length, breadth and height" of life. I almost didn't get a seat for that one. King's influence and fame had grown a great deal in recent years.

The Political Union debates dovetailed well with my Poli Sci course on international relations taught by Brad Westerfield, himself a former president of the Union. Westerfield's lectures on Alger Hiss, McCarthyism, and Soviet espionage always gave our class plenty to talk about at lunch in Commons. I admired students who had the confidence to stand up amid hundreds at Westy's lectures and ask questions. A true "weekend warrior," Westy often traveled to D.C. to advise politicians on managing the Cold War, in particular (it was discovered years later) clandestine CIA missions in Latin America.

Loaded onto a bus one afternoon, a bunch of us motored off to an evening "mixer" at Wellesley College outside Boston. I met several stuck-up girls who'd gone to Miss Porter's School at Farmington, a Connecticut prep school with an outdoorsy, fox-hunting chic-ness. But I also met a nice girl from the Collegiate School—located near Lincoln Center and catering to New York society types.

I'd had bouts of homesickness throughout the fall, but the feelings kicked in big-time during the long Thanksgiving break. Misery loves company—and food—and so I ate turkey and six slices of pie at Freshman Commons with other scholarship guys who lived too far away to go home. We wretched-of-the-earth gathered around a few tables in one small corner of the cavernous Commons, commiserating and trying to explain Thanksgiving to a number of foreign students who'd joined us.

After dinner, I caught up on English, which often took a backseat to my pressing Calculus and Chemistry classes. I read T.S. Eliot's poem *The Waste Land* for class and to prepare for a lecture Eliot himself would soon give on campus, a lecture I found mesmerizing and intimidating at the same time.

One day as Stark and I pushed carts laden with glass pitchers of water in Freshman Commons, I complained, "Eliot's poetry is whipping my ass."

I stopped my cart, and Stark did the same.

"Eliot's tough, Schorny. Ya just gotta translate him into English."

"I know, but maybe it's how my prof's *teaching* Eliot…or maybe I shouldn't be in sophomore English."

"In freshman English, we're having a ball reading Norman Mailer," Stark smirked. "He's making Kerouac and the Beat generation irrelevant."

Just then our supervisor, Janet—a George Washington look-alike—put a hand on each of our shoulders and said, "Cut the yakking and get to work."

We accelerated our carts so fast that a couple of pitchers fell to the floor and shattered.

"Why, thank you, boys," Georgina said. "I'm that much closer to getting stainless steel pitchers now. I don't like these heavy ones. Now, clean up the mess."

As she walked away, Stark muttered, "Georgina is so heavy handed."

"We bursary boys are the Beat Up generation," I wisecracked back.

Symbolic of our growing friendship, Stark and I took a football road trip to Princeton to see Yale lose 21–16.

While at home for Christmas break, I learned from John Hand that a mutual friend who had graduated from Paly with us had died in a car accident and another classmate had died in a hiking fall. Though I believed the Grim Reaper no longer had his eye on me, I decided I'd better follow up on my feelings for Sharon Belton "just in case." Lo and behold, she and I had a great phone conversation. So much so, in fact, she agreed to go to a movie with me despite still seeing Matt.

When I met Sharon at the Varsity Theatre, I couldn't believe that she'd blossomed into a shapely young woman. I kidded her, alluding to her statement when we first met at a Unitarian Youth party. "Guess you can flirt now."

"You better believe it," she replied.

After the movie, where I had to struggle against putting my arm around her, we enjoyed an espresso in the open-air courtyard in front of the Theatre. We talked until closing time, keeping an eye out for Matt because we didn't know how he'd react if he caught us. As we parted, Sharon said, "I've got to spend the rest of the holidays in San Diego with relatives, but promise you'll keep in touch?"

"I will."

Soon after returning to Yale, I came down with the flu. It turned out to be a highly contagious strain known as the California flu. Yale quarantined me and other afflicted Californians in the infirmary. I looked across a large room with beds and noticed swimmer Steve Clark sitting in a bed hunched over a book, looking miserable. I couldn't have been more opposite than Golden Boy Steve as a physical specimen. Still, he had an Achilles' heel and had succumbed to the nasty California flu, too.

That afternoon, I said to Steve, "Hey, 'Clark Kent,' does flu bother you as much as kryptonite?"

"No," he said with a laugh. "But I *am* anxious about exams."

"Yeah, it couldn't be much worse, having to take our first college finals in the infirmary."

"Yeah. Bluebooks and bedpans don't mix."

"Say, why'd you choose Yale over all the other schools after you?"

"Coach Phil Moriarty," Steve answered. "He's simply the best. Also, I recognized I could hide here."

"Hide?"

"With so much different talent here, I wouldn't stand out. I felt like a freak in high school. Too much attention. Too many expectations. Couldn't let off steam."

"Never occurred to me that being gifted could be a burden."

"Having a gift, like swimming talent, is like having a Ferrari in your garage," Steve said.

"Yeah, I have a Plymouth."

"What matters is how you handle your gift." Steve said, "How you drive your Ferrari. Some people crash and burn their fancy cars."

"Pressure, sometimes pain, comes with the gift?"

"For sure," he said.

"So, I might beat the Ferrari with my Plymouth some day?" I quipped.

"Don't bet on it," Steve chuckled.

"It'd kinda be like the tortoise and the hare...lip," I added.

Steve laughed.

Even though I admired athletic perfection in people like Steve and aesthetic perfection in beautiful women, I had long ago settled for *physical* imperfection in myself. However, I refused to settle for *mental* imperfection in myself. Indeed, I thought I never entered the foul swamp of murky, unclear thinking, but my professors pointed out that I ventured there from time to time. They marked me down for sloppy logic as well as for the spelling and grammar errors of my typewriter.

They also used shame to motivate students by posting grades on classroom doors for all to see, with names and grades listed from best to worst. But I'd been on intimate terms with shame before. In fact, shame had motivated me to work hard at my speech therapy and to compensate, perhaps even overcompensate, for my cleft and heart issues.

My grade point average the first semester put me in the bottom half of my class. I rationalized that Chemistry, Calculus, and Advanced English were difficult courses, but still it troubled me to be intellectually "middle of the road"—"normal," in a sense—even though I'd chased being physically normal all my life. I didn't like to think of myself as only average mentally, and it also troubled me that I'd already filled all my waking hours with study. A low-level dread of not making it at Yale began to replace my once low-level dread of dropping dead from a heart disorder. The last thing I needed was the phone call I soon received informing me of a family crisis back home.

APRIL IS THE CRUELEST MONTH

ON APRIL 10, DAD called to say Mom had suffered a "nervous breakdown."

"Jesus," I said, thinking *T.S. Eliot had got it right about April in The Waste Land.*

"She's okay now," Dad said.

"That's good."

"She's resting comfortably at a Stanford psych ward. She'd just helped clear out her childhood home in Longview."

"Had to have been a highly emotional task, given that Grandpa Stenerson just died."

"She's seen so many family members die in the past five years—both her parents within the past year, my parents before that, and nephew Jimmy. Grief just overwhelmed her."

However, Scott wrote that, to his knowledge, Mom hadn't cried or acted depressed after her dad's death in February. Scott did note that Mom had told him, just before her breakdown, "I'm not feeling well. There's a lot to do. I just don't know how I'll manage everything."

I'd always thought Mom coped well with life's ups and downs, but quite obviously, she had her limits. *Did she have other fragilities I didn't know about? Was this heart-attack-of-the-spirit a one-time event or a warning of more trouble to come?*

Long-distance phone calls cost a lot, so I talked to Dad only once more during Mom's hospitalization. (The psych ward didn't allow us to phone Mom directly.) Mom's psychiatrist, Dr.

Herbert Steinman, mentioned "depression" in passing to Dad, but nothing about whether Mom had lost pleasure in normally enjoyable activities or other hallmarks of depression. Nor did he say anything about her having had some sort of anxiety attack. Instead, Dr. Steinman prescribed talk therapy and a drug to treat "disorganized thinking."

I decided to *write* to Sharon, whose mother had gone through something similar. I wrote:

> *Mom had a nervous breakdown, a heart attack of the soul. Dad told me that one afternoon in the living room, she just found she couldn't decide whether to sew or take a nap or cook dinner. She walked a few steps toward the kitchen, then reversed and walked a few toward the bedroom. She couldn't make up her mind.*
>
> *She phoned Dad about her 'indecision,' and he called our family doctor. Dr. Robertson asked right off, 'Is there a gun in the house?'*
>
> *Dad didn't like Dr. Robertson's tendency toward alarmism, so he phoned another doctor, a Unitarian friend, who called a psychiatrist named Dr. Steinman, who got Mom admitted to the Stanford psych ward.*

Sharon wrote back saying, unlike Hollywood depictions, people as a rule don't cry, babble, or pee on themselves during breakdowns. She explained that her mother's "break" had come from emotional overload.

> *Perhaps your mom experienced momentary 'fragmentation'—couldn't pull her thoughts together—around a life-related issue and her sense of self came unraveled. As part of her recovery, she'll doubtless have to learn to talk more about what's bothering her in life, a hard thing to do sometimes.*

Sharon began to write me on a regular basis, and I reciprocated when I could.

Dad and Scott saw Mom a few times at the hospital, visiting her across a table like it was a minimum-security prison. She told them it struck her as strange not to be carrying a purse around, as she always did away from home. Scott said Mom seemed like a zombie, her flat affect caused by the drug Thorazine.

Amazingly, two weeks of medication and talk therapy helped Mom regain her balance...so much so that Dad couldn't tell the difference between her and her old self when she arrived home. At first Mom paced a bit, wringing her hands often—supposedly a side effect of her meds—but soon returned to her volunteer activities. Steinman advised Dad and Scott to "act normal" around her. Dad didn't tell Gayle about the break because Gayle was studying abroad and already had issues to deal with, like feeling homesick. Dad asked me to be more cheerful in my letters home and not complain about being homesick.

Confident that Mom's spirits had lifted, I turned my attention toward lifting my own during the upcoming spring break. I'd done well on mid-semester exams and papers, in part by using speed-reading tricks I'd learned from the Study Skills Office. (I even started getting seven hours of sleep a night instead of six.) I decided to visit Lee Sims in Stowe, Vermont, where he'd be skiing during his break. Only problem: I couldn't afford transportation on top of skiing expenses. So I hatched a plot to hitch.

I talked Ned into joining me since he hadn't seen much outside his beloved New York City. Unbeknownst to him, though, this hitchhiking trip would also be a test of my ability to break free of the need for structure and predictability I'd developed during my cardiac invalid days. Those days, I'd felt safer knowing *exactly* the physical challenges I'd face in a given situation or day: that way I could decide if I'd be pushing my heart beyond its limits. Conversely, hitchhiking often required walking untold miles, waiting extra hours for meals, being out of one's cold or hot comfort zone.

On the outskirts of campus in the biting cold, Ned and I counted the cars that passed our extended thumbs for more than an hour. A former submarine corpsman gave us our first ride. He drove us along the Connecticut shoreline to New London, where he showed us the Coast Guard Academy and the nuclear sub, *Seawolf*. Another ride got us to Warwick, Rhode Island, where we crashed at a classmate's home and later saw the Astor and Vanderbilt mansions in gorgeous Newport.

The next morning, an FBI agent picked us up before Ned could finish a "Yale to Boston" sign.

"You guys know that bad guys kill hitchhikers," he said.

When that didn't get a rise out of us, he said, "Massachusetts is a cesspool of corruption." Ned took the bait because of New York corruption, and a lively discussion ensued.

The agent dropped us at strangely semicircular Harvard Square in Cambridge. The damp cold drilled through my thin California jacket, deep into my bones as Ned and I entered Harvard Yard via a huge iron gate.

"Just like the Old Campus," Ned said.

"But it doesn't have Nathan Hale."

"Still, it's where Washington took command of the Revolutionary War troops."

"Where *is* your allegiance to Yale, Ned?"

"I want to come here for law school," he replied.

Even more chilled after touring the Yard, we decided to visit a friend of Ned's at Winthrop House—one of Harvard's twelve neo-colonial red brick "houses" that functioned like Yale's ten residential "colleges."

Late that evening, some very funny Jewish guys regaled us with over-the-top Yiddish humor. Ned remained stone-faced while his friend and I doubled over in hysterics.

"Why aren't you laughing?" I asked.

"We'd better turn in," he said. "We've got almost two hundred miles to travel tomorrow."

Back on the highway the next morning, we hitched north and got to Colby College in Waterville, Maine, early enough to enjoy time with friends there. The following day, a cardboard sign got us a little further north to Skowhegan, where we headed west along slow, snowy Route 2 though New Hampshire to Vermont. The back roads didn't disappoint as we found New England charm everywhere, like the cafe sign: "Eat here or we'll both starve." Arriving in Stowe, we checked into Scottie's Lodge, and I arranged to meet Lee on the slopes the next morning. An avid non-skier, Ned located a stash of books at Scottie's that occupied him over the next two days.

Lee humored me during some practice runs where I revived my sketchy ski skills. Then we skied Spruce Mountain. I loved the sun beating down on my face as I swooshed down the slopes, breathing in the earthy, sweet smell of the spruce trees.

Still, Lee complained that I lagged behind him. When I told him I didn't belong in his league, he scoffed. For the rest of the day, "Simon Legree" worked me hard and even tricked me into going down several steep runs that almost killed me. One had iced over, and I skied down its entire length sitting on my butt.

When clouds blocked the sun in the late afternoons, I'd take my wet, weary body to the lodge to warm my hands and feet. At the end of the final day, I lingered so long with Lee at the Round Hearth where he stayed that I missed the last shuttle to Scottie's. I walked back to the Lodge, not realizing that trudging through two miles of slushy snow would feel like five. But walking past moonlit white clapboard houses and churches amid pure white snow and birch trees made the effort worthwhile.

After breakfast with Lee the next morning, Ned and I headed to Burlington, Vermont for the night and then south to progressive Bennington College, where we talked until 2 a.m. with girls Ned knew from Horace Mann about *cinema verité*, Sartre's existentialism, and other French imports. After stopping to say hello to John Hand and another Paly classmate, Chris Burdick, at Williams College in Massachusetts, we hitched on to New Haven, where I celebrated that I'd faced unpredictability and survived.

As soon as I could, I called home to check on Mom. She was out running errands, but Dad said she'd returned full-bore to her volunteerism. He said she was handling things fine but got sleepy after dinner from her meds.

When I hung up, Bryce asked, "Your mom still on drugs?"

"Are you a jerk or just insensitive?" I retorted.

"Both," he said without missing a beat. "It comes with being rich."

Later that evening with Bryce gone, Ned blurted out, "Listen: can you keep a secret?"

"Sure. I kept my heart issues secret for years from lots of people."

"Okay. Here goes. My folks hoped Horace Mann would strip me of my ethnicity."

"What do you mean?" I asked.

"I'm Jewish."

"Really? 'Hooper' doesn't sound Jewish."

"Of course not, that's why my grandfather changed our name from Horowitz. He wanted to make it big in America and thought America rife with anti-Semitism—"

"There does seem to be more of it in the East than on the West Coast."

"I don't look Jewish 'cuz I'm taller than most." He paused, then added, "And I had a nose job at sixteen."

"Coulda fooled me. Anyway, I could use a nose job myself."

"You could 'pass,' ya know, Karl. Grow a mustache to cover your scar. Then tell people you broke your nose playing baseball," said Ned.

"You know about 'passing,' then?"

"I learned that early. No one here knows I'm Jewish, so don't tell anyone."

"I won't," I assured him, pleased that he trusted me, and now understanding why he'd not liked the Yiddish humor at Harvard.

I saw Steve Clark in Poli Sci class the next week and heard about his swim-filled break. Aware of his knowledge of swim coaches around the world, I told him about Walter Hewlett's upcoming high school graduation gift: a summer of training in New Zealand with renowned track coach Arthur Lydiard. We chuckled about Walter's good fortune but his poor judgment in choosing to enter Harvard next year.

The minute we finished finals that spring, Secret Service agents kicked us off the Old Campus so they could check out every suite, as Yale planned to award President Kennedy an honorary degree. When the academic hood slid over Kennedy's shoulders, he quipped, "Now I have the best of all worlds: a Harvard education and a Yale degree."

Back home for the summer, I found Mom no different from usual. Thorazine hadn't put pounds on her, caused puffiness, slurred her speech, or caused her to walk with a shuffle, as it often did with patients. Mom continued to work part-time at a yardage store, and busy days stressed her out a bit. Just for fun, though, she enrolled in an anthropology course at Foothill College in Los Altos. However, at exam time she commented, "Remembering stuff like this was a lot easier twenty-some years ago at the University of Washington."

I dated Sharon from time to time, but we both trod lightly since she still saw Matt when he came home from college. He still hated me, and told her so in no uncertain terms when he'd been drinking. I dated other girls besides Sharon including a recent Paly grad, quiet but sexy Sarah Hoffman.

Because I hadn't taken any electrical engineering courses at Yale, Hewlett-Packard busted me down to assembly-line work, where I put together oscilloscopes all summer. I got to know many fellow workers, since we all conversed a lot to manage the monotony of the assembly line.

Back at Yale, Ned and I, along with fellow dining-hall bursary boy, Stark, had bundled our names together for random assignment by the University to one of its twelve residential "colleges," which provide an intimate built-in community for eating, studying, partying, and engaging in cultural and athletic activities for three years. We got assigned to a college named after Jonathan Trumbull—a governor of Connecticut and a man George Washington relied on for advice during the Revolutionary War. One of Yale's smallest colleges, Trumbull College promised to give us that "small college experience within a larger university."

To shame my body into behaving in a normal manner, I did not request a lower residence floor in Trumbull, and, sure enough, Lady Luck shoved a fifth-floor suite in my face. I swallowed hard, knowing I'd have to huff and puff several times a day to get up to my room. As compensation, though, I could walk a short distance to one of Yale's greatest assets: massive Sterling Library, planted right next to Trumbull.

"Hey, Brainbox," Stark said to Ned as we climbed up the circular stairs to our suite for the very first time, another common room with two bedrooms. "Tell us again why *you* need the single bedroom. Was bunking with Karl a bust?"

"Naw. It's 'cuz I'm a History of Art major. I've got a lot of history and art slides to master."

"Oh my God!" Stark exclaimed. "You must just be so beside yourself."

"I've never had a room of my own in my life," I said, a bit out of breath, "so why change now."

"Okay, okay, I'll bunk with Schorny," Stark said.

"Thanks, guys. Gotta run to an Alley Cats' practice," Ned said, rushing off.

"Dang that Ned," Stark said in mock anger. "He sings, too! Hate him, hate him, hate him!"

Our common room had dark-paneled wood surrounding a fireplace on the far side. A dozen two-foot-wide leaded-glass windows above a long window seat looked out on Trumbull's largest courtyard, which featured a Frisbee-friendly lawn framed by Sterling Library, our baronial dining room, and the master's residence.

I checked out the metal bunk bed in the room Stark and I would share. A flip of a coin awarded me the farther of two desks built into the wall, which meant I could gaze out a leaded window onto another of Trumbull's inner courtyards, this one presided over by a gargoyle sitting on a toilet.

As we unpacked our stuff and talked about buying used furniture and rugs, I told Stark about my new bursary job with the Study Skills Office.

"No more slinging hash or bussing dishes!" I crowed.

"You dog, I'll be serving *you* in the Trumbull Dining Hall tonight…and every night!"

"You'd love Norman Fedde, the Study Skills' guy—bowtie, mustache, glasses, huge shock of hair," I said. "He's got us Yalies pegged—like what we read first in a newspaper. Guess."

"The stocks page?" Stark answered.

"No. I guessed that, too. Fedde says it's the editorial page— 'cuz we love to debate. Speaking of which, I'm going to hear Buckley tonight."

"That right-wing economic nut?"

"Buckley's not just about economics. Certainly…

ahhhh…you jest about him being a wing-nut," I said, "because…ahhhh…he's entertaining."

"I hate the disastah that is America," Stark said with a straight face.

As I watched Buckley handle questions that night—many of them hostile—I realized his guttural pauses gave opponents a false sense of confidence. His hesitations gave him an extra microsecond or two to choose the perfect words to chop them into pieces. Without a doubt, he was a true verbal swordsman.

Inspired by Buckley, I signed up for inter-college debate the next day. I planned to hone my argumentation skills during daily dining hall discussions where I could match wits with fellow students, and even faculty who ate in Trumbull from time to time.

All of my courses stretched out over two semesters. Madame Regalado may have loved my nasal vowels, but she didn't like the way my French r's taxed my scarred soft palate. I enjoyed introductory economics, mostly because the class, which met in Trumbull's seminar room, involved lots of interaction with our instructor. Hajo Holborn, who had fled the Nazis and worked in wartime intelligence, made European History resonate with authenticity. Dynamic Richard Bernstein breathed life into philosophy, and Arthur Galston made biology interesting, as did the cutthroat pre-med competition in the class.

Early in the year I decided it was "high time" to "get high," since I'd never drunk to excess before. And so I went to a Trumbull dance and watched people rock out to a band's ten-minute version of *Do You Love Me, now that I can dance?* After consuming three huge brews, I sought the dining hall bathroom with considerable urgency. I continued to drain beer cups and drain my bladder throughout the evening.

When the keg dance ended, I staggered out to the main courtyard. Two campus cops watching from Trumbull's gatehouse noticed I couldn't find my entryway (all four entries looked alike that night) and helped me up to my suite—whereupon I promptly threw up on myself. Luckily, the cops had bigger fish to fry that night. A student whose father advised the DuPont family about finances and served on the boards of ballet and opera companies displayed *his* drunkenness more disruptively. He held his latest bottle of scotch with aplomb out the window of his third floor suite and dropped it, just to hear the tinkle of glass on the paving stones below. Work hard, play hard—that epitomized the Yale style.

I drank with moderation after my squalid gag fest. I hated feeling nauseous, needed my senses to study, and believed I'd worked too hard in speech therapy to revert to rubbery, incomprehensible speech while high. And so most Sundays I woke up clear-headed and ready to hit the books, while some of my confreres confronted the day with yammering hangovers and blinding headaches—preferring froth and foam to Freud and Faulkner.

The inter-college debating program fit in with my heavy pre-med course load. In three-on-three contests, with the same rules as the varsity program, I debated all manner of weighty resolutions—such as "American corporate capitalism works" and "A little knowledge is a dangerous thing"—as well as lighter ones, such as "Better bed than wed," a takeoff on the "Better dead than red" debates sweeping the country.

Mother Yale provided rich extracurricular opportunities for debate and declamation, and Professor Rollin Osterweis, with his signature bowtie, coordinated them all. That year, the history prof kept his eye on a freshman named John Kerry, who did well in both freshman debate and Political Union face-offs.

I enjoyed the electricity of the various "Better dead than red" debates featuring Buckley and journalist Fulton Lewis, III, on the right against Norman Thomas, Gus Hall, and Herbert Aptheker on the left. Whenever I watched Buckley, I couldn't believe English was his second language. (He'd spent his early years growing up in Mexico and France). While his accent seemed cultured and upper class, it was unique to Buckley—as were his trademark jabs in the air with a pencil and his habit of grinning with eyes wide open when skewering an opponent. I imitated some of his verbal tactics in my own debates, hoping his style and charisma—but not his politics—would somehow rub off on me, not unlike soldiers of yore eating their dead enemy's bodies for their courage.

One day Steve Clark, who lived across the street in Saybrook College, showed up in our fifth-floor bathroom in Trumbull, shaving his arms with an electric razor.

"What're you doing here? You're in the wrong college, Swim-Dog," I said, grinning.

"Been studying Poli Sci with Tim Garton downstairs and realized I had to shave down for tonight's meet. Since my bursitis last year and my third place at Nationals, I need all the help I can get."

"I still use a blade," I said.

"I have to shave my *whole* body. Tim's GE razor helps."

"My condolences. An electric may be okay for you, but guys like Richard Nixon and me, using one of those, we'd have to shave five times a day."

Steve laughed and said, "My dad works for GE, in fact."

"How's that gorgeous Julie back home?"

"She's discovered other fish in the sea."

"You can out swim any fish—"

"It's hard, being 3,000 miles away," he lamented.

"I know. I like a girl back home, too."

"Want to come to the Mount Holyoke mixer next week? My sister's a senior there. She can introduce us to some girls."

"Great idea. Thanks."

Steve and I and a bunch of other Yalies took a "mixer bus" to Mount Holyoke, the oldest women's college in the U.S. The classic leafy green campus featured gothic revival stone structures amid beautiful turreted New England red brick buildings.

Once inside Chapin Hall, Steve's sister, Sally, led us to a cluster of young women she knew and introduced us all around. This head start over other guys did wonders for my self-confidence, and I talked and danced with as many in the cluster as I could. Except for a few gals from the haughty horsy set, I found most of the Holyoke women nice—more scholarly and less artsy than the Vassar students I'd met at a previous mixer. At midnight, I ended up with Suzi, a girl who hadn't used up her Holyoke-allotted "overnights," and I invited her down for Princeton Football Weekend before having to scramble to the mixer bus before it departed.

On the way home, Steve and I and anyone else who wasn't sleeping, either bragged about our successes or whined about our failures. We all agreed, nonetheless, that women's colleges constituted a veritable goldmine for us girl-crazy Yalies, and especially the Preppies among us who'd spent their entire lives in all-male schools.

ON THE ROAD

BEFORE FLYING HOME FOR the holidays, I chained myself to my desk to prepare for major exams in Bio, Econ, and Philosophy. Once they were finished, I could move freely about my life again. For all that, on my flight home I found myself buckled up once more, waiting to be allowed to move freely about the cabin again.

The "miracle" of a multi-ton behemoth becoming airborne always thrilled me, even after I learned the physics of it.

"Looking out the window at buildings and cars becoming small dots makes me feel like God," I told my seatmate.

"Pardon?" he said.

"I mean, makes me feel like I'm above all things petty. I enjoyed my model train layout as a kid for the same reason. I could 'soar' above that little world and be in control—something I'd missed growing up."

"I understand now," he said, hastily burying his head in a magazine.

Flying meant having food served by stewardesses, just like being waited on in a restaurant—also something I'd missed growing up. The one downside to flying for me: my ears ached after each take-off and landing. Neither yawning nor swallowing nor gum chewing let my cleft-scarred Eustachian tubes assist my ear drums in adjusting to changes in the plane's cabin air pressure.

Once I arrived home, I heard that Mom had backslid a bit from her astounding recovery, so Dr. Steinman had her coming to therapy more often. To me, though, she didn't seem much different from her usual self.

I enjoyed the warm California weather and saw Sharon several times. During a visit to her house one evening, with her family gone, she put on her new Shirelles album. *Dedicated to the One I Love* played as we started kissing on the living room couch. Worried that Matt or a passerby might see us through the large picture window, I suggested we go to Sharon's bedroom.

"A Pi Phi doesn't entertain gentlemen in her boudoir," she declared.

"So I'm up against a whole sorority?"

"And the Episcopal church!"

"C'mon, just pretend I wanna see your etchings. Anyway, Matt might see us."

"I do have some of my watercolors in there. Oh, all right."

Before long we were kissing again, and her breasts pressed against me. Instead of feeling her breasts through her clothing, I tried to unbutton her blouse for some reason.

"Stop! No buttons," she said.

"But seeing you in your bra is just like seeing you in a bikini."

"Nice try, Buster. You've seen my watercolors. Now back to the living room."

Will You Still Love Me Tomorrow? played in the background.

As soon as I returned to New Haven, I developed a cold and sore throat, exacerbated by my being a mouth-breather due to my cleft and malfunctioning turbinates. I studied hard and enjoyed corresponding with Sharon through the long winter.

When winter melted into spring break, countless Yalies left for Florida or Grand Bahama Island for sun and general craziness. As scholarship boys, Stark and I settled for an island closer at hand that enticed us west coasters: Manhattan. Ned arranged for us to see it up close with a distant relative—the brother of Kathryn Murray of Arthur Murray Dance Studio fame.

We stayed with Mr. Kohnfelder and his wife in their Sutton Place South luxury apartment that straddled East River Drive with constant traffic moving noiselessly fifteen stories below our bedroom. The first day, Mr. Kohnfelder showed us Manhattan's iconic tourist sites, as well as its slums and decaying waterfronts. We puffed up our chests at times and slunk down in our seats at others while riding in his newly-minted Cadillac Eldorado convertible, with a motor-driven retractable antenna.

The next morning, Stark and I watched a Security Council debate over Syria and Israel at the United Nations—only blocks away from the Kohnfelders' apartment. We thought the debate as impressive as the U.N.'s imposing architecture. Following more days of Kohnfelder luxury, sightseeing, and fun at the happening clubs, we morphed from parasites of the rich back to poor scholarship students.

For the rest of the semester, I settled into a routine of studying, debating, exercising, and working. I still experienced intense academic pressure, thanks in part to Biology, which, like all my pre-med science prerequisites, met every day except Sunday because of labs.

Swimmer Steve Clark experienced another kind of pressure—pressure from guys wanting to dethrone him. No one deposed him at the Nationals, maybe thanks to all the shoulder massages he got from Etta, a local New Haven gal he liked a lot. He managed to win gold in the 100-meter freestyle and again in two relays at the Pan American Games in São Paulo, Brazil.

Summer soon asserted itself, and when I returned to Palo Alto, Sharon told me she'd left Matt to be with me. She said Matt cursed me and planned to get even. Walter Hewlett's father and staffers didn't like me either, but for other reasons. Since I still hadn't taken any engineering courses at Yale, they relegated me to janitorial work at HP.

One night early in the summer, Sharon and I drove into the Stanford foothills and parked in an overgrown area that still allowed peeks between the foliage at burgeoning Silicon Valley below. She and I kissed the warm, deep kisses we'd discovered earlier. After steaming up the windows for an hour or so, we drove back to civilization.

We continued to explore each other throughout the summer. I soon began to reach under her blouse and marvel at the warmth and smoothness of her skin. As the summer progressed I nerved myself to go further on several occasions, but she always said *No*.

Driving to and from our lover's lane spots, we revealed much about ourselves to one another.

"I've felt different all my life," I said, "like I work the nightshift."

"Meaning?"

"Because of my cleft, I've wanted to be normal, to work when everyone else works."

"*I* grew up wanting to be accepted by my dad," Sharon said in a wistful voice.

"Really?"

"He worked so much, and when he was home, he watched sports. So any chance I got, I watched, too; sitting a little to the side, watching the TV with my head turned away, trying not to appear intrusive."

"That's why you know so much about sports."

"And that's why I watch TV out of the corner of my eyes to this day."

"Does he accept you now?"

"I guess, but mostly 'cuz I turned into a sports nut right under his nose."

At the end of the summer, Ned visited California for the first time, and Stark flew down from Portland. I showed them Stanford and the industrial park that would soon be known as the center of Silicon Valley. The three of us set out for New Haven via New Orleans in my family's Plymouth station wagon—just painted light green—which we dubbed the "Moldmobile."

With *Surf City, He's So Fine,* and *It's My Party* playing on the radio, we sped past cheap motels, dinettes, bait shops, gun stores, and Sinclair gas stations with huge dinosaurs. After visiting my great aunts—still Unclaimed Treasures, they told us—in Omaha, we turned South, exploring Kansas City, St. Louis, and Memphis. Driving south through Mississippi, we avoided Jackson, where civil rights leader Medgar Evers had been assassinated only two months before.

As we arrived in an outlying district of New Orleans, Ned wasn't paying attention to signs and turned onto Pontchartrain Bridge while Stark and I slept, resting up for a night's revelry on Bourbon Street in the French Quarter. Normally, such a navigational error would be no big deal. Not so if you get on what's billed as the "World's Longest Bridge," stretching twenty-four miles across Lake Pontchartrain without any way of turning around.

"You idiot!" Stark yelled when he awoke and realized the error—waking me in the process. "*You* gotta pay the toll each way, now, Ned!"

"*And* you gotta stay sober tonight," I said. "'Cuz you'll have to check around to find a campsite for us after Bourbon Street."

"B-But—"

"And drive us there," Stark said before flopping down to sleep some more.

At the other end of the bridge, we turned around and drove the twenty-four miles right back again.

Once we'd enjoyed the booze and go-go dancers on Bourbon Street, we camped near Lake Pontchartrain. The next morning, we bathed in the lake, oblivious to an unusual infestation of post-storm microbes that worked their wizardry on the T-shirts and briefs we wore, turning them pink. Worried that we too might turn pink, we were relieved, after the 24-hour incubation period passed, that we hadn't developed dysentery or swamp fever.

After New Orleans, we drove back through Mississippi and into Alabama to Birmingham. We camped out in Birmingham—sleeping near the Moldmobile, which, of course, had California plates—not realizing the hatred locals had for out-of-staters agitating for civil rights. Fortunately, no one really took notice of us.

The next day, I tensed up as we drove past several "Skip School" protests comprised of hundreds of boycotting white students and their parents. They demonstrated at several schools to protest forced racial integration. Federal troops and local police encircled each of the three schools we passed.

"I can't believe the amount of hatred expressed by whites here. You'd think blacks would be the 'haters.'" I opined.

When the hate-filled eyes of a protester locked on mine from time to time, I understood more clearly the depth of emotion responsible for much of the violence of the Civil War, fought almost a hundred years ago. I rubbed my head in despair, shocked about the continued sorry state of race relations in the South.

After driving through several black neighborhoods where the disparity between Birmingham's Haves and Have Nots was dispiriting, we visited Vulcan Park and learned about the city's iron and steel industry. We slept for a second night beside the Moldmobile. When we awoke late Sunday morning, we heard on the car radio that a horrific blast had just rocked the Sixteenth Street Baptist Church. The blast killed four young black girls and injured many other people. We left Birmingham at once, fearing violence from blacks incensed by the blast and other recent bombings in the area. We heard later that day that the pastor of the Sixteenth Street Church, which had been bombed before for being active in the civil rights movement, pleaded for nonviolence.

"I'm coming back to Birmingham to fix this mess," Stark vowed. "To raise 'holy hell'…in a nonviolent way, of course."

We rolled on north to Chattanooga, at which point we poked along smaller roads to get to the Great Smoky Mountains National Park. As the smoky mist and fog of this southern part of the Appalachian Mountains engulfed us, we began to forget the troubles of the world.

The next day, heading north out of the Smoky Mountains, Stark piloted Old Moldy along a rain-slicked road while I slept in the passenger seat and Ned slept in the back on top of our luggage. Suddenly, something went haywire. The Moldmobile began to spin out of control.

Stark cried out, "Holy shit."

"What the fuck?" Ned yelled.

We're gonna die, I thought.

And then silence. Languid, eerie silence as Old Moldy rotated 360-degrees.

Ned yelled "The Court?" and later said he saw his entire legal career pass before his eyes—Harvard Law School, a great clerkship, a significant judgeship, and then appointment to the Supreme Court. By contrast, I saw Dad looking at the crumpled Moldmobile carcass with three mangled bodies inside.

Old Moldy came to rest in a shallow ditch alongside the road. I pinched myself to verify I was still alive in the passenger "suicide" seat after being swirled like a swizzle stick down a flushed toilet. Before I could count the dead and wounded, Ned materialized out of a jumble of suitcases. He, too, had survived unharmed in pre-seatbelt America. On the other hand, Stark, slumped over the steering wheel, looked to be dead.

"Stark," I said as I touched his arm.

He lifted his head, his eyes popped open. "I'm okay. I hope I haven't wrecked the car." Still ashen-faced, he noticed Ned and said, "You still have a shot at the Court."

A pickup truck stopped. "Need some help?" the white-haired driver asked.

"Yeah," I said. "Any repair shops nearby?"

"Yes, and I just happen to have some heavy rope to tow you there."

He towed us to a gas station where a mechanic fixed our flat and repaired some minor damage. Within hours we were back on the road. I couldn't believe we'd survived what seemed a catastrophic event.

We drove on to Washington, D.C., where I talked to a couple of government officials about doing an internship the following summer. After an overnight with friends of my father in D.C., we drove the last leg to Yale. There, as we unloaded our stuff from Old Moldy at the Trumbull gate, the campus cop on duty asked, "Mr. Karl, Bursary Boy Extraordinaire, does this fine-looking vehicle belong to you?"

"Uh, yeah," I said, reminded once again that campus cops knew something about almost every Yalie."

"Show me your waiver and proof of off-street parking arrangements."

"Uh, what do you mean?"

"Sorry, gotta bust you. Your keys, please."

A JUNIOR AT YALE

R. INSLEE CLARK, THE Trumbull College dean, summoned me to his office the next day. It turned out Yale forbid scholarship students to have vehicles on campus unless they had a waiver. I pleaded "ignorance" as well as "need": I had to drive during a possible summer internship in D.C.

My heart raced and my palms sweated as the Dean consulted my file and some other materials. At last, he said, "I understand your situation. I think we can work something out."

Blinking in disbelief, I said, "Thank you."

"You can keep the car if you store it off campus, *inoperable*."

"It might welcome some rest, given what it's been through."

After a talk with Ned, I devised a plan, and Dean Clark approved it. I would store the Moldmobile on blocks at the Hooper's summer home on Shelter Island.

As I walked amid the maze of rooms in the basement of the Yale medical school, my skin tingled with excitement knowing my scholarship job would be with a Psychology Department superstar.

I found the room number I'd been given but saw only a janitor working when I peered through a window. I walked farther down the hall to another lab—this one filled with activity.

"Do you know where I can find Neal Miller?" I asked.

A guy in a tweed sport coat said, "He's likely in his lab down the hall. Lives there."

I returned to the first room and asked the barrel-chested janitor in denim coveralls about the professor.

"I'm Neal Miller," he said. "You must be here for the scholarship job."

Turning red as I shook his hand, I said, "Yes, Dr. Miller. Sorry, I just finished working as a janitor where most of us wore coveralls."

"No problem. I wear 'em because the animals and gadgets I work with get my usual clothes dirty. After we set up a schedule for you to work, I'll show you around."

"Thanks. My only scheduling constraint is I'll need enough time on Organic Chem days to allow me to bike back to the campus and then up Science Hill."

Soon, Miller—author of the frustration-aggression hypothesis, which suggested that aggression is always preceded by frustration—showed me his lab and others.

"This is where Stanley Milgram did his 'obedience to authority' experiments," he said, taking me into a room partitioned in half to allow "deception" in the service of science.

"I can't believe this," I said as I touched an electronic console with dials, which the controversial social-psychologist utilized to give "pretend shocks" to see if average Americans would yield to authority figures and inflict pain on innocent people. Milgram proved that Americans had the potential to be just as "cruel" as Germans had been during World War II.

Junior year promised to be exciting because of my job in Miller's lab, and because I could sink my teeth into my Psychology major. I used to drive my parents and grandparents nuts asking them why people behaved the way they did. Philosophers and writers had advanced our knowledge of the nature of the mind mightily. Psychology—a relatively new science—had assigned itself the task of "finishing the job" and promised to lead to even greater insights into the mind. By majoring in Psychology, I could at last start to explore some of my questions in a systematic way.

Of the various psych courses I took—ranging from child psych to experimental psych—I concluded social psych would be my intellectual home. It provided me with tools, concepts, and theories to pursue behavioral questions I had about maladjustment, aggression, and violence, among other things.

Along these lines, one professor commented during office hours, when we talked about the impact of clefts, crossed eyes, and club feet on social adjustment, "Social psych has found there's no direct correlation between deformed physical appearance and social maladjustment."

Playing devil's advocate, I asked, "Isn't physicality—whether appearance, health, or strength—important in developing attitudes one has about oneself?"

"Yes, but what's just as important as one's physicality is one's perception of other people's opinions towards one's physicality."

"You mean you're socially adjusted if you dismiss any negativity people express when they look at you?"

"Yes."

Besides the issues of perception, I began thinking about "fairness," having been sensitized to "Have Nots" during my trip through the South. However, I thought about fairness with regard to the "Haves" at Yale. For example, looking out from the window seat in my Trumbull suite, I saw guys tossing Frisbees on the lawn in the courtyard throughout the day and evening, except in the depths of winter. Where did they get the time? Of course, it was usually different guys playing because Yale had enough guys that, at any moment, some of them would have time to play.

Still, the gods blessed a few "regulars" with smarts, and these had more time for play because they needed less time for study. And the gods gave some of these obscenely smart guys wealth, good looks, and interesting personalities to boot. It didn't seem fair, but statistics accounted for it: draw from a large enough pool of winners and you'll find among them some truly extraordinary people.

John Kerry may have been one such person. He impressed many of us in forensics with his confidence and skill. He held forth with ease in debates, and I liked that he debated along side of me rather than against me. In the Political Union, we elected him president his sophomore year. He majored in Poli Sci, like many of the school debaters and leaders of the Union.

While I took several Poli Sci courses—some with Steve Clark—I felt at a disadvantage in debate and in the Political Union as a pre-med Psych major and a person with remnants of cleft-palate speech. Nevertheless, I tried to compensate by studying hard in Poli Sci and History and reading The New York Times. And before debates, I used mouthwash, which I felt, for some bizarre reason, allowed me to speak faster and more fluently. My compensatory efforts did pay off in the inter-college league, where we debated, among other things, whether President Kennedy's civil rights bill should be enacted and whether a domestic Peace Corps should be created.

One Friday in late November, my Sociology of Deviance professor was leading a discussion of how veteran prostitutes stifled competition by snitching on new girls on the street.

Suddenly, a student pushed open the door to our classroom and yelled, "President Kennedy's been shot!"

Assuming this was just another Milgram-esque experiment involving the deception of research subjects, our professor joked, "Those damned social psychologists are at it again," and kept us the usual length of time. When we went downstairs and outside, people's expressions told us this was no experiment.

I wandered around the campus for a while dazed, saddened and mostly confused.

Soon, our interim president, Kingman Brewster, Jr., and Harvard's president made a joint announcement: "Tomorrow's Yale-Harvard game will be played the following Saturday out of respect for President Kennedy." It was the first delayed game ever for the ages-old classic rivalry. Harvard students had already arrived on campus as had most everyone's dates. Restraint characterized most revelers Friday night.

On Saturday, some of us sipped too much scotch. A few Yalies and Harvard "Johnnies" proceeded with their usual raucous debauchery, their dates colluding. My date didn't mind the low-key day, but like most other guests, she returned home sooner than she'd planned on Sunday.

Of note at a disciplinary hearing soon after, a not-too-bright New Haven police officer rebuked one of our classmates for a Thursday night, pre-weekend prank: "Son, please explain how you had the nerve to paint 'Hate Harvard' on the street pavement the night before Kennedy was shot?"

A few days later, Mom and Dad called me on my birthday, which fell on Thanksgiving Day that year. "Happy Birthday, honey," Mom said.

"Thanks. How have you been?"

"It's been a dreadful week, except for today," Mom said. "Of course, I've been glued to the TV all week. I'm so sad for the Kennedys, especially Caroline and little John-John."

Mom handed the phone to Dad, and he described a couple of heart-wrenching speeches he had to ghostwrite for some government officials about Kennedy.

"How's Mom getting along?" I asked.

"She's great. Today she's excited about having the Borthwicks and Clarence Johnson over for turkey dinner."

During the holidays I had a chance to confirm Dad's assessment of Mom. She seemed in good spirits, and the bustle and busyness of Christmas didn't overwhelm her. Her mother had always made fattigmann bakkels, Norwegian "poor man's cookies," for Christmas. Mom made some of the tasty treats and invited Sharon over.

When I found out, I asked, "Why'd you do that?"

"To get to know her better," she said.

"She's an art and anthro major. Likes both doing art and studying it. Might do museum work someday."

"That's nice, but I'd like to really get to know her, hear about her family, her childhood."

One dreary winter night not long after, rain tapping a poem on the turquoise-tinted copper flashing outside my desk window, I wrote Sharon. On a whim, I invited her to the upcoming Junior Prom, mostly to lift my own spirits. I knew a transcontinental jaunt was out of the question, but my Philosophy course had taught me the value of symbolic gestures.

Sharon wrote back:

> *Karl,*
> *Just a note to tell you that I will be very honored to attend the Yale Junior Prom with you!*
> *Sharon*
> *P.S. Would appreciate being your only date.*
> *P.P.S. I'd also like to extend the weekend by attending Monday classes with you.*

After rushing back from my mailbox at Yale Station—a cramped, below-ground post office kitty-corner from Trumbull College—I showed the note to Ned and Stark.

"I never expected her to say 'Yes,'" I whooped. "I can't believe a woman would fly 3,000 miles to see me."

"I can't believe it either," Ned said with a faint smile.

"This represents a substantial investment on her part," Stark smirked.

"You'd better hold up your end of the bargain," Ned said.

"Yeah, don't cheap out at the threadbare Hotel Duncan."

I opened both my heart and my wallet by booking three nights at the nearby Taft Hotel. This cleaned out my social budget for the semester.

The first Junior Prom in a long time to be held on campus, the posh event would take over Freshman Commons and parts of adjoining Woolsey Hall. Sharon arrived by train from N.Y. Idlewild Airport around noon on Friday, and I showed her parts of the campus, including Froshland, Fratland, and Tomorrowland (Science Hill). She changed into her prom dress while I put on my first-ever tux, and we enjoyed a candlelit dinner—just for prom goers—in the Trumbull dining hall. After, we walked over to Commons with Ned, Stark, and their dates. Sharon looked ravishing in her black dress, which had to fit into a suitcase, unlike most of the more elaborate dresses, some of which looked to have been created by Disney's costume department.

The Shirelles came up from New Jersey and sang all their hits, including *Dedicated to the One I Love*, and *Will You (Still) Love Me Tomorrow?*" After the singers left, we continued dancing to The Les and Larry Elgart Orchestra, and once they left, to Eddie Wittstein's Band upstairs in the President's Room in Woolsey Hall. The prom ended at 2 a.m.

Upon entering Sharon's room at the Taft Hotel, we made straight for the bed, leaving a trail of clothes behind. It was the first time for both of us, and once we figured out the mechanics of this thing that obsessed so many of us, it was not a disappointment. My emotional heart had trumped any lingering worries about my physical heart, as I was oblivious to it pounding away from…well, everything. As we lay in one another's arms, exhausted but gratified, we talked about waking up with one another the next morning—which would be almost as new and exciting as the sex.

After a leisurely Saturday breakfast and visits to a couple of art exhibits in the residential colleges, we caught the Yale-Harvard hockey game at Ingalls Rink. Later on, we had cocktails and dinner at the Fence Club—arranged by member and fellow pre-med Ed Cox—and then segued to a dance at Trumbull.

Following a concert on Sunday, we had a few brews at a keg party at Bryce's frat house.

"Chahm'ed," Bryce's stylish date said as she greeted us.

When we left, she said, "Buh-bye."

The rest of our Sunday remained low-key, as most dates had left campus. We hung out with various guys who later agreed with Lee Sims' assessment: Sharon was "a great catch—smart, beautiful, and lusty." I had to agree, since we'd twice more revisited the pyrotechnic fun we'd discovered after the Prom.

Sharon attended classes with me on Monday; then we walked to the train station where, after both of us choked back tears, Sharon went back to New York City and the big bird in the sky. I hustled back to campus to study, but it turned out for naught. I flunked my Organic Chem exam on the chemical process known as "exhaustive methylation" the next day—clearly paying for the exhaustive titillation I'd known prom weekend.

Still, I grinned a lot the next few days even though I missed snuggling up to Sharon at night and squeezing her hand while we walked the campus. Each afternoon, I couldn't wait to go to the Yale post office to get her almost-daily letters. I wrote many passionate letters to her, but soon had to rein-in my strong feelings for her.

A WASHINGTON INTERN

MY PSYCHOLOGY AND PRE-MED studies, combined with extracurricular activities, grew to be very time consuming, limiting the amount of energy I could devote to writing Sharon. I tried doing multiple things at once to free up time. For instance, I practiced my debate skills during heated mealtime arguments amid the stone arches and dark-timbered ceiling of the Trumbull dining hall. I argued with classmates and faculty about civil rights, society's outsiders, conscientious objection, guerilla warfare in Vietnam—each controversial topics of the day. Not all of these topics were abstractions, either.

Along with Yale's chaplain, William Coffin, many Yalies including Stark got involved in the civil rights movement in the South. My Unitarian minister, Reverend Dan Lion, who had joined Reverend Coffin in the Freedom Rides, registered voters in Mississippi, marched in Selma, and led antiwar marches through Palo Alto. He and Ira Sandperl encouraged me to write essays about my antiwar feelings in case I ever needed conscientious objector status.

Dad may have wished he could join his friend Reverend Lion, but his work kept him busier than ever, as Deputy Regional Administrator in charge of an alphabet soup of government agencies, mostly related to housing.

In a call home, I asked Mom, "Do you feel abandoned as Dad brings more and more office work home?"

"No. But, I truly feel abandoned by M-Mary."

"Archer? The one Jerry married after your Dorene, died?"

"Yes. Guess we haven't told you kids about her." Mom took a deep breath. "Well…she hanged herself."

"Holy Christ! Where?"

"In the San Jose Unitarian Church."

"My God! I'm so sorry, Mom. Why?"

"I don't know; she didn't leave a note. I really do miss her, miss getting together."

"Maybe one of my classes will give me some insight into suicide."

My Sociology of Deviant Behavior course gave me ideas about the role 'feelings of alienation' play in suicides, but I hoped Abnormal Psych the next year would help me figure out Mary's death at a deeper level.

I enjoyed my current Psych courses because they allowed me to dream of combining my interests in medicine and nonviolence. If psychoanalyst Erik Erikson could do psycho-biographies of Gandhi and other individuals, why not do the same with groups or communities or even nations? Psychiatrist Robert Jay Lifton did psycho-histories (along with Lloyd deMause) which suggested that a nation's childrearing tactics could affect its foreign policy. Since psychiatrists and psychoanalysts dominated the field that interested me, I decided going into psychiatry, and in particular the subfield of social psychiatry, made sense.

Yale was notorious for its Secret Societies. Fifteen-person clubs, often housed in windowless, two-story stone "tombs," kept alive a long and secretive tradition dating back to the founding of Skull and Bones in 1832. One tradition not kept secret by the Societies, Tap Day, occurred every spring when members of the seven senior societies tapped, or selected, members of the junior class to replace themselves. Skull and Bones tapped Steve Clark and other acquaintances of mine. Allegedly, they'd all be asked at their weekly Thursday dinners to confess their sexual exploits to one another and even kiss Geronimo's skull, which according to legend, Prescott Bush—patriarch of the Bush political dynasty—stole from the Apache's grave in 1918. Scroll and Key tapped New England Preppies and social register types as a rule, so Bryce found a home at last.

When Ned came back to the suite and announced Book and Snake had tapped him, I said, "So? I've been tapped by Gin and Tonic."

Ned smiled.

"I didn't get tapped," Stark said. "I'm settling for Peanut Butter and Jelly. We'll put on a big spread at our Thursday dinners."

"Ain't no big deal if Bones rejected us," I said. "President Brewster turned down Bones when they tapped him as an undergraduate."

"Hey guys," Ned said, "the real deal for me tonight: I made it into the Whiffs!"

The Whiffs, short for Whiffenpoofs, boasted they were the best-known and oldest—having been founded in 1909 at Mory's Temple Bar—a cappella singing group in the country. Composed of fourteen seniors, the Whiffs mostly sang old standards in close harmony. Past members included Cole Porter and Prescott Bush.

"Jesus, Ned, that's great!" I said and hugged him.

"I'll be hyper-busy senior year, never knowing if I'm singing at a frat party, a banquet, or a football game."

"Count on gigs on the Ed Sullivan Show and in Bermuda," Stark exclaimed.

A lot of Whiff and Secret Society wannabes had earlier joined singing groups, fraternities, or athletic teams because these organizations often led to entry into the Whiffs and senior societies. After Tap Day, all the selected guys became instant "insiders," and many "outsiders" grieved. As a confirmed outsider, though,

I could not be happier: I'd been elected captain of Trumbull's debate team a couple of days prior.

I had savored the honor for a minute-and-a-half before setting my sights on winning the coveted Adams Debate Cup during senior year. I'd also set my sights on nailing down the public health internship in D.C. I'd been working on for a while. Public service had been a strong part of the Yale ethos long before President Kennedy's appeal for civic service by my generation.

After her nervous breakdown, Mom had started working at a fabric store part time to assert some independence. She soon decided it might be more fun to sell finished fabric goods, namely dresses, at Macy's. Notwithstanding, during a phone call, Mom complained, "The darn cash registers at Macy's are giving me fits."

"Too many buttons?"

"Yes, and they've gotta be hit in the right sequence."

"I know the feeling. I've got to put my IBM punch cards in exactly the right sequence, or they won't get processed by the computer center."

"I end up calculating totals by hand."

"Takes time—"

"And I make mistakes, just like at the fabric store where I did yardage and totals by hand."

"Well, at least, you don't really need these part-time jobs."

"But I like interacting with customers," she said and then changed the subject. "How're you and Sharon doing?"

"She's annoyed because I don't have the time to write very often."

"Well, you know relationships require a commitment of time." Mom then passed the phone to Dad.

Following pleasantries, I said, "Mom's frustrations and self-doubts tug at my heart."

"I've noticed her uncertainty, too," he said, "but I don't think it's anything important."

"I hope not."

"You know, we're creating a new cabinet-level department at work. It'll be called Housing and Urban Development, or HUD."

"You're probably working as hard as I am."

Shortly thereafter, Stark and I ran into Clark.

"Congrats, Steve, on Skull and Bones," I said, patting him on his powerful, swimmer's back.

"Unfortunately, I'm gonna miss a lot of the Thursday night Bones' meetings," Steve said. "Gotta take a 'leave' next fall to train for the Olympics."

"Tokyo?" Stark asked.

"Right. Gotta train five hours a day for the next six months."

"Wow!" I said.

"Then I've got to make the team. There's this freestyler, Don Schollander, who's nipping at my heels."

"Young swimmers catch old ones sooner or later," Stark deadpanned.

"Shut your mouth, unless you want a cleft lip," I said to Stark, drawing laughs all around.

"Even if Schollander doesn't make the U.S.A team, he'll be in my face...'cuz Yale has admitted him to the Class of '68."

I admired Steve, who could train hard for fifteen years and put everything on the line for a mere 40 seconds to see if he could beat every other swimmer in the world. I wished I had the confidence to risk failure the way he did.

It turned out I took a "leave," too, but from Palo Alto that summer.

I was to be a summer intern in D.C in the Office of the U.S. Surgeon General. So I hauled the Moldmobile out of mothballs at Ned's summer place and drove to D.C. Dad supported my decision more than Mom did, since she felt I needed to pay more attention to Sharon.

Sure enough, Sharon called to scold me for my decision not to come home before the internship started. I told her I just couldn't afford to fly home.

After giving me more grief, Sharon said, "Maybe we just aren't meant to be," and hung up.

I called her right back and told her the internship only paid enough to cover living expenses, but that I'd consider a fast road trip to and from the West coast at the end of the summer. I hoped I'd bought a little more time.

I took the Surgeon General's internship because I wanted to see if the Public Health Service might be a place I'd want to work someday, especially if it someday recognized homicide, domestic violence, and gang violence as "diseases" and "epidemics."

Surgeon General Luther Terry impressed me, since he'd just facilitated the first-ever U.S. government warnings about smoking and health.

"Would you research the impact that abolishing the military draft might have on the 'draft' of Public Health Service doctors?" his people asked me.

Preparation of my position paper on this topic often took me to the Pentagon, still much-castigated for prosecuting the Vietnam War.

The Moldmobile struggled with the gridlocked commute through traffic circles to and from work. So, too, I struggled without air conditioning in Old Moldy…and in my North Capitol Street digs. Thus, one day with typical summer humidity and searing sun, I said to myself,

"I'm going to skip a commute and give taxpayers extra value for their dollar by working two days straight in my office."

I ducked under my desk around 3 a.m. for a catnap. Apparently, though—like sleeping with Lee on my elementary school roof—I'd broken more laws that night than I could imagine. Federal police officers routed me from my nap, scolded me, and told me to drive home...so that I could drive back in an hour to report for work at 8 a.m.

Though I interned in the Executive Branch, I wasn't a White House intern. Other Yale interns worked in the judicial or legislative branches. All of us interns heard and questioned President Lyndon B. Johnson, Attorney General Bobby Kennedy, and various Cabinet secretaries at periodic White House seminars—"intimate" gatherings of hundreds of interns. In addition to D.C. sights and sounds (voices speechifying in Congress and the Supreme Court), I took in a barbecue in honor of the President's daughters, Lynda Bird and Luci Baines, both with the same LBJ initials citizens used when referring to the President and his wife, Lady Bird.

At a party in July, I met Chrisi Schlesinger who'd had experiences similar to mine in Unitarianism, Quaker activities, and the Ivy League. I canoed the Potomac River with her a few times, irking my conservative housemate, Bill Rawn, who gave me a hard time about dating the daughter of a well-known liberal. Unfortunately, I came up short with Chrisi.

Amazingly, Steve Clark came up short, too. At the Olympic Trials in New York, he failed to qualify to swim any of the individual events at the Games. I couldn't believe my hero had stumbled. Apparently deep nagging pain from shoulder bursitis and tendonitis from overuse kept him from winning what should have been an easy slot on the U.S. team. He was, after all, the fastest freestyle sprinter in the world at the time of the trials—and the world record holder in the 100-meter freestyle.

I could only imagine what he was feeling after a lifetime focused on the Olympics.

Despite Steve's disappointment, he drove himself to subsequent finish lines at the Trials—the shoulder pain intensifying to sheer agony—to qualify to swim various relay events. He dug down deep and didn't let the psychic pain of missing out on a chance for individual glory defeat him. He continued to train hard the remaining months before the Games in Tokyo.

Sharon called me toward the end of the summer and confronted me, "Are you coming home before Yale?"

"Probably not," I said. "The Moldmoblie isn't up to it."

"You can't be serious!"

"Anyway, I might have to work right up until school starts."

After a pause that lasted forever, she asked, "Why not fly?"

"It's not cheap."

"I know…My dad never forgets to remind me of that."

"Believe me, I've missed you this summer!"

"I don't think I can endure another l-o-n-g absence," she said. "This summer apart will have to be the last!"

It took all my forensic skills to persuade her not to give up on me. I hung up, my shirt wringing wet from more than the humidity.

And so, without passing "Go" in California, I returned to Yale, though it seemed like "Jail." Time was running out on Sharon's relationship clock. Fate further conspired against our relationship: since winning the Adams Cup soon became my main focus, I had even less time to write to her.

To secure the Cup, I had to get my team to the debate championships—and then win. This wouldn't be easy for me because I had to do well in my courses to get into med school and because the championship debates featured almost as much talent as varsity matches did. Given that over a fourth of my Yale classmates aspired to be lawyers, many joined the inter-college league to develop their skills in oral argument. Was I—pre-med and not pre-law—presumptuous to want to win the Cup?

The resolutions our league would debate in my senior year

included "Bilingual education is an abomination," "Court penalties should be determined by judges, not juries," and other topics that would test anyone's mettle.

Straight away, I signed up the best returning debaters from the previous year's team and began courting Ned, who, understandably, claimed to be too busy. I also went after a couple of talented newcomers who'd come to Yale, in part, to debate, as I had.

I set up a meeting with Trumbull Dean "Inky" Clark to get his tactical and strategic advice regarding our debate season. He did not disappoint, recommending practice debates, among other things. And so I set up debates within our squad and got Yale Law School students to critique both our performances and the logic we used. One law student said, "Gesture as if you're a Mediterranean!"

"But JFK kept his hands in his jacket pocket against Nixon," a squad member objected.

"Big mistake. JFK lost half his effectiveness," the student said. "Anyway, you guys are debating live, not on TV, which requires less animation."

Another law student counseled us, "Avoid over-reliance on note cards. Most of all, prove your case fully when you're debating the affirmative, or else you lose."

I continued to have remarkable classes and professors in my senior year. Spellbinding Vincent Scully brought art and architecture alive in his stunning slide-show lectures. Lights down, pointer stick at the ready, every Monday and Wednesday at 11:10 a.m., Scully treated a packed lecture hall to his passion for analyzing and understanding the ideas behind works of art—be they Grecian urns, ancient ruins, seminal paintings, or architecturally significant buildings. He'd wax poetic as he shoved his stick along the white crystalline surface of an immense screen showing his color-slide illustrations: skyscrapers "thrust up into the sky," walls "engulfed" people, doorways "ate people like gaping mouths." One time, Scully fell off the edge of the stage—a victim of his own enthusiasm.

Mostly, though, I consumed a full plate of psychology during senior year with my pre-med Physics course as "spinach."

On the social front, my neediness pushed aside my guilt feelings over Sharon, and I reconnected with Blair Chapman, my Senior Prom date and cage-cleaning buddy from back home. She travelled from New Jersey where she attended Fairleigh Dickinson College.

"I call the place 'Fairly Ridiculous,'" she said, button-cute in her Sky turtleneck under a Fair Isle sweater.

At a Trumbull dance on a chilly Saturday evening, we danced to endless repetitions of the Rolling Stones' *(This could be) The Last Time* and *Satisfaction,* with its inimitable three-note riff at the start.

I relished feeling like an insider: an accepted member of Trumbull whose company others enjoyed. I also relished our school song, which described each of the years at Yale, ending with "In Senior year we act our parts, by making love and winning hearts. Fol de rol de rol rol rol!"

In Tokyo, Steve Clark faced yet more challenges during the humid early days of October. For starters, Olympic doctors almost didn't let him swim because they discovered he had an esoteric condition called "heart block." I knew from my schooldays research that this involved abnormal electric signals. When the doctors realized well-trained athletes often have "slower" electrical conduction, they cleared Steve to swim.

Still, Steve had to swallow his pride while waiting on the bench for the relays to begin. He had to watch Don Schollander—the Yale freshman from Oregon—start amassing four gold medals, more than any American since Jesse Owens in 1936.

When the relays started at last, Steve had to face his challenges by somehow putting aside his emotions and shoulder
pain. As live TV broadcasts in the U.S. from a satellite showed,
Steve won gold by teaming up with three others in the 400-me-
ter Medley Relay, the first Olympic medley ever swum. He
followed that up with a second gold (with Schollander, of all
people) in the 800-meter Freestyle Relay, driving himself to
the finish line despite his bursitis and tendonitis. And, by not
backing off at the point when pain becomes agony, Steve even
won a third gold in the 400-meter freestyle relay, again with
Schollander.

My own challenges involved med schools, which began and
finished their admissions earlier than law schools and grad
schools. After studying the pros and cons of several schools,
Johns Hopkins, Columbia University's College of Physicians
and Surgeons, and a few backups made my list. I wrote my essays about hoping to research violence of all kinds as a social
psychiatrist. I also stated my interest in treating the poor after
my internship, possibly as military Alternative Service. Eventually, I traveled to med schools for interviews.

Invariably, interviewers asked, "How did you manage to
identify all your 'unknowns' in Organic Chemistry? That's un-
heard of."

Knowing it would be months before I'd hear back from any
med schools, I focused on my classes and the debate team.

After studying about neurotics and psychotics, my Abnormal Psych class visited a bleak mental hospital in close-by Mid-
dletown. Our professor, Edward Zigler described the hospital
as "one of the best," and so I could only imagine the dreariness
of typical, less-stellar hospitals like the Stanford V.A. hospital where Mom stayed. My mood began to match the dreary
weather outside.

At the end of our tour, we saw clinicians interview four

patients. One seemingly-together patient made me think of Mom, as did an attractive patient in a film Professor Zigler later showed. It featured Carl Rogers demonstrating his humanistic therapy techniques. I hoped Dr. Steinman's sessions with Mom included such techniques.

I had plenty of questions I wanted to research after Professor Seymour Sarason took my clinical psychology class to a center for the mentally handicapped, but I had to postpone doing so because of the start of debate season and the Cup.

In my team's first debate, we argued that "America should reduce unemployment with public works programs." We won by the slimmest margin. The topic didn't inspire us, and by arguing the affirmative, we had the always-tough assignment of proving our case fully. We also won our second debate, after which I juggled our lineup to strengthen our finish since the first speaker always returns to finish for the team. This worked and we prevailed again, arguing for the proposition that "Representation in state legislatures should be based on counties, not population." In these match-ups, Yale faculty determined the winners.

During the Yale-Harvard Football Weekend in Cambridge, I checked in with Walter Hewlett at Dunster House to catch up and talk about mutual friends from back home. Unchanged by Hewlett-Packard's runaway success, Walter continued to be thoughtful and introspective. Tall and slender, he had become a star cross-country runner at Harvard and a Boston Marathoner.

"I used to get psyched out by big meets," Walter said, "but one day I wore Yale-blue socks and won. So now I wear them every time I race even though they don't match my crimson Harvard uniform."

"Your coach lets you, even against Yale?" I baited.

"He knows that's how I can beat Yale."

Before the 1964 holidays, I found Bob and Dave, two other Yalies from California crazy enough, but still responsible drivers, to drive nonstop to San Francisco…and then nonstop back to New Haven. All in a matter of ten days. Traveling this way allowed us to pocket the usual parent-paid airfare for more exciting uses. And, as a seasoned road warrior, having driven across the U.S. seven times by now, I wanted to drive fascinating U.S. routes 40 and 50 once more before boring, homogeneous Interstate 80—still under construction at the time—supplanted them.

We pushed Bob's VW Bug without mercy the entire length of the country, rotating drivers without stopping even at night, as if pilots on a wartime mission. The driver and shotgun passenger (who had to keep the driver amused and awake) would trade places by slipping under and over each other respectively, making sure someone's foot was always on the gas. Then the former driver would climb through the bucket seats to the back seat, and the back-seat guy, the "sleeper," would climb forward. We only stopped for gas, bathrooms, and food-to-go—eschewing motels and restaurants, which would have meant a seven-day rather than a three-day trip. And we didn't tell any of our parents about the risks we took on our eighty-five-hour drive, especially passing slow trucks on two-lane highways. We were crazy.

As soon as I got home, I saw Sharon and apologized profusely for staying in D.C. We saw each other daily and trod gingerly until we traded mea culpas: I came clean about Blair Chapman at Yale and Chrisi Schlesinger in D.C., and Sharon admitted she'd dated some guys to try to forget about me.

Mom was okay with my spending so much time with Sharon, but she missed me a great deal. She gave me a new Smith-Corona Electric typewriter for Christmas.

"To speed up my typing or to replace my manual that can't spell?" I asked.

"Neither," Mom said. "To keep the cards and letters coming." I visited for only a week before repeating the eighty-five-hour epic stunt to get back in time for classes. When I arrived at Yale, I learned that Trumbull classmate Ed McCarthy, the easy-going Yale QB, had just died in an auto accident. I realized how easily it could have been my friends and me.

THE DEBATE CUP

As THE SEMESTER GOT under way, one of my tasks was to replace one of the weaker of our nine debate team members, and so I got down on bended knee to beg Ned once again to lend his quick mind and silver tongue to the team.

"Okay, okay. I'll help you out, but only because I'm intrigued by the next topic," Ned said.

"That homosexuality should be legalized?"

"Yes, I love controversy, especially about meaningful issues. That's why law attracts me."

"Remember, debate's not quite litigation," I said. "You don't have to swing at every pitch or provocation."

"Got it."

"And use your opponent's points in your own case or at least show them to be irrelevant."

"Thanks for the crash course in forensics, Schorny."

Ned's presence galvanized our team, and we went into our next debate with Ned going second and George Cole, third. When we eked out a victory, I sensed we might go undefeated, even though we'd likely have to face another undefeated team, Silliman College, in Yale's North League, for the Cup. But that wouldn't be for another few debates and toward the end of spring semester. Meanwhile, life went on, providing a pleasant distraction from the Cup.

On a blustery winter day, I ripped into two formal-looking envelopes I'd pulled from my Yale Station mailbox. I stood stunned amid the hordes rushing in and out of the crowded post office. "Hallelujah and Amen!" I shouted. Columbia and Johns Hopkins both wanted me.

In quick succession, two other schools admitted me as well. I smiled a lot for a while and then grasped that I had to decide which offer to accept. My family and friends all put in their two cents. I wrote to Dr. Cox—the surgeon who had fixed my face—thanking him again as I had when I got accepted to Yale. I told him about my college activities, chiefly debating, and my decision to attend Columbia. He wrote back, warmly congratulating me.

Though excited about med school, I still had to finish the semester. In a term paper that I wrote on the social psychology of physically handicapped children, I wrestled with whether repaired clefts and corrected speech still constituted physical handicaps or just lingering psychological handicaps. In a project about the role of looks in modern life, I examined facial discrimination based on physical appearance. I discussed how youngsters as a whole coped emotionally with America's increasing obsession with appearance, especially beauty and attractiveness.

"I'm writing a paper about issues related to the quest to look perfect," I told Sharon, during a quick call to explain my med school decision. "I'll look into the importance of 'first impressions,' too."

In another paper, I delved into the "passing"—not acknowledging the truth—and "covering"—downplaying the truth—people sometimes engage in regarding their race, religion, social class, or sexual preference. Ned and I provided much of the data.

All the while I continued my job in the Psychology Lab. Professor Miller, a pioneering researcher in "biofeedback," had me, among other things, remove the adrenal glands of white lab rats so that he could study their responses to stress without adrenaline. The surgeries I performed taught me I wasn't going to med school to be a surgeon.

At one point I ran into Steve Clark at Joe Capasso's barbershop on Broadway near the Co-op bookstore. It was Steve's first week back on campus since he'd had a lot of post-Olympic obligations.

"Way to go, Swim-Dog!" I said, shaking his hand. "Comeback Kid!"

He grinned. "Thanks."

"How's the shoulder?"

"Better now that I've cut back on training," he said with a slight weariness I'd never detected before.

"You hate this freshman Schollander?" I teased.

"Naw, he's a nice guy, and he'll guarantee Yale's dominance in swimming for a while."

"Your greatest moment at the Olympics?"

"The awards cere—No, probably when some official handed me the shell casing from the starter gun after I'd led off a relay that turned into a world record time."

If his shoulder hurt or his pride suffered from being in Schollander's shadow, Steve never showed it. He did seem less tightly wound. (Maybe competitors were gunning to unseat Schollander rather than him or, more likely, he'd shown himself to be a world-class swimmer and had nothing else to prove.) I realized it might be easier in life to start at the bottom as an "unnatural" like myself and work one's way up than to start at the top as a "natural" and have the world watch, waiting for you to stumble, as Steve (or his shoulder) had at the Olympic Trials, negating a chance for an individual gold medal.

Despite all the letters from Sharon, I couldn't stop seeing Blair, who loved visiting Yale. One Saturday night she and I caught a private party with so many people jammed into a suite the host retreated to a small clothes closet to mix gin cocktails under a flashlight somebody held overhead. My saddle shoes and Blair's Sperry Topsiders got stepped on and bathed in spilled booze. Guys guarded the bathrooms on the landing as their dates went in to pee.

Bryce said, "Preposterous party, huh?"

An urban public-school "Archie" mumbled something that started with "Twentieth-century angst…"

And a Jock said, "Did'ja hear the one about…?"

During spring break, a goodly number of Publics, and even Archies, headed for Daytona Beach and Fort Lauderdale in Florida for cheap liquor, beach barbecues, and dance parties. Preppies, the Yale Rugby Club, and Ned and the Whiffs headed to Bermuda for the same, but with more cachet.

I, on the other hand, hitchhiked to Miami, where I met Stark who had the cash to fly down. We loaded scuba and camping gear (which Stark had borrowed from Miami friends) onto an Ocean Airways Flying Goose, a small amphibious aircraft from World War II. We flew to the tiny island of Bimini, fifty miles off Miami's coast. A few blocks wide and several miles long, Bimini was a poor relative to the more glamorous Bahamian islands.

When the amphibious eight-seater deposited us at the island dock, Stark and I took off our watches and "went off the clock" for a week. We camped next in a white sandy cemetery a little south of the bright pink Avis Bimini Club, where we finagled toilet privileges. We stashed our clothes, camping gear, and Stark's scuba equipment amid the gravestones—hoping the local voodoo belief in the reanimation of the dead would keep people away. It worked.

Locals we met among the 1,200 island inhabitants thought we were either brave or foolish when they heard we slept in the graveyard by the beach.

During the day I'd sleep, read, sketch, or join Stark in the

warm water, a marvelous combination of brilliant and trans-
lucent blues, greens, turquoises. Stark scuba-dived and I snor-
keled, since scuba-diving taxed my irregular Eustachian tubes'
ability to equalize air pressure. We saw endless varieties of fish,
including an occasional stingray and barracuda, which caused
my scared self to retreat to the beach until Stark gave the all-
clear sign.

Our food included pan-fried fish fresh from Stark's spear
plus delicious local bread and veggies. Stark talked of someday catching blue and white marlin sport fish—Bimini's claim
to fame in addition to being home to Ernest Hemingway for a
couple of years.

In the evening, we'd get yacht rides from rich folks at the Big
Game Fishing Club or dance with local girls at the Calypso Club
or the Famous Door which, in an unusual twist, sold soda to
people who brought their own liquor—cheap, tax-free rum in
our case. Stark and I tended to drink too much, stumbling back
to our cemetery home along the King's Highway—a paved thor-
oughfare only wide enough for bicycle traffic.

Too soon, we had to leave idyllic Bimini.

Stark flew home, and I hitched from Miami to New Haven.

"It's great to get back to familiar food," I said to Ned in our
suite.

"I like returning to the mothering of the dining hall ladies,"
Stark said.

"That must be why you're the only Bursary Boy still working
dining halls," Ned jibbed.

"Hey, I love being back with the hum of my new electric typewriter and its black box," I said.

As one of the oldest colleges at Yale, Trumbull still ran on
direct current, forcing us to buy heavy DC-to-AC converters for
our electrical gadgets.

Ned looked at our tanned faces and said, "You scholarship

boys can hold your heads up high now and say, 'I've done the Spring Break thing.'"

Hard work had begun to pay off for me and other Publics, according to a *Yale Daily News* article; since mid-Junior year, Publics in our class had been getting better GPAs than Preppies. I bumped into Bryce as he came out of Mory's.

"So, your GPA's better 'n mine," Bryce said in a preemptive strike.

"What really matters is, 'Have you learned anything at Yale?'"

Bryce laughed. "Was I s'posed to, Schorny?"

"I've learned a lot, and it's rearranged my mental furniture."

"I've wasted some opportunities here," Bryce said, turning and staggering off. But, he wheeled around a moment later and said, "I feel bad about it…though I'm not sure if I feel sorry for me or for my dad. Expectations, you know."

Our team still had debates ahead of it, and though my teammates and I remained undefeated, I insisted we prepare extra hard for our next matchup on whether the U.S. should pull out of the Panama Canal Zone. While we had defeated Pierson College in a bruising battle, I forced our team to drill down even deeper and develop some pit-bull rhetoric to beat Branford College. During the Branford debate, I had to ratchet up my own performance because Ned faltered ever so slightly. We won by a hair, qualifying us for the Cup final.

Without time to catch our breath, we had to face off for the Cup against Silliman College, led by brilliant Gerry Reinhardt from Indianapolis.

Because both teams remained undefeated and had generated substantial numbers of fans, the huge wood-paneled Common Room where we met head-on was filled to capacity. Debate czar Osterweis flipped a coin, and our team ended up arguing for the proposition that abortion should be legalized in the U.S.

I started off the debate by launching my first salvo.

"So, what do we know about American anti-abortion laws? Well, they're Johnny-come-latelys!"

I paused briefly for effect. "They've not always existed. When abortion was legalized here, we never lost our moral compass. Nor have Japan or Sweden, where abortions have always been legal."

I continued, "For starters, we should legalize abortion when a woman's mental health is jeopardized."

I looked straight at my opponents and said "This often happens if she's pregnant due to rape or incest! Are we going to let a woman's mental health, and that of her family, deteriorate because we forbid abortions?"

Some Silliman team members squirmed, but Reinhardt clenched his teeth as he scribbled on his legal notepad.

I next argued the case for legalizing abortions when fetuses are too deformed or diseased to survive, distinguishing between survivable defects like my clefts and non-survivable ones.

Reinhardt stood up and fired back, his upper lip twitching. "America has little in common with Japan, a country without moral direction. And Sweden: it's halfway between a Communist state and a bordello!"

The crowd roared.

"You expect America to turn to such countries for guidance? Japan and Sweden have no place in this discussion."

He stated that pregnancies from statutory and acquaintance rape should not be aborted. And while pregnancies from forcible rape presented challenges, "Experience shows once a child is born, reluctant mothers, and even families, adjust to the fact and soon find themselves loving the child."

Reinhardt seemed to have made quite an impression, and so I quickly persuaded Mike Castro, our next guy up, to trade places with Ned.

His eyes narrowing and piercing, Ned jumped up, grabbed

the podium, and stated, "Japan has lots in common with the U.S.—manufacturing prowess and an interest in movies…and baseball." The crowd laughed.

"And Sweden's like us, too, being a highly-developed Western democracy. Swedes came to America and formed the heart of much of the Midwest. Sweden, and Japan for that matter, have legalized abortion for centuries and their women who abort remain stable and are neither overwhelmed with guilt nor prone to suicide, according to UCLA researchers."

Fired up, Ned continued.

"And about growing to love any child that's born—Hogwash! There are too many unloved kids in America as it is. Raising a child today is costly and time-consuming. Unwed mothers in particular are often unprepared or unwilling to raise an infant. Like the right to vote, women should have the right to abort!"

Silliman's second guy took the podium and bellowed, "Women smart enough to vote should be smart enough not to get pregnant. We're talking all women here—not just women intelligent enough to attend Yale…assuming Yale goes coed someday."

The crowd howled.

I muttered under my breath, "They're grandstanding, fighting dirty."

After the second guy finished, I literally pushed Mike toward the podium, saying, "Sic 'em. This is war."

Mike began by crisply stating various arguments for legalizing all abortions. After a couple of minutes he said, "Legalizing abortion, of course, needs to take into account the viability of a fetus, which starts at six or seven months." He then explored issues surrounding pre-fetal embryos and DNA.

Then, Reinhardt grabbed the podium and countered Mike. He ended by summarizing Silliman's three main points: "Abortion's murder—plain and simple. An embryo is 'precious DNA' arranged in a unique way, like the blueprint of a building, and as such is human, contrary to Trumbull's assertions. Finally, every-one knows abortion is unsafe and dangerous!"

As I rose, the crowd became ominously quiet, knowing it was mine to win or lose. My heart started pounding, but I relished the challenge.

"Objection, objection, objection!" I shouted. "Silliman's summation assumes facts not in evidence." I paused for effect.

"First: if abortion is murder, then so is contraception. In fact, contraception is premeditated, preemptive murder—preventing life before it even starts! And by Silliman's absurd logic, menstruation is also murder. Women regularly flush out eggs that might have provided life under other circumstances. According to Silliman, all women are murderers."

"Second: the DNA blueprint mentioned is a template, not a human being. And just as the blueprint of a building is useless unless the building is built, so too, the DNA of an embryo is nothing until the strands become fully human."

I adjusted my tie and all of the grade-school teasing, the facing of bullies, the researching of my health issues came flooding back. My mother's constant care-giving, my father's "try harder" exhortations, and my speech therapists' therapeutic interventions flashed across my mind.

I grabbed hold of my suit coat lapels and scanned the crowd, knowing every pair of eyes in the room starred at my notched lip and my scars and left nostril. I could feel my once-hesitant heart beating strong, and my once-nervous knees locked confidently, ready to cash in on all the debate prep my team had done and all the effort I'd expended to learn how to speak in a commanding, persuasive manner.

The moment had arrived.

"And third: abortions in hospitals are safe. According to new research at Hopkins and Michigan, it's safer to abort a fetus than carry it to term! In fact, hospital abortions are one-eighth as dangerous as hospital deliveries! Trumbull rests its case."

As I crossed in front of the judges to sit down, the murmur of the crowd and the blank stares of the Silliman team told me I'd ended with vigor. I still worried, though, about Silliman's strong showing in the middle of the debate.

From his judge's chair in the front row, political scientist Richard Merritt said, "I listened to you gentlemen, straining to hear any misuse of facts, statistics, or experts. For veracity, and for overall performance, I give the nod to Trumbull."

Next, historian Firuz Kazemzadeh looked up from his chair, looked down at his notes, and then critiqued one of Ned's points in some detail. He finished, saying, "Trumbull didn't establish an airtight case. I vote for Silliman."

Finally, Osterweis lifted his portly frame from his chair, buttoned his blue blazer—replete with a Yale crest on the breast pocket—and lumbered to the podium, holding the Adams Cup by one of its handles.

"In my years shepherding debate, I have not seen a better inter-college championship match than this one." He turned from us to the crowd. "Don't you agree?"

The crowd applauded.

"These teams could hold their own against the best, Harvard, Oxford, anywhere. But I digress. I agonized making this decision, chiefly because of the brilliant crossfire. Still, with Trumbull's superb rebuttals—something we in forensics call 'crystallization'—I agree with Professor Merritt that Trumbull took the night. Thus, I'd like to award the Adams Cup to Mr. Schonborn and his team."

Amidst applause and shouts from the whole Trumbull squad, Osterweis handed me the cup and flashbulbs went off as the *Daily News* captured our handshake. I held the silver cup high above my head. For once, I didn't instinctively turn to show my best profile. Nor did I flinch when the flashbulbs went off. I gestured toward each member of the team, one at a time. Even Ned—no stranger to applause as a Whiff—enjoyed the attention. I kept smiling, as images of Mom and Dad and debate moments in junior and senior high flashed in my mind.

"Thank you, thank you," I said, imagining that Mom and Dr. Cox stood in front of me—when in fact I was thanking swarms of people who were shaking my hand and patting me on the back.

When the debate dust settled, Stark and I studied for our daunting three-day comprehensive exams, as did Ned who had to know every work of art from the Lascaux Cave paintings to the latest Warhol. A week later, Ned took us to members-only Mory's to celebrate passing our exams.

We quaffed a traditional "Red Cup"—one of several shareable alcoholic concoctions served in silver trophy cups—and snacked on relish trays and oyster crackers. We toasted to our futures in New York City and Chicago, where Stark would pursue a PhD in English and Ned, a law degree.

We finished the evening with Mory's legendary Baker's soup, some Welsh rarebit, prime rib, and a divine Indian pudding.

Soon afterward, I encountered Steve Clark.

"Seen *Sports Ill-stated* yet, that ill-thought-of, ill-mannered parody?" I asked.

"No, I don't trust those humor magazines. Did they skewer me?"

"No. They *did* lampoon a new craze called 'skateboarding,' calling it 'sidewalk surfing.'"

"Reminds me, gotta take up surfing someday."

"You training now?"

"Sort of. Some guys wanna race. They're training hard and may clean my clock soon."

"You're not training hard?"

"Right. If all I do in my life is train, I won't have much to say to people."

"Too much time in the water?"

"Yeah. I've logged 3,000 miles since I was five. Gotta see what life's like on dry land."

I detected a hint of regret. Could Steve have felt left out all these years—an outsider like me? I had always seen him as the ultimate insider at Yale. Maybe his single-minded focus had kept him from experiencing many of the things the rest of us did, like hanging out and experimenting with relationships and sex.

In the unhurried last few days before graduation, Stark, Ned, and I cleared out of our much-loved suite and read articles in our Class Book, the oldest yearbook in the country. Blair accompanied me to the Senior Picnic in the nearby town of Prospect. Blair and I talked, among other things, about how Easterners talk, walk and move and at a faster clip than Westerners, but keep to themselves a lot more. The one exception was West Coaster Steve Clark who moved faster than everyone who informally challenged him in the pool on the picnic grounds. That evening, Blair and I went to a campus dance, where the Chiffons sang *He's So Fine*.

Mom and Dad arrived Saturday and feted me with a New England "shore dinner" featuring Maine lobster. On Sunday, President Brewster delivered the farewell Baccalaureate address. And at the end of the Class Day ceremony, Stark, Ned, and I smoked white, long-stemmed clay pipes, which we broke—a Yale tradition signifying that the joys of college life were ending. Afterward, I showed Mom and Dad my favorite campus spots: the Linonia and Brothers reading room in Sterling Library, the courtyards of red-bricked Pierson College, and the wood-paneled, two-story reading room at the Divinity School Library.

Despite an overcast morning the next day, the commencement pageantry of heraldic flags and academic garb impressed me, as did the honorary degree recipients, which included family favorites U.N. Secretary General U Thant and baby doctor Benjamin Spock. At the end of the Old Campus ceremonies, we Trumbull seniors had a luncheon and our own ceremony in the main courtyard, suddenly spring-green for the occasion.

Just as the sun broke through the clouds, College Master, George deForest Lord, presented me with the Adams Cup which, unfortunately, stayed at Yale to be awarded again the next year. The cup shone in the sunlight, as did Mom when Dad took a picture of us with the cup.

DEAD MEN TALK

BACK IN PALO ALTO, I had to plan my dates with Sharon around my graveyard shift at Hewlett-Packard's corporate offices. HP had demoted me from day janitor to night janitor since I still showed no signs of wanting to be an electrical engineer. To HP's credit, the company knew I needed tuition money and kept a job open for me.

In the early evenings, Sharon and I would drive my family's second-hand Peugeot 404 into the foothills near where Stanford's construction of a linear accelerator to study subatomic particles struggled toward completion. Sharon and I had a favorite parking spot where we'd unscrew the backs of the Peugeot's front seats so we could lay them down, creating a bed of sorts. We'd be crazy then.

Afterward, we'd talk about all sorts of things. One evening I asked, "What do you think of Friedan's *Feminine Mystique*?"

"I agree with the assertion that women shouldn't be subservient to men financially, intellectually, or physically." She slapped me on the knee. "Makes us crazy."

"Physically, huh? If Friedan and 'the pill' hadn't come along, do you think you'd be here tonight?"

"Yes, I think so. Like a lot of women throughout time, I have a natural interest in pleasure, in sex. Don't need a book to convince me."

When 10 p.m. rolled around, I'd drive Sharon home, change into coveralls, grab makings for a 3 a.m. "lunch," and head to the foothills again for my 11 p.m. to 7 a.m. shift at HP. I cleaned and tidied up the offices of top HP officials, including a vice president who, as a onetime mayor of Palo Alto, had arranged for Oregon Avenue from Highway 101 to Hewlett-Packard headquarters to be turned into an expressway—essentially making HP "freeway close." The eerie stillness of the HP buildings at night on Page Mill Road didn't surprise me. It did surprise me, though, to find copies of *Playboy* tucked away in corners of various executive offices.

On weekends, I'd switch my sleep schedule back to normal hours, only to have to change back again on Monday. I never quite got the hang of switching my sleep around, though the extra pay I got for working the graveyard shift made up for it. I did know I'd have to endure even worse sleep upheavals during my internship and residency after medical school.

I often talked to Mom during my weekday "dinners" at 8 a.m. "It's odd eating dinner while you're eating breakfast," I said.

"Odder still that you go right to bed afterwards," she replied.

"Tell me more about you and Dad. I need to know how relationships work."

"Sharon seems like she'd make a great partner. I like her."

"C'mon. You're not answering my question."

"Well, Dad insists I line up his shoes 'just so' after vacuuming the closet."

"Really? I'd never stand for that."

"I s'pose I drive him nuts, too," Mom quipped.

After many discussions about relationships, I concluded that Mom had plenty of emotional resilience, and that I should have no qualms about heading east for med school.

As I prepared to leave for Columbia in mid-August, the Watts community in southeast Los Angeles went up in flames.

"Why would rioters shoot at cops and firemen?" Mom muttered as she watched TV with Scott and me on the fifth and last day of rioting.

"I presume to get even with cops." I said. "Not sure what their beef is with firemen."

"HUD and Dad are sure to get involved. A thousand residences, businesses, and public buildings burned or damaged," Scott remarked.

"They've destroyed their own community," Mom said.

"Well, they started by torching only white-owned property. Looting only the stores of the exploitive merchants," Scott said.

"Oh, that's so Marxian, Scott," I said. "Our country's racism is more to blame for Watts than is capitalism."

"Fact is, HUD and everybody can't bring back the dozens who died—be they black or white. It's so sad," Mom said, slowly rising from the couch, sighing, and leaving the recreation room.

As I started to pack, images of the Watts riot haunted me: desperate people doing unspeakable things—like snipers firing from rooftops, rioters torching buildings, blacks pulling whites from vehicles and beating them. While heading to the airport to fly to New York City for the next chapter of my life, I kept thinking of the innocent bystander who had died trapped between a rioting crowd and advancing squads of policemen.

While I knew parts of Manhattan from my college years, I knew nothing about the Washington Heights area, where the medical school operated as part of the Columbia-Presbyterian Medical Center, a sprawling complex of twenty-story buildings.

Full of excitement, I participated in the P&S (College of Physicians and Surgeons) White Coat Ceremony during which the deans talked to our class of 120 over-achievers. We donned short white coats and recited the Hippocratic Oath.

After the ceremony an ace backstroker from Yale, Roger Goettsche, and I looked at the Med School handbook, turning to the class mug shots with schools listed below the names.

"Most of us went to schools in the East," Roger remarked. "A smattering from southern and Midwestern schools...and a number from out your way, Stanford."

"Yeah, an awful lot of us guys are from the major and minor Ivies, with Yale and Harvard sending the most," I said.

"Say, here's a real cutie," Roger said, pointing to a picture.

"I've noticed most of the dozen or so women in our class are quite attractive."

"Looks like they're mostly from the 'Seven Sisters' colleges."

"Then the rumors are likely true. The P&S gals probably *are* smarter than us guys."

"Speaking of smarties, I've still gotta write to my girl back home, and then I gotta get settled in."

After the mostly small classes at Yale, I liked escaping into the anonymity of the topmost seats of large old-fashioned lecture amphitheaters. Or at least, so I thought, until I got called down to the lecture floor one day early on and asked:

"Dr. Schonborn, would you palpate Mrs. Jackman's calf and tell us what you think is causing her problems?"

"Well, uh," I stammered as I examined her calf and frantically tried to remember last night's reading, "I'd say the swelling and warmth, and discoloration, are from deep vein thrombosis."

Turns out, being called on without warning to perform constituted part of the socialization tactic of medical schools...like being called "Doctor" in the presence of county hospital patients, who generally did not know our true status as students.

Some in the class, fast trackers and hyper-competitive types for sure, had already set their sights on prestigious internships, residencies, and lucrative practices. But, most of us were cooperative and friendly, realizing we were all in the same pressure-cooker together.

Most of us also lived in Bard Hall, an 11-story art deco building crafted by the same architect who had designed Trumbull

College. Bard Hall stood on prime real estate that sloped down to Riverside Drive and finally the stately Hudson River. Through my room's window, the George Washington Bridge—with its two Erector-Set-like towers—spanned the Hudson, looking like a silver version of the Golden Gate. I reclaimed vital space taken by a nonfunctioning food elevator stuck in place in my tiny (7'-by-15') room, which had once been a food pantry. I used the dumbwaiter to store my hotplate and groceries for weekend meals when the dining room was closed.

I wrote religiously to both Sharon and the family every Sunday, but didn't have much to report other than the excitement of "indoor cycling"—learning the metabolic cycle, the Krebs cycle, the menstrual cycle, and the mitotic cell cycle. I did call home from time to time rather than type a master letter and carbon copies for Gayle and Scott. In one call, with Dad away on business, I complained to Mom that we had to learn almost every single chemical reaction in the human body, a sizable chunk of material.

"I'm under pressure, too," Mom replied, "with this bathroom remodel. Dad wants it a certain way, but workers cut corners I don't see until Dad points them out when he comes home."

"Kinda like taking the car to the mechanic and then having to answer to Dad?"

"Yes, but these workers are in your home. It's hard—"

"Confronting them?" I asked.

"Yes. I hate having to stand up to them. But if I don't, Jack chews me out."

"You're in a tough spot."

"Speaking of your father," Mom continued, "he got a big promotion for helping set up HUD. And, he's ghostwriting for HUD Secretary Weaver."

"The first black Cabinet member in U.S history!"

"Yes. And did you know, Weaver's only child, an adopted son, died in 1962?"

"Not a good year, 1962, as you well know."

We talked about other things, and as I hung up, I concluded that Mom likely found herself alone more than she wanted—what with Dad busier than ever, Gayle in an apartment in Menlo Park, Scott in a residence co-op at Berkeley, and me in a food-prep pantry in Manhattan.

With classes from 9 a.m. to 5 p.m. during the week and on Saturday until 1 p.m. plus unremitting study, I rarely had time to go beyond our medical complex at the upper end of Manhattan. So when I had a day to kill before flying home for the Holidays, I decided to venture to the lower end. Walking briskly to stay warm, I headed for the subway near the med school. Besides being fast and cheap, New York's subways could be instructive. Our neurology professor told us that over time we'd see riders with almost every clinical disorder we'd studied.

To get in the Christmas spirit, I first stopped to visit the Frick Collection in a festively decorated mansion featuring Old Masters paintings from Europe. Next I went to the Museum of Modern Art to pay homage to Sharon and my mutual interest in pop art. When my feet began to ache mid-afternoon, I took the subway to the lower end to wander about the SoHo Flatiron district which was beginning to attract artists.

I ate dinner at an automat whose tiny glass doors dispensed food items after customers inserted the right combination of coins. The food wasn't bad, but nothing like the food that soon would be served in a very expensive restaurant planned for the top of the north tower of a twin 110-story tower project to be called the World Trade Center. I marveled at how fast the construction was progressing as I passed the project on the way to another station to catch a subway home.

"Surprise!" Sharon shouted as I walked off the plane in San Francisco.

I gave her a big kiss and a hug, almost forgetting Mom and Dad standing next to her.

Sharon and Mom had become friends because Sharon had started dropping by the house to keep Mom company as Dad traveled more these days.

"Surprise!" I said as I opened the coat closet at our home to hang up Sharon's coat. A life-sized papier mache skeleton rattled against the back of the closet door.

"Sheesh," Sharon said as she jumped back. "To think Matt used to call me 'Bone' as well as 'Stick.'"

"Sorry. Shake and make up?" I said, pushing the arm and hand bones toward her. When I had made the skeleton for Halloween one year, I attached the bones, rib cage, and skull together with loose-enough wire to allow the skeleton to move in various ways.

It turned out Mom had included Sharon in various activities during the holiday break, pleasing me in that I could see Sharon and my family at the same time—important, given what little time I had. But it displeased me as well: I felt pressured as it made Sharon out to be a member of the family already. I liked her a lot, but felt in no position to commit. I was married to medicine for the next few years.

Back at Columbia after the holidays, my throat seized up and I experienced dread as my classmates and I gathered outside the gross anatomy lab. Once we entered, we stood in silence for a moment, honoring the dead whose bodies would teach us so much. Right afterwards, I surveyed the tables in the room, estimating that forty or so corpses lay among us.

Tony Santomauro and Bill Abernathy had joined with me earlier to form a "table group" for dissection. Our corpse, along with scores of other bodies, had been in a "swimming pool" filled with formaldehyde for two years. This was in case a malpractice or missing-persons case should develop regarding a cadaver-to-be.

Our table group had purchased a bone saw, chisels, mallets, and a pair of bone forceps to complement the sets of dissecting tools we had each bought. I treated myself to extra scalpel blades because, as I had learned from my days doing surgery at Yale, sharp blades make cutting so much easier.

Lab instructors insisted we buy gloves…mainly to prevent skin irritation and absorption of formaldehyde. They weren't worried about us contracting infections. However, the word from second year students: gloves made delicate dissection difficult, so be willing to work "nude."

After unwrapping our cadaver, we found the fourth member of our group to be a fifty-something black male, slight of build with little or no fat.

Tony rejoiced, "We lucked out. With a thin cadaver, we won't have to clear away tons of greasy fat to reach our objectives."

"They don't call this 'gross' anatomy for nothing," Bill responded, looking at an obese cadaver on the next table.

Continuing our group's zaniness, perhaps our way of coping with death, I shook the hand of our cadaver, as one might an opponent before a match. I likely did it subconsciously to tweak the Grim Reaper, whose hooded-self had haunted and, frankly, terrorized me in my youth.

We located the sternum or jugular notch and made our first incision. We then spent an hour or so dissecting chest muscles and discovering where they connected, their "origins" and "insertions."

As we left that first day, it bothered me that my worries about the inhumanness of mutilating, and maybe desecrating, a human body had been pushed aside by concerns that the distinctive formaldehyde odor wouldn't come out of our hands and forearms despite scrubbing mightily. The odor lingered for two weeks after the course ended, repulsing everyone we encountered except fellow med students.

Once we had dissected and studied our cadaver's chest muscles, we sawed through his ribcage and began our exploration of his lungs and the area containing his heart.

"I can't believe the black granules in the lungs of most of the cadavers here," Bill said. "I've heard most were New Yorkers."

"The result of smoking?" I wondered out loud. "The Surgeon General issued his smoking and cancer warning too late for many folks."

"Living in a big city with polluted air could also do it," Tony said. "I'm sure I've got New York City lungs, too."

As our table group began to study our cadaver's heart, I looked for all the defects I'd learned about in my cardiac invalid days, as well as for holes between the heart's chambers. Our cadaver had a normal heart, though other cadavers in the lab weren't so fortunate.

I also looked at heart specimens in jars stored at the lab. Armed with the embryology theories I had learned, I tried to picture how different types of cardiac anomalies might occur along with so called "midline deformities," such as clefts, which happen when embryos grow asymmetrically around the body's vertical axis.

In physiology class, I learned that exercise can help the body fill in holes between heart chambers and perhaps even close the two fetal cardiac shunts that may remain open, improperly, in some people. My youthful push to be active may have helped my body build up tissue and close such gaps, assuming I'd had any.

On some Saturdays after classes finished, I sketched parts of cadavers in the lab, especially notoriously difficult-to-draw hands. Our cadaver's hands and face were in better condition for artistic purposes than the rest of his body, which was more shriveled from the formaldehyde. When it got dark outside as I sketched, I began to feel outnumbered in that room full of corpses. The only way out was through two dark-green doors, with "No Admission" ominously stenciled on them, leading to a dingy hallway.

One Saturday, as I concentrated on a sketch, someone shouted, "Freeze!"

I dropped my sketchbook on the floor and spun around. Fellow Yalie Ed Cox, who'd hosted Sharon and me at the Fence Club during the Junior Prom, stood in front of me, grinning.

"You scared the shit out of me," I said. "When did you come in?"

"Moments ago."

"I get so engrossed when I draw. Didn't hear you."

"Channeling Michelangelo, no doubt?"

"Yeah…You know he sketched the dead to make his figures more lifelike. Ironic! What're you here for?"

"Forgot my lab book. Big test Monday, you know."

"Why not forego studying this time? You're top of the class. Give the rest of us a chance for once."

"Neurosurgeons-to-be never rest."

When it came time to dissect the brain, I felt uneasy. Dissecting the brain and seeing it under a microscope seemed invasive and sacrilegious: after all, this had once been someone's mind, somebody's spirit.

To facilitate our dissection, we each got a pan with a "fresher" brain in it, one better preserved than our cadaver's.

The irony wasn't lost on us.

"All those extra brains and no way to tap them!" I complained, scrunching up my face.

"Yeah, we only have our own brains to use to learn the countless anatomical terms," Bill said.

We had to learn not only all of the muscles, nerves, blood vessels, and structures of the body, but we had to be able to identify these structures from every possible angle, trace their course through the body, give their function, and be able to recognize them when misplaced, atrophied, or diseased.

"And now we gotta learn the brain's every nook and cranny: the fissures, sulci, and rami," Tony wailed.

I joked, "By the end of all this anatomy and neuroanatomy, we should be given honorary degrees in The Classics for all the Latin we've had to use."

When our group started to work on the neck and face, we had yet more information to absorb. Approaching my cadaver's right ear with my scalpel, I explored the eardrum, hammer, anvil, stirrup, and the pea-sized inner ear structure (with the cochlea, the hearing organ) and Eustachian tubes. I wanted to understand why people with clefts often lose their hearing due to infections or to Eustachian-tube irregularities. I also looked at our cadaver's nasal septum and turbinates to see if he might have been a mouth breather, like me.

When the time came to dissect the palate and the structures necessary for speech, I didn't know how to feel. Eager or reluctant? Happy or sad?

I held the scalpel in a loose grip, for I was now experienced in dissection. As I delved into our cadaver's oral cavity, my table mates and I quizzed each other, as we often did, to stay alert and connect what we were seeing with what we'd learned in our textbooks.

"The hard palate separates the mouth from the nasal cavity and nasopharynx?" I asked as I worked the scalpel.

"Right," Bill responded.

"And the soft palate influences speech and swallowing?"

"Correct," Tony said.

I flashed on memories of speech exercises and even Mom's stories about my childhood surgeries. How amazing to examine the tiny part of the body that had cost me and my family so dearly in pain, concern, and money.

"People also call the soft palate the velum?" Tony said, pulling me back to reality.

"R-right," I said with a slight catch.

A day later, after everyone else had left the lab, I searched the other cadavers for a repaired cleft, but only found an upper lip and mustache area that had been cut by accident by a classmate. I found a needle and suture thread and tried to repair it using the standard technique where surgeons sew together successive layers, one at a time. For some reason, the act of repairing the "cleft" did not bring me great feelings of satisfaction, reinforcing my belief that I hadn't come to med school to become a reconstructive surgeon.

I left a note next to the cadaver for its table group members so the sutures wouldn't freak anyone out. Luckily, none of my psychiatry professors walked in on my doings, mistaking them for irreverence or something worse. Had they done so, I might have been presented as a "Case" in the next lecture.

Psychiatry class met once a week for lectures and less often for seminar discussions. Besides *Modern Clinical Psychiatry*, we also read books about social psychiatry and about childhood, adolescence, and adulthood. Interestingly, professors did not deal much with depression, leaving us in the dark about a disease that troubled countless American housewives, and perhaps Mom.

If several years back, Mom had suffered depressive feelings of fatigue and inertia with periodic "blue spells," she didn't seem to be going through such feelings now.

"Lots of coming and going," she said in a light, cheerful voice during one of my calls that first winter in New York.

"I believe it," I responded. "Dad said you've entertained, or been entertained by, almost everyone you guys know."

"Yes, and I'm taking a Psych class at Foothill College."

"On top of your busy social calendar?"

"Yup. Just finished *Personality and Psychology* for it."

"By my boss at Yale?"

"Yes, Neil Miller. He writes so well. Also, I'm reading Erikson's *Childhood and Society*, which you recommended."

"Wow! What d'ya think of Erikson's life stages?"

"I thought of you, not getting enough milk—"

"The 'basic trust' stage?"

"Right. Dr. Steinman wonders why I'm reading Erikson."

"You'd think he'd like his patients looking into human development theories."

After our phone conversation, I wondered about the quality of Dr. Steinman's treatment and therapy.

VIOLENCE CHANGES EVERYTHING

A SHOTGUN BLAST AND small caliber gunfire in the Audubon Ballroom across the street from Columbia Medical School had torn into Malcolm X in February 1965. Rushed across the street, Malcolm X didn't have a prayer, even though doctors at my school tried their best to save his life. Now, a year later, as I studied large books in my small room, violence of all sorts in the U.S. made me question my decision to go to med school.

In addition to Malcolm X's assassination, there'd been those of President Kennedy, his alleged assassin Lee Harvey Oswald, and black civil rights activist Medgar Evers. And seven cities, including New York City, had undergone debilitating riots before Watts went up in flames as I had packed for med school. What's more, violent crimes—rape, robbery, assault, murder, and its new forms, mass murder and serial murder—began to grow at a scary rate in the U.S.

The escalating war in Vietnam also goaded me to think of focusing sooner, rather than later, on the study of violence. President Lyndon B. Johnson had begun to carpet-bomb North Vietnam again after a thirty-seven-day "pause" for the holidays, and he became incensed when Bobby Kennedy, then a senator from New York, criticized him for it. Senator William Fulbright began televised hearings to examine America's policy in Vietnam, and any free moment I found, I watched senators grill Defense Secretary Robert McNamara and others. All the while, and in the background, the anti-war movement grew more and more violent. I worried that anti-war violence might soon tear up the U.S.

I knew America had a fairly violent history compared to many other Western industrial democracies. On the surface, this didn't make sense because of America's generosity and idealism, and because America had been calm and peaceful at home since World War II, the years of my childhood and adolescence.

In a chat with a classmate who'd met Ira Sandperl while she was at Stanford, I said,

"Ira and Joan Baez predicted this."

"What?"

"That America's internal violence would begin to rival its external violence."

"I do sense a sea change in the amount of domestic violence," she said.

The task before me pressed with urgency; I felt I could no longer wait. Doctors repair bodies injured by violence, but I wanted to prevent the violence from happening in the first place.

And so, on a cold, overcast, winter's day, I came up with Plan B. I would fast-track my research into the causes of violence by leaving medical school and going to graduate school to study violence and conflict. I sent a four-page letter to Mom, Dad, and Sharon explaining the reasons for Plan B. I called them all a few days later.

"I'd be kinda sad if you left medicine." Mom said. "I've seen you as a budding Dr. Steinman."

"Be sure to think through the pros and cons of leaving," Dad said.

Sharon agreed with Dad. "I support you in whatever you do. Just be sure to ask yourself and others a lot of 'what if' questions."

Based on this feedback, I decided to give myself more time to consider the consequences of discontinuing my medical studies. If I was to reinvent myself, "redraw" my career, I needed a complete drawing, not just a quick sketch. I talked to faculty members, especially those in social psychiatry, to be sure I hadn't overlooked anything. Since ob-gyn had always appealed to me, I talked to a faculty member about his field. He recommended I watch a couple of babies being delivered and report back to him. A few weeks later, I told him, "I almost cried from joy during the deliveries."

"Births are awesome," he responded. "But, as I told you earlier, there are a fair share of crises requiring surgeries."

"I know. The surgeries, the crazy hours. Not my cup of tea, I'm afraid, if I'm really honest with myself."

I probed deeper into the issues around Plan B by going to Columbia's Low Library and checking out the feasibility of pursuing "violence studies." (Ironically, the library would become the site of a legendary, and violent, student protest a few years later.) I explored the library's extensive collection of literature on the UN's efforts to mitigate violence, in particular through its peacekeeping forces. Overall, the prospects for pursuing violence studies in the social sciences seemed good.

One day, I told Tony (in my table group) that I'd enjoyed seeing an obstetric delivery a few weeks before.

He responded, "Isn't childbirth just amazing? I'm sure ob-gyn is for me. It's the only happy specialty in medicine."

"All I know is neurology is nothing but misery," I said. I'd just seen two spinal and cerebral-meningitis patients in neuroanatomy class, where we also learned about polio, paralysis, and spinal cord diseases.

"Amen. And don't get me started on oncology—" Tony said.

"I'm still partial to psychiatry," I replied. "That's been my plan pretty much from the start."

As we talked, Tony said he was fine with psychiatry, but acknowledged a prejudice against it among many classmates and faculty. I reminded Tony of my goal to research conflict and aggression as a psychiatrist, and use social and community psychiatry as a vehicle to implement my findings. I told him, though, that I'd been rethinking my goal of late and hoped to talk about it soon.

"Come to my home for Easter dinner. We can talk then. My parents are dying to meet a Californian."

That night in the basement of Bard Hall, I bumped into my other dissecting partner, Bill Abernathy, as he waited for his coin-op dryer to finish.

"So," I asked, "what do you think of med school so far?"

"It could be better," he said.

"How so?"

"The rote-ness of the learning, all the memorization—"

"I know. Every metabolic cycle, every damn nerve in the body," I said. "And then some."

"Professors cram so much into the lectures. The chalkboards—"

"Yes. Using their left hand on the board to start a sentence and then their right to finish it."

"Showoffs!" he said.

"Well, can you keep a secret?"

"Sure. Sketching the dead again?"

"I didn't know you knew," I said. "But seriously: I'm thinking of transferring to grad school."

"Christ! You're kidding?!"

"No, I'm serious. I enjoy the work here, but grad school might allow me to get into violence studies sooner, which is why I came here in the first place."

"Yeah, I know your goal. But—"

"I no longer see medicine as the path to my goal."

I explained to Bill that because violence of all sorts had sky-rocketed in the last year, the federal government planned to pump money into researching and studying the causes and deterrents to violence. As a result, I could soon be studying aggression and conflict-resolution in grad school, rather than continue through more med school, an internship, a residency in psychiatry, and a sub-specialization in social psychiatry. I told Bill I didn't mind the hard work required by my original plan. What I did mind was that it would be just a prelude to what I really wanted to do.

When his clothes dryer came to a stop, Bill said, "I'd like to keep talking about this, but I'm behind in physiology."

He gathered his clothes and, as he left, he said, "I don't envy you, trying to fathom the best path to take. Only your future's at stake."

Several times while wrestling with my decision, I wondered whether an unconscious motivation to go to med school had been to confront the history of my cleft and heart. *Did I have a need to re-live various traumatic moments, but be in control this time rather than helpless; as the doctor rather than the patient? Or, God forbid, had I been attracted to med school to show those doubters, those bullies, that I'd amount to something?*

After a scrumptious Italian-style Easter dinner with Tony's family in their modest apartment in Queens, I opened up to Tony.

"I'm thinking of leaving med school."

"Wow! I know you told Bill you were debating some options, but I never—"

"I think I need to hurry up and study violence now. It's become a major social problem."

"But how're ya gonna make a living doing that?" Tony asked, always thinking of practicalities.

"Professing. Research grants. LBJ wants to fund violence studies."

"Basically, become a professor and live like a pauper?"

"Heck. Ministers and school teachers live on a lot less than professors do," I said. "But I still haven't made up my mind."

"I gotta admire your willingness to take a vow of poverty."
Tony shrugged and sighed. "I didn't grow up with much—as you
can see—so I wanna make serious money."

One weekend, I became an arms smuggler. I smuggled an arm
out of the anatomy lab, down an elevator, along a few city blocks,
and up to my fifth floor room in Bard Hall. I needed the arm to
study the complex of vessels and nerves near the armpit for an
important exam. A big infraction, I presumed, although no one
had ever forbidden us from doing such a thing—especially in
warm weather.

As Manhattan spring weather kicked in, our lab cadavers
began to stink, and ever more so when we cut them in half.
We severed their spinal cords above the pelvis, and hung them
on a frame to better dissect the groin region. Even the breez-
es through the windows in the anatomy lab on the tenth floor
couldn't keep the smell down.

Finally, when spring gave way to an early summer, humid
weather turned the dissecting room into a truly gross anatomy lab. Our cadavers' stench easily overpowered the lab's usual
odor—a mix of latex, cleaning product, and embalming fluid.

The last weeks of school featured nothing but study, study,
study. I developed the ability to learn on the run—in cafeteria lines, in bathroom stalls, even walking down the hall to
the shower. I never thought I could master so much material—almost every nerve, every artery, every muscle, and every
biochemical process in the body. (The process reminded me
of Dad's boot camp stories—people surprising themselves that
they could survive it.) When exams came to an end at last, a
bunch of us celebrated with the mother of all beer busts.

A couple days later, while many students readied themselves to
go home knowing this might be the last free summer of their
lives, I walked down Haven Avenue toward the hospital complex.

And then, just like that, I made up my mind. It resembled a come-to-Jesus moment.

I stopped in my tracks. I started to cry. The tears confused me. Maybe neither happiness nor sadness triggered them...just the magnitude of the choice I had made.

I ignored the gaze of a passersby and stared at the monolithic hospital buildings. Malcolm X had died here the year before, and now so had my plans to get an MD and become a social psychiatrist.

I started walking without direction or purpose, and hours later ended up in Fort Washington Park along the Hudson River. A shroud of mist enveloped me along with an early evening chill. The mist disappeared and I looked up at the George Washington Bridge, which I had seen so often from my tiny room in Bard Hall. The majesty of the bridge overwhelmed me. I squinted to see where the other end of the structure touched land. I knew at that moment there would be a bridge, a way to my new career and life.

The next day I walked into Associate Dean Perera's office and told him that, after much soul-searching, I'd decided not to return to school next year. I believed I couldn't continue to do well if my mind wanted to study, among other things, the causes of the interpersonal, everyday violence that brought so many patients to hospitals.

The Dean's eyes widened and he scratched the back of his head as he said, "Your grades are fine, and you've got a great bedside manner."

"This has been a hard decision," I said.

He paused, pressing the fingers of both hands together.

"Tell you what," he said. "I'll put you on indefinite leave. You can come back anytime and pick up where you left off."

"Thank you, I'll keep that in mind."

"You understand," he said, looking away from me, "I'll have to notify your draft board now."

"Yes, I know I'll lose my deferment, but I expect to do Alternative Service as a conscientious objector. I'll probably serve in a hospital, but maybe do violence research somewhere. In any case, I'll be studying violence on the side."

After listening intently, Dr. Perera leaned toward me and said, "You may not know this, but I'm a Quaker, so I respect your C.O. position. In fact, between you and me, I'm scheduled to break the law and deliver medical supplies to North Vietnam as soon as it's safe to do so."

Flabbergasted, I stammered, "What a great thing to do!"

In a weird way, his revelation validated me, made me feel I'd made the right decision.

I called Mom and Dad to tell them I'd quit medical school and delayed my flight home because I'd have to deal with my draft board in New York.

Mom hesitated a moment and said, "We knew you were pondering this, but it'll take some getting used to."

"It looks like a big change," I said, "but it's not. I have the same goal. And I'm not throwing away all that hard work in the sciences. I'm gonna be a social scientist."

"You're not one to make decisions without thinking things through," Dad said, speaking on the new extension phone.

"I'm glad you think so," I said.

"It's your life," he continued. "You made the decision to go to med school, so it's yours to unmake."

"I'm sure you've made the right decision," Mom said.

"I've polished up my C.O. essay. I'm sure I'll get alternative service somewhere."

When I called Sharon, she said, "It's hard to believe you've done this for real, even after all your talk and research."

"I'm in a state of disbelief myself," I said.

"Aren't you sad, confused—?"

"I cried at first, but not 'cuz I was conflicted. I'm very clear now."

"So, what's next?"

"Not sure. Gotta prepare for the draft board."

"And you don't think they're gonna ship you to Vietnam?"

"Not likely. After I present my case for C.O. status, they'll have to offer me Alternative Service."

"Can you get them to assign you service in the west?"

"I sure hope so. I want to be near you. Near your warmth, your love."

Eerily efficient, the Selective Service asked me to report at once to the Whitehall Street draft board. I took my C.O. essays and letters with me, ready to prove that I objected to both combatant and noncombatant military service. As I walked through the door to my assigned reporting area, an official directed me to wait in a line of young men. Before I could ask someone the drill, a man in uniform yanked me aside and walked me a short way to a small room off the main waiting area.

"S-Sir, I'm here to be considered for C.O. status," I sputtered.

"Look, son, I'll determine what status you are."

"But I've got documentation."

"Give me your draft notice…and tell me about your cleft."

"What do you mean?"

"Everything. Surgeries, severity—"

"Well, three or four surgeries."

Without asking permission, the man grabbed my face and said, "Open wide. Say, 'Ahh.'" A second later he started writing on my draft notice, muttering to himself, "Fistula—cleft still open."

"But, but—" I said, realizing he was a doctor.

"Any complications, restrictions?" he asked.

"Not that I—"

"Don't lie, tell me the truth…or you'll—"

"Well, I was restricted from phys ed," I said.

"Why?"

"Heart stuff, a murmur. Thought it might—"

"Let me listen."

He grabbed a stethoscope, listened to my chest through my shirt, and passed me on to a burly sergeant who refused to take my C.O. documents.

"But I'm a C.O.; I'm willing to do Alternative Service. Here's my essay.…"

His eyes hard and piercing, the sergeant said, "Sorry, pal. You ain't gettin' no stinkin' C.O. from this board if I can help it. Put your stupid documents on that table. Go home and wait for a letter." He then pointed to a door. "Exit over there."

It turned out the Whitehall Board had also hassled Arlo Guthrie who told of it in his rambling song *Alice's Restaurant.*

After getting over the rudeness I'd experienced, I passed time waiting for the letter by catching Robert Rauschenberg and Dorothea Lange exhibits at the Museum of Modern Art. I further cooled my heels by hanging out with Tony and another classmate who also lived in New York City. The two of them still couldn't believe I'd be missing all the "wonderful" pathology, pharmacology, and microbiology they'd be studying the second year.

I said, "I *will* miss the 'medicine' you'll be practicing at last—interviewing patients, diagnosing them, suggesting treatments."

"I'm excited about that part," Tony remarked.

"I will miss not having my own 'man in a pan,'" I said.

We all laughed about my reference to getting the dissected vital organs of a cadaver in a stainless-steel container.

When the Selective Service envelope arrived, I opened it with trepidation, only to find I'd been "4-F'd": deemed "physically unfit for service."

"No C.O.! No Alternative Service!" I screamed.

I collapsed into a chair and put my head my hands. I couldn't believe it. After my years-long effort to establish my C.O. status, the only thing that mattered was my cleft and heart murmur.

In all likelihood, the draft board stationed the doctor who pulled me aside, at strategic places so he could scan potential recruits for clefts, lameness, or other abnormalities.

"I bet the Whitehall Board never read my C.O. essays," I grumbled to myself.

The Selective Service letter said a social worker would soon visit me for a talk because being found "not up to military standards" bothered so many young men.

And I did feel bothered, but not over my fitness, or lack thereof, for duty. It bothered me that I'd missed the deadline to apply to grad school. Without Alternative Service to perform, I would have a lot of time on my hands until I could get back into school.

I stared out my Bard Hall window for hours and wondered, *how should I use this time?* After scribbling various ideas in an old lab notebook, I came up with a strategy. I'd travel to Europe to see firsthand various conflict and violence sites such as WWI trenches and WWII concentration camps. I'd also visit places like the World Court in The Hague, where international conflicts could be resolved without resorting to violence. If I had the energy, I'd also seek out some of the works of art that had thrilled me in Vincent Scully's course. All the while, I'd test my physical mettle: with money scarce, I would have to hitchhike everywhere and do a lot of sleeping under bridges and starlit skies.

I called Sharon again, knowing extra bucks for phone calls amounted to very little compared to what I'd have to pay for airfare if I traveled. After hearing my proposal, Sharon said, "I understand your travel objectives, but I'd like to come along, too."

"You're still in school."

"Puleeeese! Grace Ball Secretarial hardly counts as 'school.'"

"Be real now...it'd cost a lot more with you along, hotel rooms and all."

"Money's no object."

"Anyhow, I can't see a sorority girl, a Republican's daughter, a Virgin Mary in her church's pageant at sixteen hitchhiking and getting down and dirty."

"Just try me. You'd be surprised."

Feeling cornered, my lips tight and my breathing shallow, I took a risk and said, "I need to travel by myself, to test myself, to—"

"Just more excuses!"

"I'm already half way to Europe, being in New York."

"You're never going to commit yourself." Her voice rose in pitch. "I'm the only '65 Pi Phi not engaged, not married."

"I know, I know—"

"You *don't* know," she snapped. "It hurts."

"We can do Europe together someday—"

"Don't count on it, Buster. This may be a deal breaker."

I took a long walk around close-by Spanish Harlem to agonize over what Sharon had said about "never committing." Was I the usual young male, afraid to commit? Or was I unable to commit because I didn't "trust" enough due to my heart issues or not getting enough milk as an infant, as Erik Erikson theorized?

Or maybe I didn't want to travel with Sharon because I didn't want to marry her yet. I knew I had to travel alone to prove something—I didn't know what for sure, but I suspected it had something to do with my manhood.

When I phoned home, Mom and Dad understood my disappointment over not getting C.O. status and Alternative Service. They didn't question my travel plans, though Mom worried about all the hitchhiking I'd have to do.

"Experts say hitching's safe in Europe," I said.

"But all the weather and—"

"It can't be any worse than East Coast weather. Anyway, that's part of why I'm hitchhiking…to challenge myself."

Before ending the call, I asked them for a loan to pay for the trip. I told them I planned to travel in a frugal manner, spending way less than Frommer's promise in his book, *Europe on $5 and $10 a Day*. When we said goodbye, we all cried.

The next few days blurred into a flurry of activity—getting a passport, arranging a flight to the UK, and storing my stuff. Ned's parents let me store my boxes of unsold medical books at their summer place on Shelter Island and helped me prepare for my travels. They gave me an old backpack, a cup, and a sleeping sheet, required by youth hostels I planned to stay in when camping out proved dicey.

As I waited for my Icelandic Air flight to take off, I called Sharon at her school from a pay phone, having stacked up a bunch of coins on the phone ledge, knowing they'd soon be worthless to me. I needed to tell her of my deep feelings for her.

"Grace Ball Secretarial School. May I help you?"

"May I speak with a student—Sharon Belton? This is an emergency. I know she's in shorthand class now."

"Who may I say is calling?"

"K-Karl Schonborn."

"One moment, please."

It seemed like a long time.

"She says she doesn't know anyone named Karl."

"She…What? Maybe you asked the wrong person," I said. "Can you try again?"

"Pardon?"

"Can you ask her once more? Please hurry. This is long distance."

"I told you already. She doesn't know you."

The phone went dead.

EUROPEAN REVELATIONS

MY LOW-COST, ICELANDIC AIRLINES flight landed in Glasgow, Scotland, where the campaign to clean up the furnace soot that had blackened the city's buildings had stalled. To find the youth hostel I had to navigate along dark buildings facing narrow streets filled with edgy young men.

I wrote Sharon once I'd settled in, concerned about her refusal to talk and her "deal breaker" comment. I told her I loved her, counting the ways. I asked her to forgive me if I'd behaved like a jerk, and I elaborated on the various reasons I had to travel solo, not as a pair. And I reminded her I came to Europe to learn about violence—in particular revolution, war, and the institutions created to prevent and contain war. I closed by giving her addresses for post offices in the cities I'd be visiting. The clerks would hold mail for me until I picked it up.

I bought a Hallwag map to tuck into the side pouch of my pack along with my Frommer's guide and sketchbook. The map, perfect for hitching, had the kilometers between every little village and burg in Europe. Mixing map realities and my goals, I plotted my first moves: check out Scotland, ferry over to Ireland, return to England and drop south to catch the Dover ferry to France and go south to Spain and Morocco.

So I headed for the hills—the Scottish Highlands. On the way to charming Inverness, I walked along the edge of Loch Ness and looked in vain for the fabled monster. Despite this, I added a whimsical Nessie in my sketch of the lake. I then got a ride with a teacher from whom I learned the history of the centuries-long violent feud between the Campbell and MacDonald clans. My hitching skills soon returned to me, and my pack became one with my body as I travelled south to beautiful Edinburgh and its castle with a history of wars going back to the fourteenth century. I then turned west to Stranraer to catch a ferry to Ireland.

In Ireland I wanted a sense of Northern Ireland's "troubles" and I found it. When I arrived in Belfast, the brand new—yet heavily armed—Ulster Volunteer Force (a Protestant militia) had just fire-bombed a Catholic-owned pub on Shankill Road. This constituted a declaration of war on the Irish Republican Army (IRA), a Catholic militia. Having thrown down the gauntlet with a couple of other attacks on Catholics, the Protestants all but guaranteed that violence would erupt full-blown any moment.

A cold sweat came upon me as I walked along Falls Road, past the pro-Catholic Sinn Fein headquarters, noticing the sectarian hate graffiti everywhere and the strained look on people's faces. Then I walked, still apprehensively, through the Protestant neighborhoods of Shankill Road and Sandy Row, where murals rich with Unionist symbols abounded.

Since people recognized me as a "neutral" American and safe to open up to, I asked questions as I bought lunch makings at grocery stores and ate dinners at eateries in disparate neighborhoods.

"What's the meaning of that huge mural across the street?" I asked a diner at an adjoining table one evening.

"Ahh, that one, a fine one, celebrates William of Orange's victory over the Catholic King James II."

"Must've been recent—if it still resonates."

"Naw, the Battle of the Boyne was in 1690."

"Long ago!"

"No matter. King Billy of Orange heroically crossed the Boyne River on his beautiful white horse."

Another "informant" at a pub said he couldn't wait for a mural of masked fighters brandishing guns to be finished.

While the murals thrilled some Protestant, Unionist hearts, they chilled mine.

I asked a dinner patron in a Catholic neighborhood, "What's with all the flag murals?"

"They show Catholics are Nationalists, in favor of one Ireland," he said.

Another patron leaned over and said, "Those bloody Protestants want to remain part of England, even unite with it."

"They bloody well better stay out of my way," the first said.

I sensed that many working-class people in Catholic as well as Protestant neighborhoods had no intention of "moving on" from the past. This obstinacy would be no help in resolving their religious and political conflict. I noticed one area of agreement: both sides used the hoary "red hand of Ulster"—clenched in a fist rather than open in welcome, as it used to be depicted—to stir their followers' passion.

The more I heard and read about the conflict in Northern Ireland, the more similarities I saw it had with the ongoing Arab-Israeli conflict. Like that conflict, the two sides in Ireland appeared to be fighting about religion, but deeper down the conflict seemed to be about turf and territory. Plus, economic factors figured hugely into the mix, especially in working class Belfast.

In due course, I made for another city that knew the "troubles" centuries ago: historic Drogheda. After many truck rides south, where lorry drivers pretty much echoed the sentiments of Catholics in Belfast, I got to Drogheda. In this town in 1649, England's Oliver Cromwell and his army of 17,000 wasted no time overpowering 2,500 soldiers who refused to surrender to discourage any further attempts to defy English rule. Cromwell massacred the surviving Irish soldiers and another 1,500 civilians in short order.

I asked a lady in Drogheda, "What do you think of Cromwell?"

"I cringe whenever I hear his name," she said.

"Really? Centuries later?"

"Yes, even though I have a friend in England who reveres him, seeing him as an enemy of tyranny."

"That's still happening up north in Belfast. One man's terrorist is another man's freedom fighter."

"Yes, I know," she said.

That night I heard authentic Irish music in a pub and speculated whether anyone would sing about Drogheda. Instead, I heard songs about other long-held resentments, some over a century old. A singer with a rich, Burl Ives-like voice sang *Revenge for Skibbereen* about hunger and rebellion in 1848. And his teenage daughter sang *Lost Little Children*—a haunting tale about immigrant children unable to find their parents in New York City because unscrupulous "shippers" had put them on different ships, unconcerned how the families would be reunited once the children disembarked in the New World.

I wondered if resentments fueled emotions in Dublin as well. Despite the rain, it was an easy hitch to Dublin, where a local fellow, Sean, befriended me in an eatery. After hearing me talk about the "Temple Bar" lyrics in Yale's *Whiffenpoof Song*, Sean insisted on showing me the "original" Temple Bar located nearby and just a few cobbled streets away from Trinity College. Walking to the bar, we passed plenty of happy revelers and a few menacing ones, burly and missing a front tooth or two.

"Someone told me Dublin's the 'stabbing capital' of the world," I said.

"It's likely Glasgow, Scotland," he laughed.

"'Because they carry knives in their kilt stockings.'"

"People *here* get drunk, break their pint glasses, and slash people's faces with 'em."

"Holy Christ!"

"Don't worry. No one's gonna mess with us. There's two of us."

As we entered the bar (a corner building painted red-orange with black and gold accents), I saw numerous rooms filled with partygoers.

"These rooms just go on and on," I observed.

"The place grew like Topsy. Order a Guinness. It'll be fresh 'cuz the brewery's but a mile away."

When the pints showed up, we toasted and tasted. I looked around and pointed to a bunch of young women coming into the bar, dressed only in black with funny red hats.

"A hen party for a bride-to-be," Sean said.

Guys descended on the women in a flash, and the bar became a temple for the holy trinity of booze, babes, and blokes.

After a couple of pints, Sean and I left and crossed over the Liffey River via the Halfpenny pedestrian bridge. Suddenly, a young guy, bleeding profusely from his nose and mouth, rushed past us. Sean's presence comforted me as several of the menacing hulks we'd seen earlier streamed by. Luckily, they couldn't keep up with their prey.

While the drinkers I knew in Palo Alto and at Yale tended to be "happy" drunks, I'd heard many emergency-room stories at med school about "angry" drunks and the violence that brought them, their loved ones, and complete strangers to the hospital. Interestingly, Ireland taught me about violence of different types: that between individuals and that between neighborhoods and communities.

When Sean and I did part ways, I sought out the imposing General Post Office, eager to find a letter from Sharon. The clerk sent me outside to wait for ten minutes until she had time to go through the stacks of *poste restante* mail. I paced up and down the front of the Greco-Roman building and noticed lots of pitting in the columns.

"What're these?" I asked another person waiting.

"Oh, they're from bullets fired during the failed 1916 Easter uprising by the IRA against the English."

"Left as a reminder, huh?"

"Yeah," he said. "Just like that." He pointed to what looked like the base of a very tall column or pillar.

"It should be left. The IRA just blew up the statue of England's Admiral Nelson that used to stand atop that pillar."

"Jesus!" I said and walked a number of feet to inspect the pillar's base.

After ten minutes or so, I rushed back into the post office. The clerk said she could find no letters for me in the stack.

My shoulders slumped forward and I shuffled out of the building.

I wondered, *Will Sharon's anger toward me last as long as the IRA's anger toward England?*

Before we parted, Sean insisted I visit his friend Tina who gave private tours of her large estate in the small village of Borris, south of Dublin. After a day of miserable hitching and a night at a nearby hostel, I met fifty-ish Tina as she let three others and me inside a stone gatehouse a hundred yards from her castle-like manor. Pleasant looking, Tina apologized for taking a moment to stuff some garbage into a street-side container. She wore pants, a blouse under a rust-colored sweater, and sturdy, waterproof shoes.

Gesturing to her shoes, she said, "Irish weather goes through all four seasons in an hour."

Tina took us inside the monolithic three-story Tudor-Revival mansion where she and her husband lived. A huge rocking horse in their living room—fitted with a special saddle—had helped an ancestor, born in 1831 without arms or legs, learn to ride real horses.

"I imagine he had some of the first ever prosthetic limbs?" I said.

"Yes, Arthur MacMurrough-Kavanagh did. In time, he rode great distances."

"Really?"

"He became a member of the Irish Parliament and an adventurer, even a sailor."

"Wow!"

"And an artist, a poet, and father of seven children. When his favorite horse died, he covered this rocking horse with its skin," Tina said as she patted it. "Let me show you the rest of the place."

The interior seemed rundown, as did the exterior and several outbuildings, including a church and stables, had loose or fallen-in stones. No ordinary "fixer upper," nevertheless, the property featured Persian rugs everywhere and gilt-framed, well-painted portraits on every wall. In the library, Tina showed us the family Bible dating from 1598. She flipped its priceless dog-eared pages as if it were a phone book.

Tina's manor house stood on 700 acres, on a slight rise overlooking what seemed to be half of Ireland.

"The horses grazing in the distance allow me to call this place a 'stud' farm, and, as a 'working farm,' I can get grants to refurbish the damaged buildings."

"Couldn't you sell off a portrait or two for refurbishing?" I asked in jest.

"Oh, no. My husband would kill me."

She explained she had married into one of the four dynastic families that long ruled Ireland. Then it dawned on me: unassuming Tina was the Queen of Ireland, since the other three families had died out!

After returning to Dublin, I caught a ferry to Liverpool, England and the land of tasty Wheatabix, salty Marmite, and complicated A-level exams. Once I'd poked around the Beatles' hometown, I got a ride with a lorry driver who spent most of the time telling me of all the accidents and near-misses he'd been involved in. I bailed at the first opportunity.

I next visited fellow Yalies in Manchester and Cambridge and then hitched south to London. As I entered the vast, sprawling, fog-engulfed city, I made a beeline—as much as one could through irregular streets—for the main post office, hoping for a letter from Sharon.

This time I struck pay dirt. After the clerk handed me Sharon's letter, I muttered "Hallelujah." I decided to defer reading it until I found a nice place to sit and enjoy it. At a nearby shop, I ordered tea and opened the letter.

I've appreciated the postcards and letters you've written, and I'm sorry for my child-like behavior when you called me at secretarial school. I apologize a hundred times over. Please forgive me.

What softened me towards you is that I've grasped just how short life is. On my way home yesterday from school, I saw the remains of a woman someone had pushed in front of a train. Violence is popping up everywhere. You made the right career decision to study it.

As I often did with coffee and tea on my meager food budget, I paused to add more cream and sugar to my cup for protein and energy.

Sharon ended her long letter with these words:

I kept writing you and then ripping up the letters. And speaking of writing, why don't you keep a journal of your trip? Include, above all, the insights into violence and conflict you've had. I'd love to read it sometime. I admire

your zest for life. Be good and keep dreaming about me.
Warmly, Sharon

I sprang from my chair, ran next door, and bought a journaling book and some lightweight airmail stationary, returning before anyone could take my seat. I wrote Sharon, keeping my handwriting small so as to pack as many words as I could on a page.

You can't imagine how good your letter made me feel. Of course, I forgive you. No apology necessary. I'm the one who drove you crazy.

With each passing day I wish all the more that I'd asked you to travel with me. We can weather this time apart. Yes, I will come back a different person, but my feelings for you will remain.

During your silence, I worried you'd started seeing some of the people you've flirted with or had seen in the past— like Matt. I experienced pangs of jealousy when I pictured someone else holding you, kissing you. I know, I know... not befitting a rational man. But how can you expect me to love you and not be jealous at the same time?

Would love to draw you near and lie alongside your soft, supple self. Being around you physically quiets and settles me, and yet stimulates me. In fact, I'm sure I'd be tempted to do more than just appreciate your presence and nearness if you were lying next to me now.

I love how we undress each other so creatively and then passionately indulge ourselves. I miss this 'show' that we are. It's free entertainment, and we can see the same show time after time and not be bored.

Miss your concern and care, your charms and your chassis (had to throw that in). Think about you always.
Love,
Karl

When I'd finished my letter and mailed it, I contacted another Yalie, George Frampton, studying now at the London School of Economics. He showed me around the city and we found that the English line up, queue up, everywhere except at pubs.

Before leaving London, I visited St. Paul's Cathedral—Sir Christopher Wren's masterpiece and "the heart and soul of London," according to Professor Scully. After eavesdropping on a tour for a while, I took out my journal and wrote:

St. Paul's became one of the miracle stories of World War II. Hitler's Luftwaffe targeted it often during seventy-six nights of bombing raids and succeeded in destroying most of the surrounding buildings, but not St. Paul's. Later, Hitler, an amateur architect when he wasn't trying to destroy other countries' architectural masterpieces, decided St. Paul's could be used as the Third Reich's U.K. headquarters once he conquered Britain.

I caught the Dover-to-Calais ferry and hitched north along the French coast to Dunkirk, where I read various plaques and talked to volunteer guides. I noted in my journal:

In 1940, more than 300,000 mostly British troops used 800 nonmilitary small boats from across the Channel to escape oncoming German soldiers, giving an important morale boost to the English in the early, dark stages of the war.

Still, England suffered over 68,000 casualties and heavy matériel losses (ships, aircraft, supplies) in the battles that raged during the evacuation. Even morale boosts come at a high price during war.

Like the Brits who left Dunkirk by boat, I found leaving Dunkirk by car difficult. I had to walk for miles before snagging a ride to Vimy, the site of several historic World War I battles in which thousands of French and Canadian troops endured poison gas, shell-shock, and rats in their trenches during the final year of the war. I spent some time wandering through the well-preserved trenches trying to imagine the tedium, punctuated by horror, of trench warfare.

After a night in a youth hostel in nearby Arras, a jolting truck ride got me to the outskirts of Paris. Contrary to their rumored rudeness, Parisians treated me with warmth and generosity, starting with the bus driver who let me stay on board all the way to the center of Paris even though I told him I'd run out of francs to pay the fare.

My usual bright spirit had dimmed during my week of travel since Sharon's letter in London. I realized I missed her. And so her letter waiting for me in Paris excited me a great deal. I began reading it—slowly, to savor each line while sipping an espresso at a Champs-Elysees outdoor café. It disquieted me that she enjoyed hearing about my adventures, but thought I might become a travel junkie.

That night, I wrote, among other things:

I am undone not only by your beauty, but by your insight: your thought that I might become addicted to travel is perceptive. Travel can be a heady, powerful drug. And I know I have a tendency to get carried away. So I could get travel obsessed, like some I've met at youth hostels.

Still, I can't see that happening. I want to get back home to you and start the career this trip is helping to sculpt. Seeing the places in Europe where conflicts and wars occurred makes an indelible impression. (Your journaling idea makes great sense, though, 'cuz memory does fade.)

You may think this trip an excuse to avoid commitment. I don't think it is. But it is something I had to do by myself. Please don't think, either, that I'd want a marriage, like our parents,' where the male does most of the traveling and the female stays at home. We can travel together a lot someday. It'll take a while before we can afford to stay in real hotels and take trains instead of hitching—which, by the way, proved wretched between Dunkirk and Vimy.

If only we could communicate through touch and lingering looks rather than aerograms and lightweight stationary. Can't get you off my mind. Am learning what love is. I hope it's not too late to learn how to love you the right way.

XXO,

Karl

From Professor Scully's course, I knew Paris would be a visual feast. I visited Notre Dame, the Eiffel Tower, Sacré Coeur in Montmartre, and, of course, the masterpieces in the Louvre. But I hadn't realized Paris would engulf my other senses, too, with the sounds of strolling musicians, the aroma of fresh-baked croissants, and the eye-stinging cigarette smoke that came with indoor cafes on the Left Bank, where Sartre and other existentialists argued over the human condition.

After several days of sensory experiences in Paris, I got a quick ride to the Palace of Versailles ten miles west of Paris. The palace and its Hall of Mirrors beckoned me, just as it had the statesmen in 1919 negotiating the peace treaty at the end of World War I. Walking through the Palace prompted me to write:

The great hall built by Louis XIV witnessed and reflected, in its 357 mirrors, German signatories giving up their territory and colonies to the victorious Brits and French over the misgivings of many. According to historians, the humiliation of Germany caused by the Versailles Treaty and the stiff war reparations sowed the seeds for World War II.

The next day, en route to Bordeaux, I found myself abandoned to the elements for six hours outside one particular town. No one would give me a ride. The stark, disinterested stares of passing drivers didn't help, either. Nothing worked: signs, pleading gestures, a small American flag pinned to my backpack which often did the trick in a Europe that still loved Yanks. I had some French bread in my pack and, using a little water in a stream, made myself a cup of cold instant coffee. Ugh! Eventually, a battered red van stopped to pick me up.

After a day in Bordeaux and a ride across the border into Spain, I ended up walking some hilly terrain in Basque country in wind-driven rain. The locals' wariness, especially toward non-Basques, had made hitching difficult. My spirit was tired. Hitching Europe differed greatly from the Grand Tour wealthy young Europeans used to take. Nor was it like the tour freshman-roommate Bryce and his moneyed friends took right after graduating from Yale.

As time wore on and no rides came my way, my body ached, reminding me of how I had felt during my dehydration and anxiety attack in Mexico. But, of course, things were different now. I had a better understanding of my body from medical school, and I had tested my constitution's stamina more than once. While concerned I might have to walk for hours without adequate food, water, and rest, I wasn't frightened, as I once had been, that my heart might seize up and I'd collapse and die.

"No, no danger of that," I told myself. "These are roads that Don Quixote popularized."

No matter how hard my heart pounded as I walked, tired and alone, through the rain, I said out loud to myself: "I will not die, not today, on these Spanish roads."

As night fell, I entered a small village. I splurged on a prepared dinner that didn't break my budget because of the small portions.

"We call these tapas," the craggy restaurant owner said.

The next day, hitching remained difficult, but I made progress. Arriving in Madrid at last, I inhaled a fabulous paella dish for dinner at 10 p.m. with all the other late diners. After kicking around the city and visiting The Prado museum with its Goya and El Greco paintings, I headed to Seville to visit its Alcazar palace (originally a Moorish fort) and its immense Gothic cathedral with its smell of tallow candles and ancient mustiness.

Pushing on south to Algeciras, I caught a ferry bound for Tangier, Morocco. As the ferry got under way, a Brit pointed out Algeria in the distance.

"Isn't that where an Italian film director is shooting *The Battle of Algiers*?" I asked.

"Yes. Why?"

"I'd love to do something like that someday: the perfect combination of my interest in violence and the visual arts."

"What d'ya mean?"

"The film's a pseudo-documentary about the lessons learned about guerrilla warfare."

"In the war involving France and Algiers?"

"Yeah, the one that just ended with the guerrillas, the insurgents, winning."

MOROCCO, A WALL, A LETTER

A COLD, HARD STARE pierced my soul. I thought: Is another military man examining my face? For what seemed like an eternity, a Tangier customs official looked me over from head to foot. Then, hearing an offhand "Non," it dawned on me I'd just been refused entry into Morocco.

"But, Monsieur, I have plenty of money," I pleaded, pulling out bills from my hidden money pouch, "and I promise to spend it all!"

After consulting his superior, the official told me if I really wanted to visit Morocco, I could take a boat east to Ceuta, a Spanish enclave in Morocco, and enter through that customs point. I quickly agreed to this solution, figuring that someone's brother must own the boat service to Ceuta since I looked more substantial than the hordes of hippies being admitted.

Following the boat trip to Ceuta and a bus trip back to Tangier, I went straight to the medina, or old town, where I was captivated—and often held captive—by a maze of uneven medieval streets and alleyways with irregular arches and stair steps everywhere. I enjoyed getting lost, most of all when I smelled saffron, cinnamon, and other aromas emanating from brightly-colored spices displayed in cone shapes in open-air markets.

After several days in Tangier, I hitched to Rabat, a port city on the Atlantic Ocean, and then southwest along the coast, arriving at Casablanca, which smelled variously of mint, fish, raw meat, or garbage when unpredictable thunderstorms taxed street drains. Despite ubiquitous "water sellers," who wore bright red tunics and leather water pouches, I often battled thirst because I never trusted the water they offered me in shallow silver cups. I spent a couple of nights in my sleeping sheet on a Casablancan beach under dramatic Moroccan skies. As my eyes closed each night, I remembered people's warnings about desperate shepherds swooping down on unsuspecting campers and slitting their throats for a dirham, twenty-five cents.

My petty concerns about water and shepherds paled next to the drama that drew me from Europe all the way to Casablanca. As I wrote in my journal after being briefed by the local tourist office:

The battle to break Nazi Germany's hold on Europe and North Africa began on the beach where I camped. In late 1942, American troops landed here as part of Operation Torch, which in due course took back North Africa from Hitler.

In 1943, FDR and Winston Churchill met in Casablanca, where they decided to invade the underbelly of Europe via Italy, seek unconditional surrender of the Axis Powers, and assist the Soviet Union. Thus, Casablanca played more of a role in the war than its well-known nonviolent role: being a way station for smuggling (mostly Jewish) refugees out of Europe, as suggested in Bogart and Bergman's Casablanca.

I soon set my sights for Marrakesh, knowing its reputation as a place of mystery and wonder long before Crosby, Stills & Nash popularized its charms years later in song.

On one occasion, I hesitated to enter the backseat of a large beat-up Ford sedan that had stopped. Two Arab youth—high from hashish and marijuana cigarettes—grinned at me. The smoke overwhelmed me, and before I could decline the ride, the youths pulled me inside.

The driver sped off. He kept turning his head to speak to me in the back seat, extolling the virtues of America. Being distracted, he continued to almost hit chickens and even children in the streets of the small villages we raced through.

The eyes of one of my backseat companions glazed over, but the other man stared at my backpack on the floorboards. I slowly maneuvered my pack between my knees.

Then, abruptly, the driver asked, "Avez-vous beaucoup d'argent?"

I responded, "I wouldn't be hitchhiking if I had money."

He sighed in disgust, realizing I wouldn't be worth more than a few dirhams. He couldn't wait to drop me off at the next village. I fell or got pushed out of the car. For a moment, I sat on the ground in a cloud of dust pondering my "close call."

Soon, the red, iron-rich soil of Marrakesh, the wailing "oooh-eee" of Moroccan music, and the monkeys and cobras in the huge Djemaa el-Fna market square captivated me. I hung out in the square. Locals bartering with merchants in open-air stalls populated the vast square—redolent of dust, spices, and body odor. After a while I sought out the security of a hotel, settling on Hotel Chellah, which, though rundown, constituted a step up from a youth hostel. I also ate a hearty meal of tajine (a magical stew of lamb, couscous, prunes, and spices) and pastilla (puff pastry with roasted almonds and honey). Delicious.

After switching to less-pricey digs the next day and spending time in the sun-parched old city, I ended up at a gathering with a couple dozen youth hostellers on a remote, dune-like hill outside the city. The smell of marijuana permeated the air, and I enjoyed a few tokes from the joints and hookahs on the scene. As night fell, flirting and dancing by the light of a large campfire ensued. A feeling of communal one-ness permeated the air, reminding me of beach parties in California. As people started pairing off and drifting away, an attractive Dutch girl I'd danced with approached me and said, "I want for you to lay with me on sleep sheet."

"Thank you, but I just put my sheet down."

She grabbed my hands and tried to lead me away, saying, "I don't have any—how you say—birth controls? But my period is start tomorrow."

I remembered from medical school that that was "safe." Still, I resisted her powerful allure by taking small steps as she pulled me along.

"I think you're beautiful, but—"

"Is that how you want it? Separate sleepings? Is not necessary."

"Yes, I think separate is better," I said, wondering what Sharon was doing at that very minute.

"But I have kief. I buy it just a week ago."

"What is that?"

"Like hashish. I just make kief cookies. Me, by my own self."

"Well, I can help you with those," I said, not having had a cookie since the states.

We stopped in a very isolated place, where the moonlight illuminated her soft, pleasing features, and we ate the cookies and let them take effect.

"Very good stuffs?" she asked.

"Wonderful."

"Glad I eated all them with you."

After much giggling and playful kidding around, we held each other and talked until the moon slipped behind the Atlas Mountains. In the darkness, we continued to play…under more stars than I'd ever seen.

For the next few days, my new Dutch friend and I explored—Koutoubia Mosque and the maze of streets around the Marrakesh market square. Then we bid a sad, almost tearful, farewell. She had to go south to Agadir, and I had to head back to Tangier via Beni Mellal, nestled at the base of the Middle Atlas Mountains.

I ruminated during my travels to Tangier about the emotions stirred up by the Dutch girl. *What did it all mean? Was I revert-*

ing to my adolescence where any passing skirt turned my head? Why hadn't I thought of Sharon, even once, during my time with the Dutch girl? Was I incapable of keeping a commitment to Sharon, though in truth I'd only committed myself to her on paper and flimsy aerogram paper at that?

All I knew for sure: I felt happy, excited, sad, and guilty— all at the same time.

I had just boarded a night ferry from Tangier back to Spain when authorities kicked me off. I had to race back to passport control on the pier because their officials had used the wrong authorization stamp. I barely made it back to the ship in time.

I soon grew to like the vibration of the powerful engines propelling us at a slant across the Strait of Gibraltar to Algeciras. Oil freighters glided low and slow through the glassy waters around us, silhouetted against Moroccan and Spanish land masses.

When fatigue overtook me, I sought out floor space in a nook by a wall and curled up, away from the hordes on the ferry. With one hand on my hidden money pouch and the other grasping my backpack straps, I dozed off despite the din of people talking, eating, and laughing.

Upon disembarking, I walked along the seedy and dirty waterfront of Algeciras to find a road north. Thumb out, I tried to catch a ride along the Costa del Sol road to Málaga. I lucked out with a long ride that took me past Málaga and sleepy towns like Nerja that intoxicated vacationers with their mix of sun, cheap wine, and good Andalusian food.

I focused on getting on up the coast to Barcelona, in part because I'd given Sharon the *poste restante* address in that city. Hurrying through Barcelona to the central post office, I noticed that Antoni Gaudí's quasi-gothic, organic curvy cathedral and other buildings provided a fitting backdrop to the city's mix of aromatic paella and big city exhaust, machinery, and people perspiring from intense heat.

Almost running into the post office, I floated on cloud nine anticipating another letter from Sharon. I slipped down to cloud seven as I opened her letter and noticed she didn't start her letter with "Dearest" or "Darling One" as she sometimes did. Also the ardor I'd sensed in her prior two letters appeared to be missing. After finishing her letter, I found a spot on the post office steps and wrote her. I concluded with:

> *Your letter seemed cool. Have you met a prince or a stock broker who's more promising than this journal writing, would-be grad student?*
>
> *Am going to keep my eyes peeled for scanty French lingerie for you when I get back to France. However, lingerie I buy might be confiscated by puritanical countries. Customs officers are so unpredictable, as I've told you. They sometimes search backpacks.*
>
> *Am eager to hear from you. Your letters satisfy my emotional self, but my physical self needs to be in your arms. Cheap wine won't do the trick, either.*
>
> *Miss you. Perhaps too much for my own good.*
>
> *Love,*
> *Karl*
> *P.S. The hard thing about getting a letter from you is I have to wait a period of time for another.*

I traveled on to Marseille and the French Riviera, with its impossibly blue water and beautiful hills that had attracted and inspired Matisse, Chagall, and Picasso. I enjoyed poking around Cannes, Nice, and Monte Carlo in Monaco—but couldn't find lingerie that I could afford.

As I waited for rides east to Genoa, Italy, I had plenty of time to think about Sharon. One thought kept bugging me: *Did at-*

traction lapse if unattended; that is, Did love have a "Best if used by" date, an "Expiration Date?"

At the Genoa post office I picked up a letter from Sharon with eagerness, but, wanting to savor it, carried it unopened to the youth hostel in nearby La Spezia on the Italian Riviera. The hostel, costing only 350 lira, 50 cents, a night and once a hoary castle, overlooked yachts in the spectacular coastal cove below. I started reading Sharon's letter. As I read through it, while enjoying the rooftop sitting area, any momentary sense of being a castle baron in control of things left me.

Sharon had written that she would soon fly to New York to catch the *SS Atlantic* to cross the ocean and cruise the Mediterranean. At first I thought, *I can join her, and we can enjoy the spectacular Mediterranean together.* Then my heart sank. She had listed the post office addresses of the ports she'd be visiting—and the dates. Either the ports were on costly-to-get-to islands like Corsica and Crete, or she wouldn't arrive at them for another month. By the time she got to Naples, Italy, for example, I'd be well on my way to northern Europe.

Although trying to enjoy the sunset before me, I attempted to sort out my conflicted emotions. *Should I be flattered that she'd decided to become a fellow traveler? Or was she planning to give me a taste of my own medicine?* I composed a letter to her.

Dearest One,

What a surprise! Your trip sounds like it'll be an amazing adventure.

At first I thought I could join you here and there, but then I realized I couldn't. Our timing, once again confirms what our friends have asked, 'Will they ever be in the same place at the same time?' I console myself by remembering we can continue writing and can compare our impressions of the places we've both visited.

Just be careful. I'm concerned about you walking alone in certain cities. And about guys seeing your beautiful face at mealtimes, your body at the ship's pool, and your Yale Prom dress at ship dances. Please try to resist men coming on to you. I'm worried about losing you.

My apologies for any double standard that's crept into my ramblings here—you know, it's okay for me to travel alone, not okay for you.

Have a safe flight to New York and oceanic crossing. Remember, I love you.

Karl

As I headed south through the picturesque Cinque Terra coastal villages and into Tuscany, I found astonishing beauty everywhere—especially around the hill towns with their towers looking out at gently-rolling fields of yellow rapeseed flowers. The next day I went to Montaione to see a high school friend, Ann Frye, who had just married P. P. Giglioli, an Italian she'd met while at Berkeley.

"How's married life so far?" I asked.

"Going well, despite occasional language mishaps," she answered.

"Do you think cross-national marriages help prevent war?"

Laughing, she said, "Not sure. They do build bridges. The U.S. and Italy fought each other just twenty-three years ago."

"Well, let's just say, P.P.'s study in the U.S. facilitated healing—and a marriage—between two cultures."

"So, how're things with Sharon?"

Ann probed gently as I related the saga of Sharon and my arguments about traveling together, our aerograms back and forth, and her decision to see the Mediterranean on her own. I relished talking about Sharon to someone who knew her.

The Giglioli extended family came to P.P. and Ann's converted Tuscan farmhouse to celebrate Feast Day. After a fabulous four-course meal, for dessert we mixed wine with shredded ricotta cheese in small bowls, added honey and coffee grounds—yes, coffee grounds. Assolutamente delizioso!

In Rome, I hooked up with Carter LaPrade, a Yale classmate on summer break from law school. We rented bikes and cycled around the Eternal City for several days, visiting the usual tourist places, as well as sites and artworks Professor Scully had talked about. We thought Bernini's immense twisted baroque canopy over the altar compromised St. Peter's Basilica at the Vatican. And the gold decor in the Vatican and other churches we saw made us wonder if there'd been Blue Light Specials on gold leaf centuries ago.

Leaving Rome, I stuck out my thumb and soon heard the familiar screech of tires and the opening of a door. Off I sprinted, as usual, so as not to hold up the driver offering a ride. This particular driver knew English well, and I loved being able to speak English instead of the schoolboy French which I often used after exhausting the basic phrases of various local languages.

When I questioned the ethics of my driver's occupation—buying surplus military equipment in one country and selling it to the highest bidder in another—things got tense. A German, he was in Italy to ferret out Allied jeeps and halftracks for an upcoming multi-million-dollar sale to Turkey.

"Gottverdammte! It's just good business," he insisted.

"You should be converting the half-tracks into tractors," I said.

"Don't give me that swords-into-ploughshares crap."

I refrained from arguing with him, knowing we'd be together all the way to Venice. I owed it to drivers to be civil. After all, they were doing me a favor.

Venice had been bereft of tourists of late, and so the pigeons in the St. Mark's Basilica plaza looked hungry. I fed them, paying homage to St. Francis, a nonviolent bird enthusiast and namesake of San Francisco back home. I'd just passed his birthplace, the town of Assisi, en route to Venice. I didn't press my cardiac luck by climbing the 400 stairs of the Basilica's nearby tower. Instead, I explored hidden streets and canals in the intoxicating city and bought Sharon a silver pin. It did bother me the next day—after striking out at the Venice post office—that I hadn't heard from Sharon since she'd started her cruise.

While hitching across the top of Italy's boot to Switzerland, a land of neutrality and war-avoidance, I stopped off in Milan to be mesmerized by Leonardo da Vinci's "Last Supper." In Geneva, I visited the *Palais des Nations*, which once housed the League of Nations, predecessor of the U.N.—both organizations in the business of implementing St. Francis' and other religious leaders' exhortations to "Love thy enemies."

I wrote:

Today the Palais hosted meetings of key U.N. commissions, and because I could flip among five languages on my headphones, I heard Secretary-General U Thant speak and then heard delegates from France and Panama get into a nasty debate over disarmament issues. When the debate got too technical, I sketched the proceedings.

I later visited the World Health Organization and the International Red Cross, which has its hands full dealing with POWs in the Vietnam War.

After leaving Geneva, I hitched around Lake Leman to Lausanne and then on to another city with a well-preserved "old town," Zurich. When I'd had my fill of low-to-the-water bridges and high-to-the-sky prices, I left Zurich, setting my sights on West Germany. Two locals picked me up and dropped me at the Swiss–German border where the skies had just opened up.

While I was showing my passport, a couple in a VW bug drove up to get clearance, too. They displayed telltale blue-green American passports, and so, amid the downpour and the disapproving looks of the police, I begged the couple to give me a ride. They agreed, saying they'd take me to Stuttgart.

As we passed fairytale castles shrouded in pale clouds and mist, perched high above the autobahn, I learned my driver hailed from Latvia and his wife, Germany. After meeting in a German hospital during World War II, they had married and moved to the U.S. When we arrived in Stuttgart around dinnertime, they insisted I have dinner with them at her father's home. They dropped me off at an elegant house and told me to make myself at home while they picked up more dinner guests.

A servant sent me down a long, dark hallway in the house, lined with vertical glass cases containing wooden spears and, to my amazement, shrunken heads. At the end of the hall, an outrigger canoe hanging from the ceiling distracted me so much that I almost bumped into a man standing in the darkness.

A taller version of Winston Churchill, he growled at me in German, though in a soft voice. When I realized he owned the house and wanted me to follow him, I walked into a better-lit study filled with books and more South Sea relics. The man's maroon smoking jacket and the glasses of cognac he poured for us did not seem out of place in this room with its dark mahogany wainscoting. He wasted no time quizzing me, in broken English, regarding what I was about, what I believed, and why I bothered to breathe or live at all.

After satisfying himself with my credentials, the man showed me room after room of skulls, bones, weapons, war drums, and primitive art and artifacts—some of which he claimed the Smithsonian wanted for its collections.

About this time, the couple returned with three others, including a tall man named Rudy who had been blinded by an explosion in World War II. The gray of his face was the result of the blasting powder and the silver nitrate used to treat his burns.

It didn't take long to figure out that Rudy had fought for the Nazis. Angry feelings welled up inside me, especially when I realized he bore arms to legitimize Hitler's campaign to exterminate kids with birth defects. Still, as a guest, I felt I shouldn't express my feelings and rock the boat. I made an effort to find something redeeming about this handicapped man.

I soon learned that Rudy, though blind, had climbed a smaller version of the Matterhorn in Switzerland a year ago. He also ran after buses to board them on his way to work. And once, on a dare, he had ridden a motorcycle for several miles, guiding himself by extending his right leg so his foot could follow the road's curb.

All of us soon entered a large dining hall for a sumptuous dinner, during which we talked about art, politics, medicine, and chess. My driver spoke of winning several national chess titles. When the evening ended, he drove me to the Stuttgart youth hostel and revealed that his maroon-coated father-in-law had retired a short time ago as chairman of the board of Mercedes-Benz.

I told my astonishing tale that night to the hostel crowd and the next night to friends at Stanford-in-Germany's campus in nearby Landgut Burg. Hitchhiking has its rewards.

After playing cat-and-mouse with police determined to keep a bunch of other hitchers and me off the autobahn, I landed a ride heading north to Gottingen. Intrigued by how the abstract Cold War notions of communism and capitalism got translated into concrete reality, I asked Gerhardt, my driver:

"Could we look at the Wall, the Iron Curtain dividing the East from the West?"

"Ja, it's nearby as you probably know."

Gerhardt exited the autobahn and drove down a secondary road through a rolling, dark green, forested landscape to the border with East Germany. The sky, filled by heavy gray clouds with ominous black accents, weighed down on us. The trees and occasional houses with red-tile roofs ended suddenly, and we came upon a swath of cleared land. We faced a fifteen-foot high wall of concrete, stretching to the north and south, ribbon-like in the distance.

As we got out of the car, Gerhardt explained, "All the interesting stuff and potential 'action' remains out of sight, hidden by the wall."

He told me on the other side of the wall was a second, much lower "wall" of jutting iron girders that prevented vehicles containing "escapees" from crashing through the concrete wall to where we stood. A paved road paralleled the iron girders on the other side and allowed East German dog-and-jeep patrols along the wall. Beyond the road, a wide strip of fresh-tilled soil could reveal footprints and slow down runners. And beyond that existed an extremely wide strip of grass laden with mines.

"All these components keep East Germans, except the most desperate, from trying to escape."

We walked to somewhat higher ground, where I could see the top of a watchtower in the distance on the other side of the wall. Guards scanned the entire area, instructed to shoot to kill if someone somehow made it to the wall itself. Both Gerhardt and I retreated into silence as we walked back to the car. The barking of a patrol dog in the distance jarred me out of my reverie as I got into his car.

As we left, I had a terrible feeling in my stomach. I'd touched a continuously hot burner on the Cold War stove.

On our drive north, Gerhardt said, "Very few have managed to escape the East."

"How many?" I asked, hoping to lift the pall cast over my soul.

"We may never know for sure. More have made it across in Travemunde, up north, where the Iron Curtain disappears into the Baltic Sea."

After thanking Gerhardt for the tour and the tip about Travemunde, I hitched north to that small coastal town. Walking on the beach, with a chilly wind blowing in from the Baltic, I got close enough to a multilingual sign to read:

"Attention! Danger of life! If you pass the demarcation line, soldiers will shoot."

As I stood there looking for a line drawn in the sand, a guard and his German shepherd came up to the other side of a near-by cyclone fence topped with razor wire. Through a bullhorn, the guard told me in German and broken English to get off the beach and pointed to another sign, which said, "Stop! Border Zone."

I saw in the distance a round tower with observation windows and shooting slots, as well as small boats with huge floodlights patrolling the waters. Just as on Spain's Costa Brava, where I had seen fish hunted using bright lights, so too were hapless East Germans hunted if they tried to swim to West Germany.

I left the beach a different way than I'd come, passing a primitive wooden cross with a dried-up wreath nailed to it. I learned later that relatives of murdered escapees put up such memorials if their loved-ones were killed.

I wrote in my journal:

Saw the Iron Curtain today. Terrifying experience. At the very least, it must be an emotional nightmare for citizens along its length and along the Berlin Wall as well.

World leaders should visit these walls and contemplate the consequences of war and the importance of conflict resolution. Visits like these during cold wars might be akin to visits to the wounded in hospitals during hot wars.

I got letters from Sharon in Hamburg and again in Copenhagen, but I detected even less ardor than in previous letters. I chalked it up to the distractions of travel, which may've caused me also to write letters long on information and short on passion. I responded to her letters, sharing, among other things, my ongoing sadness that our timing had been off for seeing southern Europe together.

I thought of the Dutch girl I'd met in Morocco when I entered Holland, who—if she'd stuck to her plan—would be as far south in Africa as Dakar or Lagos. Connecting with her seemed so simple and straightforward compared to Sharon. Of course, marijuana had played a role.

After seeing battlefields from both world wars, I didn't need any more evidence of human beings' capacity for violence. Nonetheless, I headed for the Nazi S.S. camp in Breendonk, Belgium, on a cold and windy day. I wrote:

A shocking and sobering place! Nazis killed hundreds of the 3,500 prisoners at this camp. Information posted along narrow hallways connecting dreary concrete cells and dormitories documented the horror and cruelty, not only of this forced labor camp, but also of Buchenwald, Auschwitz, and other camps in the service of Nazi genocide.

As I walked the grounds of the camp, I saw where S.S. guards had beat and tortured prisoners by hanging them on hooks. I pressed against one of the many wooden posts where S.S. soldiers shot inmates and touched the worn steps leading up to the gallows at the "execution site." I felt nauseous. The horror of the Holocaust had hit home, and I had to leave.

On my way out, I hurried across a drawbridge over a moat designed to prevent escapes. I didn't feel like eating my usual lunch and decided to walk to the nearby cemetery, stepping into a shallow water-filled ditch along the way. I experienced, if only for a moment and at a very much reduced level, the cold that prisoners must have endured twenty years ago living in damp, concrete spaces.

Of course, I knew nothing of their real physical distress or the mental turmoil they must have endured. I wandered around the cemetery for some time, hunched over, hands in my pants pockets, shocked at man's inhumanity to man—a phrase I'd heard and used often, but had not appreciated in full until that moment.

To get a better sense of how American soldiers in Europe experienced World War II, I hitched to the Battle of the Bulge memorial where almost 8,000 Americans lie interred in a sprawling cemetery. I journaled:

The "bulge" happened in 1945 in the densely-forested mountain range of the Ardennes, when Germans tried to break through the Allies' advancing line. The Allies had created the counter-offensive line in Belgium six months after D-Day, the Normandy landing. With over 800,000 Allied troops committed, and over 19,000 Americans killed, the Battle of the Bulge was the single largest and bloodiest land battle fought by American forces in World War II.

Just as in Breendonk, I left the huge Henri-Chapelle cemetery and its informational plaques with a heavy heart. By chance, an upbeat civil engineer named Georges Oger gave me a ride to his apartment in Brussels, where he and his wife cooked me a filling dinner before taking me to the local youth hostel. The next morning I went to the post office and picked up an envelope from Sharon. Little did I know, it contained a "letter bomb."

COMPETING WITH ADONIS

Sharon's "letter bomb" went off in my hands:

I've fallen in love with Greece—Corfu, to be exact—and I've fallen in love with a Greek, Christos Constantsis, who is more olive-complected than you. He swept me off my feet in Italy, Yugoslavia, and now Greece.

My eyes and mouth widened, and I almost fell backwards as I gasped for air. But, I forced myself to read on.

Christos works on the ship as the purser, managing the money. We plan to disembark in Lemesos, Cyprus, on Oct 12th, where he'll start a much-needed vacation and decide whether to stick with the cruise line or head for Athens, where his parents live.

I'm not sure what life will bring, but I foresee living in Greece for a long time. I can still visit the U.S. Christos has relatives in America. He's older, suave, and knows what he wants in a woman. I'm not sure you do. Sharon

Despite the light rain, I went outside the post office for fresh air. My head started to spin, and my knees weakened. I sank down on the steps. Unlike when I passed out in Mexico in my youth, I now knew a different kind of heart condition. Tears came that wouldn't stop. They flowed to the steps, mixing with the rain.

I walked back to the hostel with a mood to match the rainy,

overcast sky. As I walked, I thought, *Sharon is the only girl who ever really liked me. It's not like I have lots of options.*

Straight away, I sought out an American whom I'd known from other hostels. I told him my longtime girlfriend—an Audrey Hepburn look-alike—had run off with a Greek Gregory Peck—just like in *Roman Holiday*. I summed up my situation by telling him, "I can see Sharon holding on to her handsome, dark, Greek god on the back of a Vespa, along the Amalfi coast."

"I've got the picture," he said, "loud and clear."

"Do I throw in the towel, or do I fight for what I want?"

"Well," he said, pushing a chair toward me and grabbing one himself, "you need to tell me more."

And so I told him how Sharon had been the girlfriend of a guy who'd bullied me in public school. As I described how I got to know Sharon, it seemed as if the Karl I spoke about was quite a different person from the Karl of today.

"So, she accepted you from the get go." He paused, thinking on it briefly before saying, "That's huge."

I told him how fate conspired to keep Sharon and me apart, but somehow we kept being drawn to each other, like the tiny magnetic Scotty dogs I had as a kid.

I amazed him when I told him about Sharon's gutsy trip to Yale when we both lost our virginity, and he agreed my summer in Washington right afterward must have strained our relationship.

"We each sowed some wild oats during our senior year," I said, "but we got into car sex in a big way during the summer before med school."

I concluded by telling him how I hemmed and hawed about our relationship even as I prepared to come to Europe—refusing Sharon's request in the end to "do" Europe together.

And then I related how during my hours of soul searching in Europe, I had come to understand how accepting Sharon really was of me. I based this on the fact that I'd met and talked to hundreds of different women, in hostels and while hitchhiking.

"I also began to understand Sharon's talent," I said. "I think all my exposure to art here has made me value Sharon's artistic talent more."

"And value some of your own, too, I hope. I've seen your sketches," he said.

"Thanks." I thought a moment. "You know, Sharon and I could certainly share a lifetime together. Art, travel, babies— cleft-palated or not."

He looked at me and grinned. "I think you've made up your mind!"

He was right: I had. After taking in Europe, I'd come to know myself better, could question my prior assumptions more. So, it was really simple. I was Sharon's. And Sharon was mine.

I needed to win her heart back!

I decided to intercept her in Lemesos and plead my case.

Once I'd made my decision to fight for Sharon, the skies outside thundered praise.

I checked maps posted in the hostel and located the large island of Cyprus—tucked under Turkey, with Lemesos on the island's southern coast. Staff at the hostel desk showed me schedules for ships that ran from Marseille to Cyprus, which had become popular due to newly developed beach resorts. I decided to head directly to Marseille to catch the one ship that would get me to Lemesos by October 12, just over a week away.

Aphrodite, the Greek goddess of love, and Adonis, a shepherd so handsome the goddess fell hopelessly in love with him, both came from Cyprus. Although the storyline augured ill, I vowed to show Miss Aphrodite that I knew what I wanted, and Mr. Adonis that he wasn't the only suave guy on a ship.

As soon as I could, I sent Sharon a shore-to-ship radiogram

that read, "Need you. Love you. Will meet your ship in Lemesos. Karl"

I also wired Gayle for a small loan for the ship passage to Cyprus. I had but a handful of French francs to fund my dash to Marseille. But I figured it would be an easy hitch to that port city—it being an almost direct shot south from Brussels.

In spite of this, Dame Fortune—who'd smiled in general on me in France with Citroens driven by engineers, salesmen, journalists, and students—now hid her face. No one would stop for me the first several hours. Even vacationers with sports gear in their cars amused themselves by waving at me as they passed. At length, though, I got a ride with an Israeli businessman, and followed that up with one from a former Algerian freedom fighter, making it to Champigneulles-Nancy, where I slept outdoors to save money.

Hitching to Dijon the next day took even longer because of short, infrequent rides, and it required another whole day to get to Lyon, only 120 miles farther. I grew increasingly anxious about my progress.

Time kept slipping away and I had made it only two-thirds of the way to Marseille. I spent all but my last few francs for a cold and crowded overnight bus to the port city. Would I make it in time to get aboard the last ship scheduled to arrive in Lemosos on the 12th?

Hours later, it thrilled me to see the sun slowly rise over Marseille. But even though I craved a real bed and a shower to remove days of grit, I spent my last francs on a tram through town to the port and the shipping office. The office had received Gayle's money-gram, and I got processed just in time to board the ship to Lemesos.

We steamed out of the beautiful yet busy port, and if all went smoothly, we'd arrive in Lemesos in five days, just a few hours before Sharon's *SS Atlantic*. I enjoyed showering and catching up on sleep the first day. As the days went by, though, I became ever more concerned we'd arrive in Lemosos too late. I began to pace the deck.

After stopping in Crete, rough weather threatened to delay us even more. I dreaded each passing hour, worried sick that Sharon would disembark and disappear forever with her Adonis of Accounting. Once we got within sight of landfall, we seemed to inch forward. Time was running out.

At last I disembarked and saw the *Atlantic* in the distance. I sprinted the length of the wharf, my pack banging against my back, to intercept the people who were just starting to come down the *Atlantic's* gangway. I'd arrived with no time to spare. I watched as a long line of people disembarked one by one. I kept watching and waiting for Sharon's face. But, after the last person had stepped ashore, I realized I'd made my trip to Cyprus in vain.

Both depressed and desperate, I noticed a skuzzy-looking attendant leaning against a gangway anchoring post.

"American Export Lines office?" I asked. He motioned toward a building down the wharf. When the clerk finished going through several long lists, she said, "Miss Belton and Mr. Constantsis both disembarked a couple of days ago in Rhodes, Greece."

My neck and face muscles tightened, and I flushed with embarrassment.

"Thank you," I said and stumbled out the door, crestfallen.

I shuffled without hope or direction around the streets of Lemosos, my shoulders drooping, and sometimes stopped to sob without restraint.

I'd lost. Game over. The furious dash across Europe and the Mediterranean had been for naught. Nice try, Buster. I hung my head low. I'd survived a cleft palate, but could I survive a cleft heart?

I drifted to the city's outskirts, and when someone offered me a ride to the next town, I accepted, if only to put distance between me and the city in which I had invested so much hope and found so much disappointment. An hour later I found myself in Larnaca, and after dinner, I hitched to the center of Cyprus and its capital city, Nicosia, arriving after nightfall.

The next morning, I recognized that the barbed wire and observation towers around the city meant peace still eluded Cyprus. At lunch, in part to mask my pain, I pulled out my journal and chronicled my morning activities:

I ducked into a bookstore, and its British owner reminded me that ever since the Brits granted independence to Cyprus in 1960, there'd been clashes between indigenous Greek and Turkish Cypriots, fueled in part by meddling from nearby Greece and Turkey.

The owner said, "After one bloody clash in 1964, the British and the UN created a 'green line.'"

"To keep Greek and Turkish communities separate?"

"Yes, to keep 'em from cutting each other's throats."

I talked to several blue-helmeted UN soldiers and numerous Greek and Turkish Cypriots. The dynamics of the conflict resembled what I'd seen in Belfast.

With this latest lesson in conflict and conflict resolution, I realized I'd accomplished my key goal in traveling overseas. The time to return home had come. One problem, though: I'd run out of money again.

I remembered a help-wanted sign on the docks at Lemesos for a French cargo line and tracked down the line's local shipping office.

After questioning me in Franglais with a British accent, the swarthy office manager said, "On the basis of your dining hall

job in college, you can work a reduced shift on our next ship due
into Lemesos, the SS *Indochine*."

"How soon, and what would be my pay?"

He checked a schedule and said, "Four days. You'd get room,
board, passage to Yokohama, and fifty francs a week."

"Let me think about it," I said.

I asked around at the youth hostel about working on an updated version of a tramp steamer. The enthusiasm people expressed lifted my spirits for the first time since my undoing in
Lemesos. I figured once I got to Yokohama, I'd get a job on a
California-bound ship, but if I couldn't, I'd hit up Gayle for another loan.

Without any other options, I returned to the shipping office
and signed on the dotted line. I hitched back to Lemesos to catch
the SS *Indochine*, an aging ship bound for the Orient.

THE LONG WAY HOME

I BOUNDED UP THE gangplank, eager to get on with my future, though anxious about it as well. Within an hour, the SS *Indochine* steamed out of Lemesos, heading for the Suez Canal and the Far East. Unlike a tramp freighter, the *Indochine* had a fixed schedule and published ports of call. As a passenger cargo-liner, she carried more cargo than passengers.

After giving me a crash course in working the dishwashing sprayers and machines in the ship's huge kitchen, my Ceylonese boss, Thissau, said, "Most of your co-workers speak Vietnamese, Cambodian, or Tagalog. A few of the crew also speak elemental French or English."

"I'll search those guys out when I need a helping hand or information," I said.

"Like lifting beverage tanks into dispensers and hooking them up right," he said.

Most of the crew seemed pleasant despite years of doing scut work, though some of their frequent smiles, like mine, covered for embarrassment over our language barriers. Of course, language barriers were nothing new to me, including the ones between males and females.

Two days into the trip, while subbing for a waiter in the dining room where servers had to know French or English, I met several of the paying passengers. One female I couldn't keep my eyes off introduced herself as Ellen Nettle. Her back was straight as she sat in her chair. She had the tawny complexion of a movie star and swept-back short black hair.

"I grew up in Cincinnati and majored in French at the University of Ohio," she said, looking at me with bright blue eyes. "That's where I met Janice."

"I'm Janice Seldine," her pleasant-looking table mate chimed in. "We're on our way to Tokyo. Got jobs lined up."

I soon learned the two had travelled Europe and the Mediterranean and had roomed together in Paris for two years while working for IBM. I judged them to be a year or so older than me.

After dinner, I joined them to talk about "home" since we'd concluded we were the only Americans on the ship. Having come on board a week before me, they showed me the ins and outs of the ship, and above all, how to sneak from the lower deck where I bunked through the infirmary to the top deck to visit them.

The next day, Ellen and Janice showed me the paying passengers' quarters and took me to a couple of top-deck events, where I met Gerhardt Schack from Germany and Mena Mendelowitz and Fran Bending from Australia. In return, I introduced them all to a few of my co-workers. That night after work, we crew guys went back to the top deck, taking wine and cheese to share with everyone.

"You know," Ellen said to me after several glasses of wine, "My immigrant parents named me 'Elida,' Norse for 'winged sailor.' But I wanted to be an American, not a Norwegian."

I told Ellen I found her to be "charis-magnetic"—a word I'd just made up with a little help from the wine.

The demands of my kitchen duties meant I had only a short time to visit Port Said, Egypt—the gateway to the Suez Canal. (This motivated me in the future to trade shifts with long-time crew members who had tired of certain ports.) Port Said straddled two continents, and I enjoyed sketching its fascinating mix of docks, desert plants, mosques and churches. Meanwhile, Ellen and Janice had paid to be driven two and a half hours west to Cairo and Giza to see the pyramids. They'd rejoin the ship a day or so later at the other end of the Canal.

As the *Indochine* eased into the Suez Canal, brutal heat descended, as if a barbecue lid had been lowered over the ship. I could only stand being on deck for five minutes at a time to watch small, slant-sail boats pass by; I mainly stayed in the semi-ventilated confines of the ship. The heat remained with us for the day it took to navigate the Canal, which was only 500 feet wide—the God-forsaken Sinai Peninsula on one side, the Egyptian desert on the other, and the Red Sea at the far end.

During our two days traversing the long, narrow Red Sea, I looked forward to our stop at Aden before we'd head out into the Arabian Sea. I loved exploring Moroccan Kasbahs, the old fortresses surrounded by crazy-quilt streets, and knew Aden would be the last Arab city I would see. I hustled down the *Indochine* gangplank at daybreak—the only person at that hour. I walked as fast as I could along the wharf road to find a post office before heading to the Kasbah.

"Kef! Kef!" a soldier yelled at me.

"What? Wha—"

The crack of a rifle stopped me cold.

"No can go ashore. No can—"

"Why? *Why?*" I said as I kept walking.

CRAAAACK. A closer rifle warning.

I froze.

"Trouble in streets—no can go ashore."

"Jeez! I just want to go to the post office."

"Go back ship. You go back."

Dejected, I turned and retraced my steps. My disappointment reopened recent wounds from my big let down in Lemesos. I might never see another Arab Kasbah again just as I might never see Sharon again. Back in my dormitory, I pulled a tattered photo of Sharon out of my pack. My eyes moistened.

That evening as we left port at an accelerated clip and headed for the Arabian Sea, I still ached for Sharon, but I missed my family members, too. I hadn't heard from any of them since informing them of the "Dear John" letter I got in Brussels.

In due course, I sneaked upstairs and found Ellen and Janice playing cards with a married couple from Bombay.

"I'm interested in Gandhi," I said during a lull. "I want to visit his historic home when we stop in Bombay."

"Wonderful," said the husband. A broad smile broke out on his wife's face.

As the night progressed, the five of us talked among other things about French and British colonies and Gandhi's use of nonviolence to win independence for India.

Our passage to India would take five days across the Arabian Sea. At one point Ellen and Janice invited me to a top-deck dinner, and I arranged for a substitute to take over my duties.

"Mmm," I kept saying.

I still remember that divine dinner: chicken liver paté, pureed soup, sautéed mountain trout, roast potatoes, Spanish salad, and black-walnut ice cream. No surprise after living on sardines and French bread for most of my European trip and then, as a crew member, eating broth, celery sticks, kidney beans with bacon, and canned fruit every night.

I reciprocated, in my own lower-deck way, by treating the girls to wine, French bread, and cheese at midnight under an incredible star-scape.

Emboldened by the wine, Ellen asked, "Did you break your nose playing football?"

"Yes," I said, then quickly, "Really, no, though that's a manly explanation."

My cleft lip and palate story interested Ellen. Her concern

and sympathy touched me. No wonder I felt drawn to her. But I knew I had better not act on my feelings, given my still-cleft heart over Sharon's rejection.

Long, languid days ensued, inflicting boredom on some top-deck passengers. I worked hard, though, and met Ellen and Janice as often as I could. One evening after talking alone with Ellen about our respective families, I said, "My mom had a nervous breakdown a while back."

"What caused it?" she asked.

"Officially, 'depression,' but I think it had something to do with her father's death."

"Well, I just read that 'longing' is the most common response to a loved one's death."

"Longing?"

"For the loved one to return."

"Longing's more common than depression?" I wondered, wide-eyed.

"Yes. And interestingly, the longing peaks a few months after the loss."

"Wow! That would be just about when Mom had her break."

"So, maybe longing triggered it," Ellen suggested.

"Maybe yes. Yes. Yes!" I hugged her in appreciation.

After disembarking in Bombay and passing the Gateway to India and the Prince of Wales Museum—all fascinating because of the many monkeys chattering in the surrounding trees, I continued to Gandhi's Malabar Hill home to pay homage. After touring the home, I wrote in my journal:

Guides reminded me that Gandhi created the notion of "satyagraha," the philosophy and practice of nonviolence as a political force. MLK, Jr., Joan Baez, and others try to follow "satyagraha" in their antiwar and civil rights struggles in the U.S.

The next day Ellen, Janice, and I walked around the mobbed

indoor Crawford Market, with produce spread out across count-less stalls and every customer noisily intent on getting a deal. Outside, children played in garbage stored in half-covered ox carts, even though we could see that rat poison had been sprinkled on the refuse. Their mothers watched them play.

"It's mind-blowing," Janice said, "the children appear cheerful and happy despite the filth and reek of garbage."

"Even more astounding, their mothers seem at peace, serene," Ellen said.

"Maybe their spiritual beliefs explain their serenity," I said.

The next day, I hung out in the heart of Bombay with Ellen; Janice had discovered a young man, Alain Lucas, who'd just boarded the *Indochine*. Ellen continued to amaze me.

"You're so unflappable," I said to Ellen as we took care not to step on people lying on the sidewalk.

"I just assume they're all sleeping."

"But it's late in the morning."

"I try to look on the bright side."

"Some may be dead. It's not unusual for people to lie down and never wake up due to untreated diseases, like tuberculosis."

"Thank you, Dr. Schonborn," Ellen said.

I saw all manner of physical deformities—open clefts, club feet, eyes clouded from cataracts and glaucoma—and also the tell-tale symptoms of starvation: bulging stomachs, wide open eyes, gaunt ribs and cheeks.

You'd think seeing these problems would have kept *my* anxi-ety over my appearance at bay, but no. After an aromatic dinner of sizzling tandoori chicken and basmati rice, I asked Ellen as we strolled back to the ship under a purple and pink sunset, "Do you think I should grow a mustache?"

"Why would you do that?"

"To cover my hare lip."

"Then you'd have an h-a-i-r lip instead," she said with a grin. "I actually like men who are clean shaven."

I nixed the idea of a mustache at once.

After another stop in India, the *Indochine* steamed on to Ceylon, a huge island at the bottom of India featuring a rugged shoreline and much virgin jungle. I left the ship early to hit the post office in Colombo. Walking alone along Colombo's long wharf, I dodged laborers using huge hooks to carry sacks of rice and large clusters of bananas. When I got to the post office, I found—Eureka!—a letter awaited me.

It came from Ellen and Janice.

Apparently I had so fretted over not receiving letters that they had mailed it to me from Bombay. The girls wrote sweet sentiments and praised our mutual friendship, but also recommended I stop patching the seat of my shorts and buy new ones.

I raced back to the ship and gave the girls big hugs.

"Who's exploring Colombo today?" I asked.

"I can't," Janice said. "Drank too much last night."

"I can," Ellen declared. "Maybe I can help you buy shorts."

Ellen and I walked around Colombo in a dull, heavy heat that gave a hazy yellow color to the buildings, including the city's iconic clock tower, which we climbed for its panoramic view. We sloshed through puddles from a tropical downpour to get to the Pettah Bazaar, where mud and muck—along with ox-drawn carts—gave off a musty, dank stench. Men wore skirt-like sarongs and went barefoot, in spite of the sludge. Many had dark skin and called out, "Hello, white man" or "Hey, white girl."

The next day, Ellen, Janice, and I took a long bus ride to Kandy, situated at the center of the teardrop-shaped country. Thatched houses where naked people nonchalantly used outdoor showers gave way to tea plantations dotting the beautiful countryside. As we climbed into rugged mountains, palm, banana, and rubber trees ceded to verdant, gravity-defying rice-paddy terraces—truly man-made wonders.

"I can't wait to partake in the festivities" Janice said.

"We're almost there," a local on the bus said.

After innumerable hairpin turns, our bus arrived in Kandy at sundown. We'd traveled here for the annual Esala Perahera Festival to see and celebrate a relic of the Buddha that, most of the year, rests on a solid-gold lotus flower in a sacred shrine.

We had only just gotten our bearings when three huge elephants bore down on us. Several handlers alongside tried to control them with eight-foot-long sticks. Red fabric—inlaid with jewels and small pieces of sparkly tin—covered the enormous, wrinkled creatures from head to foot; large eye cutouts in the fabric enabled them to see. The middle elephant carried on its back a cupola with a pillow that bore a glass case containing the famous relic: one of Buddha's teeth.

After jumping clear of the magnificent beasts, I whipped out my cheap camera to photograph the scores of other elephants marching behind. Suddenly, a police officer in dark pants set off by a white tunic jacket yelled at me.

"No picture. No picture!"

"Why?" I asked.

"No like flash!"

"But there are flaming torches everywhere," I protested.

"Flash stampedes elephants!"

When each elephant reached the "Temple of the Tooth," it got down on its knees and bowed its head three times. I stood transfixed, slack-jawed.

"They're beyond amazing," Janice said.

Ellen's eyes remained wide-open. "A wonderment."

Our trio spent the rest of the night bedazzled as the pageant of locomotive-sized beasts, as well as flutists, drummers, and swirling dancers, engulfed us. Toward the end of the evening, while feasting on an array of savory exotic foods served up by street-side vendors, we debated the genuineness of the tooth relic and whether camera flashes in fact spooked the elephants.

Finally, gas lanterns replaced torches, and handlers chained their elephants to palm trees. Since the last buses and trains had left Kandy, we decided to sleep in the open-air train station. Ellen leaned her head on my shoulder and soon fell asleep, her head slipping into my lap. She beguiled me to no end. But conflict reigned supreme: my head liked her a lot, but my heart kept pining for Sharon.

An inhuman shriek jarred us all awake. Two policemen had brought a man into the station to catch the train we would be taking back to Colombo. We ended up in the same third-class carriage with the man, who lay on the floor, his hands and feet shackled to the iron leg supports of a train seat. I didn't mind the man's periodic shrieking and his struggling against his restraints, but I strongly objected to the officers' behavior.

I stood up, saying, "Please stop kicking him!"

Nothing but blank stares followed by more kicks.

Out of desperation, I made the same request in French, "S'il vous plaît arrêter lui donner des coups."

Knowing that some Ceylonese spoke Portuguese, I hoped the similarities between the two romance languages would allow them to understand.

Still nothing but blank stares.

I sat down, defeated, realizing our language differences meant I couldn't protest with any real effect. The officers continued to kick the man—to the delight of most of the people in the coach—whenever he uttered a sound. He continued to froth at the mouth.

En route to Singapore, I'd visit with Ellen whenever I had a free minute from work. If we got shooed away from the top-deck lounge or game room, we'd talk in either her small cabin—sharing it with Janice and her new friend Alain who occupied it

24/7—or in my dormitory, where we always got interrupted by various crew members.

We bounded off the ship the minute we docked in Singapore. Close to the equator and hot, Singapore struck Ellen and me as a wealthy, cosmopolitan melting pot—the result of having one of the busiest ports in the world. At the post office, a letter from Mom awaited me. I skimmed it, reading it to myself without showing emotion since Ellen waited nearby.

Scott ran into Sharon's brother a while back who said his family had 'grudgingly' sent boxes of Sharon's stuff to Athens for her new life with Christos. We all knew Sharon planned to stay in Greece, but the finality of 'sending boxes' hurts. Hope you're getting over her, Karl, and moving on. As for me: thanks to therapy, I'm in better touch with my feelings these days. I just have to start sharing them now with Dad.

I jammed the letter into the back pocket of my new shorts and said, more to myself than to Ellen, "Time to embrace independence."

She looked at me funny. "Independence?"

"Yes, Singapore's a newly independent island state."

After we visited the classically beautiful Old Parliament House and the stately Government Offices next door, we meandered through the garden at Raffles Place. Since men, even policemen, often held hands while walking in public, we held hands. I loved it.

We walked through Tiger Balm Gardens and its huge, garish, weird plaster statues. The statues illustrated characters in Chinese folklore and history, and the "blood" flowed a bit too freely for this sometime-devotee to nonviolence—especially in the "Ten Courts of Hell" where the punishment for the "crime" of breaking a promise entailed having your lip split by Hell's henchmen.

"I won't break any promises," I said.

"I know you're sensitive about lips."

"Surgeons re-split my lip every time they operated. I never liked it."

After some light chit-chat at Ellen's cabin door that night, I tried to kiss her on the lips as we said "Goodnight." She turned at the last moment. I wondered, *Am I moving too fast for a newly independent soul? Is she reacting to my lips? What?*

As the *Indochine* fought a wet monsoon on its way up the Chao Phraya River to Bangkok, Thailand, I stood on its outdoor bridge, pretending to command the ship. With my face swept by wind and rain, I surveyed the river and the occasional stilt-houses carved into a jungle that came right to the river's edge. But, like first mate Jim on the bridge of the *SS Patna*—in Conrad's novel *Lord Jim*—I wondered if I'd ever redeem myself for hesitation during a moment of truth—my hesitation to commit to Sharon.

When we arrived in Bangkok, Ellen and I disembarked together again. We paid a young boy in a narrow *klong* boat to take us down a canal to one of Bangkok's floating markets and marveled at how he darted and zipped around slower boats loaded with produce.

After carefully clambering off onto a ramshackle pier, we visited one of the shops perched precariously on the edge of the canal to watch girls weave Thai silk. We walked through the royal family's Grand Palace compound, full of magnificent three-story temples with multi-tiered roofs punctuated with numerous gold-leaf spires. I felt so good at one point that I grabbed Ellen and kissed her on the mouth, feeling I had to fight my tendency toward hesitation in "affairs of the heart."

She didn't kiss me back.

Was Ellen conflicted? I wondered. Then again, *Did my heart beat too passionately? Was I coming across as needy? Maybe I was just trying to replace Sharon or get back at her for leaving me.*

At a restaurant near the Grand Palace that smelled like ginger, I asked Ellen, "Do you have a story I don't know about?"

"No," came the answer from behind a giant menu.

"I'd like to know more about you."

"You know all there is to know."

Feeling brushed off and confused, I kept silent for a bit—forcing Ellen to raise my spirits again, which she did.

After our meal we walked to the Democracy Monument, where Easter Island meets Stonehenge in the middle of a traffic circle. Farther along in our wanderings, we stared in awe at two classic statues of Buddha—one reclining, 150 feet long, gold plated; the other upright, two feet tall, pure emerald. Incense-laden Temples Wat Pho and Wat Phra Keo held these treasures, and under a cloudless sky we walked their sprawling grounds—amazed by many different-sized, all-white structures featuring roofs of bright red and green with gold leaf accents.

We started our return to the ship on a city bus with loose metal chairs for seats. Focused on staying upright in the chairs, we missed our stop for the Snake Farm Park, known for its collection of poisonous snakes. Ellen didn't regret missing it.

At her door Ellen said, "Today was magical," and kissed me on the lips.

I put my arms around her and we embraced with passion before she slipped inside her cabin.

I couldn't believe how high I felt—compared to my earlier low—descending the stairs to the *Indochine* dormitories. I hummed joyously as I undressed and brushed my teeth.

The next day I had no time to drift into romantic reveries. The *Indochine* kitchen kept me busy, making up for shifts I'd skipped. Washing dishes as we left Bangkok that evening, I saw through a porthole the 270-foot Wat Arun tower—like an overweight obelisk of heavy stone—pierce a gold-and-pink sky. Further down the Chao Phraya I watched the sun set over the river and jungle, darkness soon swallowing them up. I wondered what occupied Ellen top deck.

As the *Indochine* glided across the sometimes mirror-like South China Sea en route to Manila in the Philippines, I had plenty of time to think about my relationship with Ellen. We had shared travel adventures; had shared our minds with one another. And now it seemed only natural, I thought, that we share our bodies. But if baring of bodies was to happen, I first had to bare my soul. I needed to tell Ellen about Sharon and my ill-fated race to Cyprus to win her back.

As Ellen listened to my story, she put her hand on mine, saying, "It's hard losing love and letting go."

"It *has* been difficult…even telling you has been hard."

"I don't like talking about the trials and tribulations of love, either," Ellen said.

"I'm over Sharon now."

"Emotionally available?"

"Yes. Question is, are *you* emotionally available?"

She blushed.

Then I took a chance and said, "I love you, Ellen."

She smiled, but said nothing.

When I couldn't bear the silence any longer, I said, "Sometimes I feel our relationship is like this ship: in the middle of nowhere, without markers in any direction."

"I like you a lot, Karl. I'm just not sure of my feelings.".

"Then, maybe we should try being apart tomorrow. Maybe that will clarify your feelings."

Since I had already planned to look up a friend in the Peace Corps in Manila, I knew I was being less than straightforward.

"Okay, if you think it's best," she said with an enticing smile.

We hugged and briefly kissed. Then I made my way downstairs to the galley to work.

The next day, after the *Indochine* docked, I hurried off the ship to visit college buddy Nick Guthrie. I caught a flamboyantly painted jeep, called a Jeepney, from the pier to the Peace Corps office. My spirits dropped, though, when I learned that Nick had just been reassigned to a post hundreds of miles away. Disappointed, and sad to be without Ellen, I shuffled along Herran Street, my shirt dripping from the high humidity.

Then I remembered more World War II history. Corregidor, an island in Manila Bay, saw two protracted battles during the war. I searched for a boat company that serviced the island and engaged a guide. I later wrote in my journal:

I learned that when Japan invaded the Philippines in 1941, American and Filipino soldiers retreated to the nearby Bataan Peninsula and to Corregidor. After Japan defeated the Bataan contingent of soldiers, they forced them to march sixty miles without food or water. Over 10,000 perished in the Bataan "Death March." I imagined the suffering as I sweltered in this climate that my guide described as "hot and wet."

Relentless Japanese bombardment forced Allied troops to surrender this strategic island in 1942. Two years later General Douglas MacArthur made good his promise to return to the Philippines, and the Allies recaptured the island after ferocious fighting.

Back on the ship, I searched out Ellen.

"On Corregidor today I learned about the Bataan Death March," I said. "I hope grad school helps me and others figure out how to prevent such atrocities in the future."

"Diplomacy and conflict resolution," Ellen said.

"Speaking of diplomacy, I've brought a peace offering."

When I handed her a dozen roses, she took them, whirled around, and kissed me.

"Well, I've got a surprise, too," she said. "I've made arrangements for us to eat on shore tonight."

We had a few drinks containing Tanduay Rhum. As we finished our meal, while enjoying another round of rum, I leaned across the table.

"Ellen, Ellen, Ellen!" I exclaimed.

"What?"

"I love your spirit."

"Well, I love your adventurousness."

"I also love your face...and your body."

"Now you're being really adventurous."

A while later, as we staggered along a back street, I maneuvered Ellen into the foyer of a modest hotel. "I think if we want a safe, private place, we'll have to pay for it."

"You might be right, Bad Boy," she replied.

I asked the desk clerk for a room for two, and he pushed a registry form toward me. I looked up at him when I saw underneath the first line: "Must share last names and show ID if a couple."

"You need our ID's?"

"Yes, Amerikano, the law says couples must be married."

"Geez, Manila's a major port."

"That's the problem, Kano, too many GI's with prostitutes."

"Well, thank you," I said and escorted Ellen out the door.

"I'm sorry, Bad Boy," Ellen said, squeezing my hand and putting her arm around my waist as we walked. "We shouldn't blame the GI's. We should blame the Church."

"Yeah, I forgot. Roman Catholic priests run the show here."

The next morning, some kitchen crew members accused me of being a lovesick puppy. I ignored their gibes and sought out Ellen after my shift. She and a stylish woman from Sydney were just finishing a late morning coffee.

"Gotta run!" the woman said. "Janice and I have a date to shop on shore in five minutes."

After she left, I said to Ellen, "What if we take advantage of a rare opportunity?"

"I thought the same thing. Janice and Alain treat my cabin as their private preserve."

We almost ran to Ellen's suite and, after adjusting the small room's lighting, sat together on her bunk. I put my arm around her and cherished the feeling of being alone with her at last.

I looked into her beautiful eyes, cheered that desire was evident in them.

We kissed for what seemed a luscious eternity. Our hands explored our bodies underneath our clothes. We then stood up, and I pulled her silk shift dress up over her head. Her tanned skin glowed, the tawniness contrasting with her bright white bra and panties.

"You do have protection?" she asked.

"I'd be a true Bad Boy if I didn't."

She helped me take off my shirt, and I reached both arms around her to unhook her bra.

All of a sudden a strong knock at the door caused both of us to freeze.

"Anyone here?" said a voice I recognized as belonging to my boss, Thissau.

"Yes, I am," Ellen answered.

"I need Mr. Schonborn. Thought he might be with you."

We looked at each other in silent terror.

"He's not here."

"If you see him, tell him there're big problems in the kitchen. We need him to report to work at once."

"Okay."

We both sat back down on the bunk, our heavy breathing returning because of the close call with Thissau.

"You'd better go," she whispered.

"Yes, I can't risk getting fired."

I dressed, kissed her goodbye, and left—feeling stymied and frustrated.

The kitchen emergency entailed a shortage of workers. But the cabin incident showed we had to be extra cautious onboard because Thissau was onto us now. The *Indochine* forbid relationships between passengers and crew, at least in writing.

Once the *Indochine* berthed in Hong Kong, Ellen and I took a rickshaw cart, powered by a barefoot young man, into the heart of the dense, teeming city.

We explored the Wanchai district and Ladder Street, so named because it is a narrow lane with numerous steep, crooked flights of stairs lined with a haphazard patchwork of shops. Free enterprise also flourished on neighboring Cat Street. As the story went, one could buy anything on Cat Street: drugs, elephants, even the Hope Diamond at one point—45 carats of curse according to legend. I bought Mao's *Little Red Book* of quotations for Scott back home and a beautiful jade-like necklace that I hid from Ellen.

A tram carried us to the top of Victoria Peak for a breathtaking view of greater Hong Kong, whose geography reminded me of a larger version of the San Francisco Bay Area. As we sat, soaking up the view, I said, "I've got a gift for you."

I handed her the necklace.

"I love it," she said, putting it on. "The perfect shade of green for me."

She leaned over and kissed me. Some of the Chinese tourists around us giggled.

"Someday, I'll buy you a real jade necklace." I said.

The next day, we took a train to the last railway stop going north to visit Shenzhen, a town in mainland China. "To see communism in action," I told Janice. When we tried to walk past the sentry building outside the train stop, Red Chinese guards grabbed each of us by the arm and swung us around, saying, in strongly-accented English, "No entry!" "No pass!"

I thought, *A new version of the Great Wall of China? Another demarcation line, another Iron Curtain, another Green Line?*

Back on the train and figuring we had an unexpected chunk of free time on our hands, I said, "Maybe we should try to get a hotel room."

"I read yesterday that Hong Kong's just as uptight as Manila." Ellen sighed. "Pre-marital sex is considered a 'theft of virginity' by a man from the woman's father."

"Your father is back in the States," I quipped.

"Hong Kong police would arrest you on his behalf."

"You're worth being thrown in jail for," I said, hanging my head, rubbing my eyes. "Bad luck has danced through our days, wreaking havoc. We've stopped at all the wrong ports."

Ellen massaged my shoulders and kissed the top of my head.

"Even if we could get a room," I added, "you'd have to pay for it. Your necklace cleaned me out."

Realizing I should rise above my frustrations over sex and Shenzhen, I suggested we visit an area in Hong Kong called Typhoon Village with its countless sampans and junks. A world unto itself, the Village—where people travelled only by boat—had its own language as well as food, songs, superstitions, and wedding rituals. According to experts, some in the Village never set foot on land throughout their lives: conceived and born on boats, maturing and aging on the water, and then buried deep within it upon death.

After leaving Hong Kong, the *Indochine* passed the island of Okinawa, and I wrote that I thought of

—*the tens of thousands of American and Japanese troops killed here during the final battle of WWII: the largest land, air, and sea battle in all of history.*

—wheelchair-bound vet, screenwriter Dave Lewis stricken here.
—Dad reporting on Japan's surrender of Okinawa in 1945.

During the long passage to Japan, I didn't see Ellen often since she and I and most everyone else on board became violently seasick. The deep Mariana Trench at the intersection of the East China Sea and the Pacific caused rough seas that rocked the *Indochine* without mercy.

The night before arriving at our last stop, Yokohama, Ellen and I—joined by friends—talked, drank, and danced to music that a crew member had hot-wired from the top-deck lounge down to the ship's stores. (Despite our remote location, we all took turns being look-outs for Thissau or ship officers.) Then, after sad farewells to new friends and crewmates, Ellen and I left at the very end to pack for final disembarkation the next day.

In the early morning at Yokohama, I hustled off the ship alone to follow up on two leads for work-as-you-go ships to San Francisco. Finding neither ship's schedules workable, I settled with reluctance for a conventional passenger ship, the *SS Cleveland*. I wired my sister Gayle for another loan, offering to pay her interest this time. She wired the cash forthwith, becoming the most reliable, go-to female I knew besides Mom. I loved my "banker."

Ellen, Janice, and I took a train to Tokyo and, after storing our belongings at the train station, visited the Eiffel-esque Tokyo Tower and the first kabuki theatre in Japan. We then took a monorail to Yoyogi Park and the iconic swayback, suspension-roofed arena where Steve Clark had won his gold medals in 1964. I later journaled:

Here I stand, feeling successful after struggles with birth defects and speech communication. I've seen much of the world and feel like a winner.

And here stood the Golden Boy, once the world's fastest swimmer, perhaps feeling like a loser after Schollander earned more

Olympic gold than he. And perhaps feeling that nonstop swimming had caused him to miss out on some things in life, especially at Yale. So, if losers and winners sometimes trade places, is it just an irony or is it part of the natural scheme of things?

And had Mom, the Golden Girl winner, traded places with me, the loser? Was her nervous breakdown an indication that—like the doctor and his patient in Fitzgerald's Tender Is the Night*—she had lost her way while helping me find mine?*

Once we got back to the train station lockers, I hugged Janice goodbye and wished her the best in her new job, along with Ellen, in the executive offices at Tokyo's Bridgestone Tire Company. I pulled Ellen to one side for a private goodbye. Taking hold of both her hands, I said with a catch in my throat, "I've loved sharing so many incredible experiences with you."

Tearing up and lips trembling, she responded, "I've loved that, too, but—"

"But what?"

"I've been conflicted all along....I've hesitated to get completely involved with you because I-I have a boyfriend back in the states."

I gasped and let go of her hands. I couldn't believe what I'd heard. Then, after what seemed like forever, she said, "I haven't seen him for two years."

I blurted out, "Well, I haven't seen Sharon for a year."

"I didn't want this to end up as a mere shipboard romance."

"Me neither," I assured her. "I wanted the real thing."

"My Midwest upbringing makes me more conservative than some of the women you've dated."

"Sleeping together would've changed things?" I asked.

"Probably....I know it would've ended things with my boyfriend."

"Well...thank you for coming clean. It'll help me figure things out."

Ellen drew me close and looked me in the eye. "I was torn ever since I met you. Janice had to listen to me agonize over the months."

Not able to process all this, I just said "Okay."

Then, her eyes moist and glistening, she said, "I not only like you, Karl, I love you."

She kissed me deeply, and I kissed her back with passion.

"We have each other's addresses," she said.

I nodded. "Time will tell what happens with us."

The station clock edged toward my train's departure time. I didn't know what else to say or do. I cried, and Ellen cried, too. We hugged one last time. I boarded the train, and as it pulled out of the station, we blew kisses to each other.

On the trip back to Yokohama, I watched in numbness as scenery passed by, punctuated by flashes of baseball games being played on countless fields.

The *Cleveland* featured four classes, with big spenders shelling out for their first-class cabin six times what I had paid for my economy-class dormitory. And, even though I heard the ship's engines grinding away behind my bunk at night, I did have assigned tablemates during quasi-formal dinners. This made me feel first class in spirit, since others now served me rather than, as at Yale and on the *Indochine*, me serving others. Waiters brought spectacular food to our table, and I hoped I could gain enough weight so that Mom would recognize me after half-a-year on a sub-Spartan diet.

Some of my tablemates intrigued me. Sam from Australia had a prosthetic arm with a hook for a hand, and Daryl, a Harvard grad my age, kept putting his eyeglasses in a case and taking them out again as he snobbishly pontificated on all sorts of issues. He struck me as an intellectual version of my freshman roommate, Bryce.

After several meals together, Sam and I spoke about disabilities and adjusting to them.

"Growing up with a hook prosthetic probably would have been a lot harder than getting one later in life, as I did," Sam said.

"Because of bullying?"

"Yeah, and all the limits imposed. Ya know, girls, sports, coaches. People don't give ya a fair go of it."

"I know what you mean."

"Of course, a later-in-life disability ain't no picnic, either. Amputation memories and Korean War trauma still haunt me."

"Imagine all the traumatized and disabled vets the Vietnam War is generating for Australia and the U.S."

The horizon stretched forever in every direction, and I had as much time to reflect on my failed relationships as there was green and pewter-blue ocean around me. Ellen's last-minute revelation of her stateside boyfriend had begun to eat at me. I resented that, whenever she'd hesitated or pulled back, I'd beaten up on myself for not being attractive, charming, or something enough for her, when, in fact, I had undisclosed competition.

It dawned on me that just as Ellen's reactions to me often had not been about me, so too other people's disdain for me growing up may have had nothing to do with me. *Was I getting a better perspective on myself?* I wondered. *Sharon's honesty about us— despite the bumps it caused—looked very good compared to Ellen's withholding tactic.*

I began to read the *Ship of Fools*, a loan from the ship's library. In the book the novelist explores the human condition with all its frailty, pride, and class and ethnic biases. I looked among my fellow passengers for "fools" just as the novelist had aboard her ship. I identified a few types in addition to Sam and Daryl, including a failed alcoholic artist and a number of selfish rich women. *But wasn't I the greatest of the fools for leaving Sharon behind in the states and then falling for the nearest girl at hand?*

I ruminated on how much my stalling had contributed to Sharon's decision to start a new relationship. *Had I stalled because I thought I could do better? Did I devalue the bird in hand, thinking others in the bush might have more striking plumage? Was I so ambitious in love that my wings had melted as I reached for some "perfect woman" and then plummeted to earth? Had I thought Sharon was second best, ignoring the fact that she had loved me?*

On our sixth day at sea—after repeating one day at the international dateline—the Hawaiian island of Oahu appeared in the distance. We docked near the Aloha Tower in Honolulu, and I hitchhiked past Hickam Air Force Base to Pearl Harbor. I wrote:

A Navy launch took me to the USS Arizona *Memorial, which spans the sunken battleship's hull resting in the water underneath it. Inscribed on a marble wall inside the memorial are the names of the almost 1,200 killed on the ship on December 7, 1941. I almost wept thinking of the thousands of other servicemen also resting in underwater graves beneath the remains of other U.S. ships and planes lying silent in the harbor.*

The study of conflict and conflict resolution should show me and others ways to minimize the bloodshed of war in the future.

As I left Pearl Harbor, I noticed a Del Monte Foods cannery and thought of Sharon; her dad worked at Del Monte's HQ in San Francisco. And later, while swimming at Waikiki Beach, I saw the Royal Hawaiian Hotel—a study in pink and the epitome of elegance and class—and again thought of Sharon, who, I knew, had stayed there a week as a teen while her Dad did Del Monte business. Then I wondered, *Had she married her Greek god?*

As time expanded itself like the almost limitless ocean, I settled in for more time at sea—reading, visiting shipmates, thinking about Sharon. I thought about the stages people go through when they are abandoned: protest, despair, and detachment. I may have got only to despair when Mom and Dad left me at hospitals for surgeries, but when I left Sharon once too often, she got to detachment without a doubt.

After five days, one last, glorious sunset showered the *Cleveland* with color as the red-orange sun sank below the horizon. San Francisco would be at the other end of the long, dark night, and then I'd be home. As the *Cleveland* passed under the Golden Gate Bridge the next morning, I reflected on the fact that, since flying east to medical school over a year ago, I had traveled around the entire world.

KEEPING UP APPEARANCES

I RAN DOWN THE gangway ramp and hugged Mom first. She started crying and said I looked malnourished.

"Eurobics," I said, with a laugh. "Walking across Europe takes off the pounds."

Mom looked great. Not dark or depressed as I'd half-expected.

Dad hugged me next, followed by Gayle and Scott. After a gush of news, we all piled into the car and talked nonstop the thirty miles to Palo Alto.

We had all missed Sharon's buoyant presence at the pier. Even though family members knew the details of how Sharon had bolted and settled down with Christos in Athens, they persuaded me to call her house, just to see how her parents and brother were doing.

And so, a few hours after we arrived home, I picked up the phone and dialed the Belton's number. For some reason, my heart started pounding as it hadn't since I first started calling girls in my teens.

"Hello?" said a voice.

I hesitated before responding. Was I hallucinating? I opened my mouth but no words came out.

After almost dropping the phone, I asked at last, in a whisper, "Sharon?"

"Karl?" the voice responded. "Karl! What a surprise!"

"I...I thought you and...Christos...the Greek guy—"

And, as I listened, caught between shock and relief, Sharon

told me, in a sometimes faltering voice, that Christos' temper and machismo had shown itself once he'd dropped his crew officer's role and felt comfortable on his home turf in Greece. She'd left him, fearing his shouting and shoving would escalate.

From out of nowhere, I asked if I could visit her to finish the conversation.

She said, "Yes."

After hanging up the phone, I experienced every emotion imaginable—my mind whirling 'round and 'round—as I dealt with the astounding news that Sharon had returned home. Though I off-loaded some of my excitement on my astonished family, I still couldn't sleep that night.

The next day, I raced to Sharon's house, and after some awkward moments at the front door, I followed her to her backyard patio, fragrant with honeysuckle. At first we talked in a polite way about our respective travels. Sharon's arms—and legs—remained crossed much of the time, and I stroked my chin as I listened to some of her stories.

She set me up when she said, "You've got to go to the Azores, Majorca, and Naples someday."

"Yeah, you've seen a lot of places I haven't."

"I'm not some stay-at-home wuss, you know."

I changed the topic by describing in dramatic detail my frustration at not being able to intercept her in Cyprus. As that seemed not to elicit much sympathy from her, I described a few adventures I'd had while working my way east on the cargo-liner.

She switched the topic in a big way. "I've changed since you last saw me. I'm 'grown up' now and not needy for a man."

"I can tell."

A bit later, when I sensed she might be receptive to another visit, I said, "I'd love to see you again."

"That *might* be possible," she answered.

We parted without hugs or kisses, but on my way home I

couldn't stop smiling as I thought, *Maybe I still have a chance with Sharon.*

I decided not to write Ellen for a while and concentrate on the challenge at hand. When I had my first alone time with Mom, I asked about her emotional state, and she claimed to feel fine. She still found it helpful to see her therapist, Dr. Steinman, though. "Although expensive, he seems worth it."

"If you're happy with the results and have rapport, that's what's key," I said.

"Yes. And maybe I can pick up pointers for our marriage. Dr. Steinman has time for fun outings with his family."

I knew where she meant to go with this: Dad had little time these days. He'd been caught up launching HUD, working late every workday to meld several once-distinct agencies into a cohesive whole.

Mom added, "By the weekend, Jack's tired and just wants to stay home."

I didn't have much time for fun, either. I began exploring grad schools and the application process, which—as I had suspected—would take half a year and force me to put off my studies until September 1967. I also began looking for a job to cover rent at home and to repay my creditors.

In time, I found work at Stanford Medical School researching violent offenders and social psychiatry issues as well as psycho-architecture.

"What's psycho-architecture?" I asked Dr. Rudolf Moos during my interview.

"The study of the effects of prison walls, mental wards and such, on people."

"Fascinating! My brother plans to be an architect someday."

One of my first assignments involved researching the effects prison wall colors had on juvenile delinquents. I enjoyed working for the "Red Moose," an affectionate name we researchers gave our boss.

As Sharon and I talked on the phone that fall, I learned more details about Christos' abusive behavior, as well as about the job she had gotten at *Sunset* magazine as the editor's assistant. I also finagled a brief visit with her on Christmas day. I asked her out on our first real date, a New Year's Eve party, where she let me kiss her—on the cheek—at midnight. Her hair smelled of lilac.

In January, as part of my charm-offensive, I took her to the 57-variety Scandinavian smorgasbord at Rickey's, a fancy local restaurant. Over dinner, we compared notes about the great paintings we'd each seen in Europe and about our culinary adventures overseas and on board ships.

All of a sudden, with a flourish, she said, "I'll cook you a gourmet dinner and show you what I've learned about food and wine at *Sunset*."

"I'd love that," I said. *She likes me again,* I thought.

Still, she left me discouraged that night. She only gave me a quick hug when I dropped her off at her parents' house.

After chiding me about neglecting my dental hygiene during my travels, my dentist told me my wisdom teeth had to come out.

"You don't need them anymore, now that you've gained some wisdom circling the globe," he said.

"How 'bout removing my 'stupid' teeth as well?" I asked.

"Sorry! Don't have the tools for that," he said with a smile. "But, on a serious note, you should have a surgeon examine that cleft gum—the fistula—and the uneven 'alar wings' of your nose."

I took my dentist's concerns to heart, but after seeing a few surgeons, I wondered about the motives of those who had ambitious plans for me because I knew, as they must have known, that facial symmetry would forever elude me. Anyway, I had no money for surgery.

My visits to surgeons started me thinking about the *behavioral* version of *visual* symmetry: namely, perfectionism. My family had problems with perfectionism.

"I'm seldom satisfied with my sewing and weaving projects," Mom once said. "I often tear a dress apart and redo it if it has the slightest imperfection."

And perfectionism bedeviled Dad, too. He tried to take the perfect photograph, build flawless furniture, and construct perfect scale models with me.

He often said, "If you're gonna do something, do it right."

In seeking the perfect woman, the perfect face, the perfect drawing, was I a perfectionist, too? I didn't feel good about the possibility.

In my planning for grad school, I'd concluded that an urban university—close to a troubled, violence-prone city—would give me more opportunities for research, but I still had to decide whether to pursue my PhD in psychology or sociology. I had majored in psychology, and it had more standing as an academic field. Yet, its division into many subspecialties meant it would be difficult to study an overarching phenomenon like violence.

By contrast, sociology would give me more latitude to study violence in an interdisciplinary and wide-ranging way. Sociology, too, had a tradition of examining variables such as gender, class, race, and ethnicity—important variables that affect violent behavior. So, after a week of agonizing, I chose sociology and jumped on my grad school applications, but not before getting Sharon's input regarding cities, since I still hoped she'd accompany me.

While clearing the table after her promised gourmet meal, I said, "Philadelphia's a contender. Gets a little snow, lots of humidity. What d'ya think of Philly?"

"It's on the East Coast and near the ocean, real pluses."

"Another plus, in a weird way: it's a violence laboratory," I said.

"But, you said the University of Pennsylvania campus was crime free."

"It is. It's an oasis in a sea of crime."

"What do you like about Penn?"

"It takes a qualitative, theoretical approach to violence, unlike the University of Michigan, which takes a quantitative, methodological one."

"So you like Michigan, too?" she asked, after closing the door on the dishwasher we'd filled.

"Yes, that's why Ann Arbor's the other main contender. Number two city, in fact."

"Lotsa snow. Cold, right?"

"Yup and humid summers, but with Detroit, another violence lab, forty-five minutes away."

"And U of Michigan's great because?"

"It's got conflict-resolution superstars like Kenneth Boulding, Anatol Rapoport, and Robert Angell," I said as I started to wipe off the kitchen counter.

"And who's at Penn?"

"Penn's standouts include Thorsten Sellin and his protégé Marvin Wolfgang who runs a center that studies crime. Oh, and Digby Baltzell and—"

"I don't know any of those guys," Sharon interrupted, "but, if I had a vote, I'd vote for Philly. Better weather, close to the ocean, and near New York City."

"Thanks. It also doesn't hurt that Philly's close to Swarthmore and Haverford, towns that also have colleges with Quaker roots and an interest in nonviolence."

The next day, after raving about Sharon's culinary wizardry, I explained to Mom about the application essays I'd started.

"The easy part is writing about wanting to study violence and conflict across a wide spectrum, from the interpersonal to the international."

"The hard part?"

"Well, I'm still stuck on how to prove I have a 'sociological mind' when in fact I took only one sociology course as an undergrad."

Mom thought for a moment, then said, "Why not tell them you used to drive me—well, everybody—nuts asking 'Why?'" I hugged Mom and lifted her off the ground. "You're a genius! Thank you."

I ran back to my room and wrote that I'd had a sociological mind-set from my earliest days, asking my parents and grandparents nonstop about social matters, about rules, roles, norms, and rituals. Of course, I left out my questions about how alarm clocks work, why water's wet, and whether God is an American.

Whenever I bought books at Kepler's Books, I'd chat with bearded Ira Sandperl, whom I had gotten to know well during high school Quaker-affiliated retreats. As a rule, Ira steered me toward books on nonviolence and always kidded me about selling out to the "elitist," diploma-driven education establishment. (Ira, for all his brilliance, had dropped out of Stanford.)

This visit, I eagerly listened when Ira described the battle he and Joan Baez had just waged to establish, with Roy Kepler (a pacifist and World War II draft resister), the "Institute for the Study of Nonviolence" in Carmel Valley.

"Three hundred people packed a tense hearing room, where county supervisors had to decide whether to allow us to set up shop," said Ira.

"A big turnout!"

"Folks from Fort Ord came in opposition, fearing Baez activist-types would block convoys from the army base, like demonstrators did to the troop trains through Berkeley in '65."

"I remember. They did that several times," I said.

"Other locals said they feared 'Pied Pipers' and 'people with beards' would run down property values in their little bit of paradise."

"Did they look straight at you?" I joked.

Ira chuckled, "Joan testified that she, if anyone, should worry about property values since she owned two parcels in the Valley."

"I'm sure Joan's charm prevailed."

"It did," he said, smiling. "Check out the Institute. Come down for a seminar."

That spring, I signed up for a weekend seminar to discuss classic writings on nonviolence by Thoreau, Tolstoy, and Huxley, as well as contemporary works by Thomas Merton and MLK, Jr.

During the seminar, Ira wore Levis and a blue Oxford-cloth shirt rather than the suit and tie he frequently wore. Like Joan, he sat on the floor with the rest of us participants, his eyes often twinkling with mischief despite the seriousness of our discussions. The son of a wealthy St. Louis surgeon, Ira had come west to study at Stanford.

He told us, "I lived a playboy's life for a while until I saw a book about Gandhi in a bookstore window."

"And then?" I asked.

"Gandhi, the rat! He ruined my life." He grinned, waved one arm, and threw his head back.

As we discussed Thoreau's book, Joan appeared to enjoy the intellectual give and take among the eight of us. While she might have recognized me from brief encounters over the years, I kind of doubted it. She looked at me with her beautiful, heavy-lidded eyes and agreed with me often during the liveliest moments of the debate. During the lunch break, she and I laughed as we exchanged Paly High stories.

"Call me 'Joanie,'" she said.

The afternoon session dealt with classic tests of using nonviolence in response to violence or its threat: assailants about to rape someone, snipers about to shoot, nations about to attack. Ira recounted that during a trip to New York City, a young man with a weapon had tried to rob him. Ira talked his assailant into having lunch with him, and after a long conversation, managed to convey his concern for the man's welfare. They parted friends.

Commenting that we might not all respond to violence as nobly as Ira, I brought up my father's dilemma after Pearl Harbor.

"In college he had signed the Oxford Pledge, which constituted a promise not to fight for 'King or Country.'"

"That's an odd mix," someone said.

"The Pledge started in the U.K.—hence, King—and got Americanized—hence Country. Anyway, Dad wrestled with his pacifist feelings after the attack, concluding in the end that Pearl Harbor—by unleashing the fury of outraged Americans—made pacifism no longer an option."

"Booo, booo" a person said.

"Well, when drafted, Dad fought using a pen rather than a sword—as a journalist." Later, when someone proclaimed, "Pacifists make the fiercest fighters," Joan and Ira smiled. Joan admitted she had a competitive streak and hated being on the losing end of anything—an argument, a political battle, a love affair. She had just emerged from a prickly relationship with Bob Dylan.

Hanging out after the day's seminar session, Joan and I talked about our mutual interest in sketching. (Her whimsical line drawings decorated one of her later record albums.) She also revealed that music was not her only passion.

"I care deeply about nonviolence. I've obsessed about it since I was ten."

Joan and Ira each had evening obligations, so I spent time with the Institute administrator, Holly Chenery, whom I'd known from Palo Alto and had respected for years. She told me bits of gossip about Joan and Dylan's failed romance. She also answered a question many people had wondered about: Ira's slight limp came from a bout with polio.

The next morning, Joan and I kidded around while waiting for the seminar to begin. I enjoyed the repartee between us. Later, while Joan and I were alone making sandwiches in the kitchen, she suddenly kissed me on the cheek. I kept talking and making my sandwich as if nothing had happened. When I'd finished it, I bit into it. The die had been cast, my mouth was filled with sticky peanut butter and I could hardly talk, let alone consider returning any kind of kiss.

Alluring, powerful, and funny, Joan attracted yet terrified me. I didn't want to assume anything about the kiss. *She's just an affectionate person. She likes to flirt in a playful way*, I thought. Still, I wondered what if this peck on the cheek meant something. Was I crazy not to respond to a woman who sang like an angel, charmed audiences ten thousand strong, and stood for— and acted on—gutsy things she and I believed in? I rationalized my behavior by concluding that I had my hands full, just trying to win Sharon back. I couldn't keep my mind from wandering during the afternoon session. I guess I was already under Joan's spell. When she excused herself early from the session and drove away in her Jaguar, I experienced a complex of emotions, including both relief and disappointment.

After the Institute, I got Mom's permission to invite Sharon over for Easter dinner, and Sharon seemed to enjoy being at the family table as much as we enjoyed having her.

At the end of the dinner, I said to Sharon, "All good things don't have to end. Let's watch the Easter special on TV."

"Let's help with the dishes first."

We held hands through much of the TV program. As I said goodnight to Sharon back at her house, she let me kiss her on her lips, though she kept them pretty much closed. It bummed me out that she still had me on probation, but I sensed her old feelings for me were returning.

Besides taking art classes, spending time with the family, and fighting to become important in Sharon's world once again, my life consisted of my work at Stanford Medical School.

One morning, out of the blue, the Red Moose said to me, "Please search the literature and do a report on the tactics community psychiatrists recommend for schools, factories, prisons, and hospitals."

"Sure thing. Something right up my alley."

In the hospital section of my report, I discussed recommendations for dealing with suicidal patients. One such suggested that doctors and nurses should avoid playing into a patient's sense of hopelessness by writing "Take suicidal precautions" on patients' private charts. I knew this advice to not label a patient might avoid a self-fulfilling prophecy between doctor and patient, but it seemed unrealistic with regards to suicide, self-directed violence.

Violence of other sorts dominated the news, making the study of violence even more compelling to me with each passing day. In early June, Israel launched a pre-emptive strike against Egypt for amassing a thousand tanks and a hundred thousand soldiers on Israel's border. In just six days, Israel captured much Egyptian land, including the entire Sinai Peninsula—the desert I'd seen along the Suez Canal and assumed to be worthless. The Israeli's wanted it as a buffer against land invasion.

Just before the Six-Day War started, a riot broke out in Boston's Roxbury neighborhood. Soon, city after city in the U.S. exploded in racial rage: over 150 riots in all, leaving hundreds dead, thousands injured, and untold millions of dollars in damages. As I watched horrific news footage of brutal police and troop behavior, I began formulating ideas about how governmental authorities could manage violence without themselves using violence.

"My mind boggles at the contrast in the U.S between lower-class frustration and middle-class idealism," I said to Sharon on the phone one evening.

"It's uncanny," she said.

"Yeah. As political and racial hate pour out across America, so, too, in many cities love flowers."

"They're calling it 'The Summer of Love' in San Francisco."

"I hope some of the 'Make love, not war' sentiment rubs off on you."

"Shut up!" she said with a laugh.

After a string of dates, we felt relaxed enough with each other one Saturday to drive west over the hills to the ocean. Shrouded most of the time in fog, San Gregorio Beach heated up enough that day for us to take off our shoes, roll up our pants, and wade into the surf. After our splashing one another got out of hand, we realized we'd have to retreat to our beach blanket to dry our shirts and pants, which clung to our bodies leaving little to the imagination. Since we'd placed our blanket in a natural cave opening in one of the sheer cliffs facing the beach, we had enough privacy on the almost deserted beach to get playful in our efforts to dry each other off after we'd stripped down to our underwear.

"We should've brought bathing suits," she said as we both dropped to our knees.

"I'm glad we didn't. You're so sexy in wet clothes."

When we'd run out of friskiness, we held each other to keep warm.

Soon, we kissed fervently...and then made love.

We lay together, spent, unwilling to break the silence, interrupted only by the gentle crashing of waves in the distance. Over and over, I caressed the soft skin of her now pinkish porcelain cheeks. She kept running her long fingers through my hair. I thought: *She loves me once more. Home at last.*

"I've never been happier," she whispered.

"I love you," I said as elation gave way to contentment in my soul.

As we drove back to Palo Alto along La Honda and Woodside roads, we scouted out new trysting places to add to our favorite haunts in the hills from long ago. Sex in the hills soon became as good as it had ever been before our breakup. And it became more frequent once Sharon moved into her own apartment in Menlo Park close to *Sunset's* offices. I loved that passionate physicality had returned to our relationship.

Not far from where I worked, Steve Clark had started a summer coaching job at the Alpine Hills Swimming and Tennis Club. We met for a meal there. I learned he had married his New Haven girlfriend after graduation, coached the Peruvian National Swim Team, and had started Harvard Law School. Writing a book about swimming kept him super busy the rest of the summer, so we couldn't talk often. The few times we chatted, we compared notes about our adventures abroad.

Whenever I thought about Steve's marriage in 1965, I marveled again at his ability to focus and commit. It made me wonder why, after winning Sharon back, I did not ask her to marry me right away. While I rationalized that grad school would take a lot of my time and force me to live a "starving student" lifestyle, the real reasons eluded me. I suspected they involved, at minimum, a combination of a "grass is greener" mentality and a kind of "risk aversion" stemming from enduring a lot of psychic and surgical pain as a kid.

After paying off my travel debts and bankrolling wisdom-teeth extractions, I had money left over to undergo surgery to close my cleft gum and to even up my nostrils. Even though I went to a surgeon recommended by my speech therapist from years back, I ended up with disappointing results. Despite the Red-wood City surgeon's best efforts, my cleft gum remained open and my left nostril reverted to its pre-op asymmetry even after I wore a temporary stent inside it to force the cartilage to maintain its shape.

"The pathetic surgical outcome upsets me and makes me mad and despairing at the same time," I told Sharon at one point.

"Remember, you've said yourself, there are no guarantees," Sharon said.

Dejected, I nevertheless decided to try one last time, even though it meant borrowing money from Gayle. With great care, I checked out several oral-facial surgeons in San Francisco and chose Dr. Zyler. He had repaired countless clefts in underdeveloped countries and learned the wily ways of shape-determining nasal cartilage. Dr. Zyler unsettled me, though, when he refused to show me sample "before" and "after" pictures, saying, "Every patient is different."

"But how will I know you're as good as people say?" I protested.

"Because I treat each case with utmost seriousness. And because I drink and fall down every night before surgery!"

In an odd way, I felt reassured by his humor.

Because Sharon had taken time from *Sunset* to drive me to and from my Redwood City surgery, Mom insisted on doing the honors the second round. As we drove to the hospital in San Francisco, I said, "I appreciate all the time and money you and Dad have spent caring for me and 'patching me up' over my lifetime, using resources you could have spent on yourselves and others."

"We wouldn't have had it any other way," she said. Her glistening eyes caused mine to well up, too.

"It had to have taken some toll on you guys. I think I should write you a thank you note as I have Dr. Cox a couple of times."

"You don't need to. I still remember the day you thanked me when you were six."

"But you keep on giving. I'm twenty-three, and you're still giving."

"Well, you've taken so much responsibility for yourself of late; maybe I won't have to for much longer."

As I lay on the operating table, Dr. Zyler walked up to me, another surgeon at his side.

"Dr. Coulson's a resident who'll assist our team," Dr. Zyler said. "We won't put you all the way under. You'll be able to see, hear, and feel except in your oral and nasal areas." Waving a small contraption, he continued, "I'm going to use a modified Kilner-Dott gag to keep your mouth open and your tongue out of the way."

I soon experienced a dull, dragging sensation along my gums, my upper-lip area, and around one nostril. Dr. Zyler described to me how he had hidden the nostril incisions in the folds where my nose met my cheek. No doubt trying to reassure me, he made me even more tense. For a while, I sensed the rubberized touch of his hands. Then I heard the crunching of bone as he broke off some of my fan-shaped turbinates, which filter air entering through the nose. The crunching and cracking terrified me.

Later, I heard Coulson ask, "Aren't we awfully close to the brain?"

"Don't *ever* talk that way in surgery again!" Dr. Zyler snarled. "Ever!"

A chill went down my already-cold spine. Had they nicked my brain? Anxious and worried, but fading in and out of consciousness, I let myself succumb to sleep. Next thing I knew, I found myself in a regular recovery room, thankful that brain damage hadn't entitled me to the attention and amenities of the Intensive Care Unit.

After being sent home with bottles of painkillers, I took a

long nap. When I awoke, my face seemed to have doubled in size and my eyes to have sunken into deep, black-and-blue sockets. A gauze dressing and white adhesive tape crisscrossed my face. Even though Dr. Zyler had straightened my deviated nasal septum to facilitate easier breathing, I could only breathe through my mouth, which had become dry and sore like my raspy throat.

As I reached for another pain pill, I wondered how I'd survived my surgeries as a baby, some of which featured much more painful procedures. Maybe my infant self was one tough trooper. Still, I thought, *It's a good thing the brain represses a lot of scary stuff from those infant years.*

Two days later, after Mom drove me again to San Francisco, Dr. Zyler removed the stitches, staples, and packing from my nose. He re-dressed my nose and upper-lip area so fast that I didn't get a look at my face.

I frowned.

"The swelling needs to go down before you take a look," he said.

As the days went by, I worried that I still couldn't breathe through my nose, but I had to wait a full two weeks before I drove myself to my next office visit. After Dr. Zyler removed the bandages, I took the handheld mirror he offered me, but for some reason, I raised it with deliberation—more afraid of success than of disappointment. My eyes widened; I couldn't believe what I saw.

"My whole nose is pulled over to the side!" I yelled.

"You're right," Zyler said, "but your nostrils are a tad more even. And the tip of your nose is much higher."

"So?"

"That's good from an aesthetic standpoint, trust me."

"My cleft gum is still open!"

"I can refer you to another surgeon—"

"No more surgeries."

"I don't blame you…"

"*And* I still can't breathe through my nose!"

"Now, *that's* not good." Dr. Zyler rolled his chair closer to me, putting a viewing scope into my nose. The nurse looked anxious as he reached for pincer forceps and inserted them deep into my nose.

"I don't know what to say, but this may be the reason," he said, as he pulled out a two-foot-long strip of packing-gauze.

"I neglected to remove the deepest gauze strip last visit. Sorry."

"Wow!" I said. "That's 100 percent better! I can breathe—I can *breathe!*"

I wanted to hug and strangle Dr. Zyler at the same time.

With my whole nose skewed to one side, I realized I had to give up the dream—subconscious or not—of ever having a normal or symmetrical face. This bothered me even more because I had read of late that "symmetry" is DNA-speak for biological quality and helps drive mate selection. When Sharon assured me she didn't mind my asymmetry—nor the fact that I might carry cleft genes—my heart leapt for joy. I thought, *How had I been so blind for so long to Sharon's great qualities?*

To cover up the cleft that defiantly remained open at my gum, I arranged for a prosthodontist to place an oversized cap on the peg tooth that had erupted decades ago to the left of my cleft gum. Sharon, my family, my coworkers, and I liked the way I looked now.

Often after dinner, I found Mom sleeping upright in the living room with an open book on her lap. I figured Thorazine, which she still took, caused her drowsiness. But that didn't prepare me for what I saw one evening.

With Dad off on a business trip and just Mom and me at home, I got up from a brief evening nap and walked into the living room. To my surprise, I saw handsome Erik Gaspar, from our church, sitting next to Mom on the sofa in the living room in dim light. For married acquaintances, they were sitting very close together, I thought. I didn't notice whether they were touching or holding hands. *Of course, they might have just been talking, but then why weren't they sitting across from each other? And why were the lights so dim?* None of us spoke, and I pivoted and returned to my bedroom.

My face flushed. I sat for a few minutes, dumbfounded, confused. *Was this any of my business?* I wondered, *Should I protect Dad's "turf?" If so, how?* Soon, I heard a car drive off. I stayed in my room and never said anything to Mom or anyone else about the incident.

The Unitarian Church had helped Gaspar and his wife settle in the U.S. as "displaced persons" from the Hungarian revolution. The Soviets had arrested, imprisoned, and then released Gaspar for passing out leaflets calling for free elections. My mind went in circles: *Had Mom found a "freedom fighter" more intriguing than Dad? Was she lonely with Dad gone so much? Or was I guilty of an overactive imagination?*

The incident got me thinking about another time—earlier in the year—when I noticed Jed Palmer at our house one mid-afternoon. (The glad-handing husband of my pock-marked kindergarten teacher, Palmer had dinner with us every year when he came to San Francisco for trade shows.) I remember Palmer bragging about his store sales that year, flattering Mom, and touching her on the arm a time or two. I left to have dinner with Sharon later in the afternoon.

Nobody mentioned the next day whether Palmer had dinner with Mom and Dad the night before. I concluded my imagination got carried away, just as it had as a kid when I'd feel jealous about Mom kissing people outside our family circle—at, say, our front door at the end of a party she and Dad had thrown.

When Penn offered me a fellowship before Michigan did, I knew at once I'd be packing my bags for another Ivy League school. Mom gave me a congratulatory hug, and Dad patted me on the back. His approval, so rarely given, meant a lot to me. I also knew how I could now answer Lee Sims' mom, who'd often asked how I'd ever support myself while saving the world: I'd become a professor.

Gayle had news of her own. Her husband of a few months had just accepted a job at Temple University, and they, too, would be moving to Philly. She'd be back next summer, though, to finish up coursework for her masters at Stanford.

That night on the phone, after hearing Sharon's profuse congratulations, I asked her, "Does the fact that Gayle's going to Philly, too, change your mind about relocating with me?"

"I like Gayle a lot, and I'd like to go to Philly with you. But I can't leave *Sunset* so soon after starting," Sharon said.

"I'm worried going our separate ways might have dire results like before."

"I know, but it'll kill my parents if I live with someone again before getting married."

This disappointed me. I wondered, though, *Was this a hint that she'd go with me if I asked her to marry me?* Still, I couldn't bring myself to propose.

BEFORE THE STORM

ARRIVING IN PHILADELPHIA IN September—where trolleys screeched in their metal tracks, cabs honked nonstop, and the sultry humidity engulfed as it did in D.C.—I *still* felt good about Philly. Larger than New Haven but smaller than New York City, Philly seemed just the right size.

At Penn I loved being surrounded once again by classic campus architecture. I rented a studio apartment in West Philly seven blocks from the Sociology Department in Dietrich Hall which buzzed with excitement. I couldn't wait to get on with my studies.

Many, but not all, of my fellow first-year grad students sought out Penn because of concerns about violence and curiosity nonviolence.

"I came in part to study with Sellin, an expert in the codification of violence," I told a cluster of students.

"Sellin, with Wolfgang's help, essentially established the field of criminology," one responded. "Many of us are here for both men."

Another student chimed in, "I came because of Erving Goffman, who pioneered the sociology of interpersonal behavior."

"Baltzell's my guy," another said. "He coined the term White Anglo Saxon Protestant, and though he's a WASP elite himself, he goes after them for their reluctance to share power with others."

My first semester courses included sociological theory and

methods, social psychology, and a book-a-day reading course for those of us who hadn't majored in sociology in college. Besides getting to know my current profs, I sought out professors William Evan and Walter Isard, who researched international conflict and conflict resolution. I got along better with Evan—a prolific writer who had just co-edited *Preventing World War III*—than I did with Isard who, as an economist, approached conflict issues the same as the Michigan scholars: in an ultra-quantitative manner.

I called Sharon and implored her to come to Philly. I told her about the charms of the City of Brotherly Love, like Boathouse Row on the Schuylkill River.

"I think about you far too much," I continued. "I want you in my arms and need your body close to mine."

"While I'd like to do naughty things with you, I've been burned once cohabiting with Christos."

In a follow up letter, she explained the Christos fiasco again as well as why her parents disapproved of premarital cohabitation. She added that she liked her job at *Sunset* and, anyway, had developed a crush on her older, long-married boss.

"He looks and sounds like you," she wrote. "Has your sex appeal. Full of your zest for life, too."

Far from feeling jealous, I took her remarks as an indirect compliment or "a kiss through a veil" as I'd heard Muslims say during my travels.

I got to know some wonderful women in the Department, but didn't date any of them as I didn't want to encourage anything I couldn't follow through on…as perhaps Ellen Nettle had.

Not long afterwards, Mom phoned and, after a few pleasantries, said, "Sharon stopped by Sunday. She misses you a lot."

"I miss her, too. I worry she'll find another guy."

"I don't think you need to worry. You just ought to propose."

I gulped. Nothing came out of my mouth.

Mom changed the subject. "I've begun group therapy, facilitated by a Dr. Hardy. I didn't utter a word the first session, though I cried when a woman poured out her soul."

"Doesn't sound like you to cry," I said.

"Tears come easier without Thorazine. But, I've been out of synch all week, ever since Dr. Hardy suggested I go off Thorazine for more than a day or two. He wants me to check in with the 'real me.'"

Reading Goffman's bestseller *Asylums* in my book-a-day course reinforced the conclusion I'd reached during a college field trip years ago: that Mom's stay at the Stanford psych ward, though short, must have been hard. Goffman's descriptions of "total institutions" like mental hospitals made them sound oppressive. If Mom had ever felt constrained by Dad or a Betty Friedan-type patriarchy, the psych ward must have felt doubly stifling.

Goffman's insights also helped me understand Dr. Steinman's possible logic for prescribing Thorazine for Mom. Heavily drugged, numbed-out patients in psych wards feel less rebellious than drug-free patients, making it easier for them to adjust to the routine and rigid scheduling. After reading *Asylums*, I started to see Thorazine and other psychiatric meds in a new light: as emotional lobotomizers and chemical straitjackets.

I never discussed Mom's emotional issues with my professors, though my theory professor, Philip Rieff, might have been the logical one to approach. In class one day, he said, "'Therapeutic man' has triumphed over 'religious man' as well as 'economic man' in today's western culture."

I raised my hand. Rieff acknowledged me, saying, "You, the one without a tie."

"What's wrong with 'the triumph of the therapeutic,' as you call it?"

"Since the mid-1940s, people's mindsets have become more

Freudian than Marxian or Judeo-Christian. The problem is that Freudian thought—the therapeutic—undermines important features in cultures, especially 'authority.' Your lack of a tie demonstrates this. It shows disrespect for my authority."

Rieff intimidated most of us grad students who had to take his course in sociological theory. His course caused more frustration than enlightenment. Though strict and demanding, Rieff seemed uninterested in teaching theories other than his own. Well, mostly his own. The open secret we grads knew: his ex-wife Susan Sontag had researched and written parts of his highly acclaimed *Freud: The Mind of the Moralist*.

Several of us had to sit in on an undergraduate theory class to learn the sociological theory we needed to know. Rieff *did* provide us an example of how to "do theory"—if reading one's latest writings to get class feedback during lectures counts. Though the Department assigned me to Rieff for academic advising, I relied on other faculty for help because Rieff would often open junk mail as he talked to me in his office. A dapper dresser, he'd begun to call me "the man in the collarless shirt."

Having tired of wearing jackets and ties at Yale, my "uniform" in grad school turned out to be banded-collar "collarless" shirts and khaki pants. Growing up, I'd had no say over the appearance of my face; now at least I could control my "threads."

I didn't buy into the counterculture and its long hair, flowery shirts, and bell-bottomed trousers. But I *did* have one foot in it. Sixties fashion had started off with the Ivy-League, tailored style of the Kennedys and ended up mired in the hippie look of Haight Ashbury and Woodstock. I hewed a middle course, having been a believer in "extreme moderation" since my cardiac invalid days.

So I chose medium-length hair and a clean-shaven face to show off my various surgeons' skills. And the banded-collar shirts? Old-fashioned, American, detachable-collar shirts were sold for pennies at dry cleaners in Philly when older custom-

KARL SCHONBORN

ers died, leaving their shirts unclaimed. The shirts reminded me of peasant shirts in India and Mandarin-collared ones in Hong Kong. In all, my counterculture-Ivy look expressed an image I could live with.

In a flash of inspiration one day, I wrote Sharon with an idea of how to resolve our "cohabitation" conflict. For some reason, my apartment building had two entrances, and the bottom floors had one address and the top two had another. I wrote:

> We could store some things in an apartment—yours!—
> on the top floor and live in mine on the second floor. Your
> folks would think we lived in separate buildings. Brilliant,
> no? I'm learning conflict resolution fast.
>
> I respect your parents' values, and I want you to make
> the decision, not me, dependent on your moral compass.

Sharon responded, saying deep down she believed in "cohabitation," but wanted a face-saving solution like this for herself and her parents. She agreed to move to Philly.

I waved her letter in the air, shouting, "All *right!*"

Sharon had one condition, though. Knowing I'd be preoccupied with my studies, she wanted to attend art school. (She hoped to go from doing small watercolors to large Precisionist oil paintings in the style of Philadelphian Charles Sheeler.) Philly had several well-regarded schools. I looked into their tuition charges and wrote that, in all likelihood, we could co-habit on my fellowship if we tightened our belts. The Ford Foundation might even increase my stipend if we got married, and of course she might be able to get a fellowship herself for her art studies.

In her letter back, Sharon wrote:

> Dearest,
> I think the finances are do-able and I quite expect to
> contribute to the pot, too, by working part-time. I know

my market value dropped awhile back, but my mistake matured me.

Been missing you more than I ever thought I would. Miss your physical nearness. Miss having your arms around me.

I want to talk with someone who understands me, and you've understood me better than anyone I've ever known. Love is not just a part of my life, it shapes the whole thing.

Love you terribly,

Sharon

P.S. Doesn't hurt that my current landlady is bonkers. Rent changes every week. Utilities arrangement keeps varying.

P.P.S. I've stored up enough frustration to keep you from your studies the first week I'm in Philly. My salacious thoughts are with you tonight.

I wrote back, ending my letter:

Counting the days till you arrive. I think you're part of my relational DNA 'cuz I need you to survive.

I love you,

Karl

P.S. Bet you thought I'd never put that in writing?

Sharon flew out two weeks after giving notice at *Sunset*, having shipped her personal effects to 313 40th Street. She moved into my studio apartment at 311 40th Street, and we shared my pull-down Murphy bed. She only used the apartment upstairs for storage or when she needed to cool off after a lover's spat.

"I can't believe the sirens screaming night and day," Sharon said early on.

"It comes with the territory," I said, frowning.

Fire engines did race around West Philly, since some of its

grimy, run-down areas—heated by oil and coal—saw many fires. And police sirens did frequent the night as shootings bedeviled Philly's slums, some of the worst in the country in 1967. The dangerous areas didn't start for about ten blocks in each direction from our building. (The three-day race riot in 1964 had occurred in North Philly, across the Schuykill River and well north.) We lived close to the campus which was, in some ways, a privileged white cocoon. All the same, we had to be vigilant, chiefly after dark and in the subway, which didn't bother this student of violence or his well-traveled girlfriend.

While waiting for admission to art school, Sharon found a secretarial job at the Wistar Institute—an independent, biomedical research enterprise close to the Department—which meant she and I could walk to campus together in the morning and connect up at lunch, too. In her free time she drew and sketched in the apartment or looked at TV on my little 4-inch black-and-white, which she still watched from the side, out of the corners of her eyes.

One morning, Sharon's personal phone in my apartment rang. She answered, listened, gasped "Okay," and hung up.

"My father's at the airport! He's catching a taxi to come visit," she wailed.

"Holy Christ! We'd better get your stuff upstairs."

"Gimme that suitcase," she barked. "I'll get my clothes. You take the other suitcase. Fill it with pots, pans, toiletries, anything…"

After making several trips carrying stuff upstairs, we positioned it in the nick of time just as her father knocked on her apartment door. We hoped, with some naïveté, that he would be distracted by the cockroaches that always scampered across the floor and not notice that the apartment didn't appear lived in except for the unmade pull-down bed. It seemed to work.

When we went with him from her apartment to mine, we exited to the street and entered via the other entrance, and whenever he seemed to sense something fishy, we changed the topic fast, as we'd seen actors do in sitcoms. We figured in the final analysis, though, that he saw through our ruse, but decided to play along, turning a blind eye to our cohabitation.

"Please take us to Bookbinder's, Dad," Sharon asked during a lull later on. "Anything to get us out of the building," I whispered to her.

We had a great dinner at the iconic Philadelphia restaurant, which we never could have afforded on our own. We talked mostly about the social movements sweeping the nation. In a stroke of diplomatic genius, Sharon gave her dad a "CARE package" filled with goodies she'd baked earlier and a crossword puzzle book for his train ride that night to New York City.

As fate would have it, Joan Baez performed at Penn's Irvine Auditorium while we ate dinner. We had tickets for her show, but missed it.

When we had the chance, Sharon and I attended late Friday afternoon student-faculty sherry parties, learning to thrust and parry verbally in academic and sexual innuendo fencing matches. It didn't take much sherry to lubricate everyone well enough to bring about fierce academic debate, as well as sexual double and triple entendres. One of the stellar married faculty, distinctive for his sharp facial features, was also known for his sharp tongue—and womanizing. He managed to smoke, drink, make a debate point, and hit on a female student all within the confines of one spoken sentence.

Sometimes the academic culture of the Department overlaid other cultures. Our cohort of grad students included several nuns and priests, plus a few hippies who kept us careerists in touch with contemplative culture as well as the counterculture. This was not always appreciated.

One female friend said to me, "What a waste. The two best looking guys in the Department are priests."

And a male friend echoed her sentiments, "It's nice that Sister Marie is out of her habit, but she's also out of circulation."

Some Department hippies got burned by their association with a charismatic Penn grad active in the university community. Ira Einhorn, a colorful counterculture character in West Philly and a self-proclaimed flower-power guru, dominated the local antiwar scene and efforts to save the planet. A hidden propensity for violence emerged, though, and he killed his girlfriend Holly Maddux, stuffed her body in a trunk, and used chemicals to keep it from rotting for a year. In due course, police found the trunk in a closet in his apartment. Known as the "Unicorn Killer," he jumped bail, hid out in Europe, and wasn't brought to justice for decades.

I continued to read sociological classics nonstop for the doctorate-qualifying exams. And I studiously prepped for my foreign-language proficiency test before my travel-enhanced French faded to black. Thus, I was taken aback when Lee Sims called.

"We need to march on the Pentagon," my boyhood chum said, on the East Coast after finishing grad work at Stanford.

"But I can't devote a full weekend to do it," I protested.

"Organizers bill the march as a chance to take nonviolence and civil disobedience to new levels."

"I guess I'd better not miss it, then."

Sharon signed on, too, and the three of us drove down to D.C. in my just-acquired used VW bug, a car fast becoming a symbol of a mobile and rebellious generation.

Before marching on the Pentagon, we listened to speakers at the Lincoln Memorial rail against the fact that U.S. troops surpassed 500,000 in Vietnam; 13,000 had already died there. Benjamin Spock—the baby doctor blamed by some for creating '60s protestors by advising "permissive" parenting—spoke, accusing LBJ of breaking his campaign promise not to escalate the war.

I marveled at the twenty-somethings who also spoke at the Memorial, confident enough to address a crowd of 70,000. Even though people increasingly told me I had normal speech, I didn't believe them, and speaking in front of large crowds still scared me. As I listened to the young speakers, I resolved to get a voiceprint as soon as I could. I hoped the newly developed gadget could reveal any nasality in my voice and lay any uncertainty I had to rest once and for all.

The speechifying done, the three of us marched with hordes of people toward the Pentagon. Then we sat down along with hundreds of others who sat just before the rise in the middle of Memorial Bridge, which connects Washington to Virginia and the fortress-like Pentagon.

"I'm not sure why we sat down," Lee said.

"The rise impedes my view," I said, "so I can't tell whether the leaders want us to block traffic or the police have stopped us from progressing further."

The "thump," "thump," "thump" of newly arrived police helicopters kept us from hearing one another, and the noise intimidated us—just as helicopter gunship noise did in Vietnam—but we continued to sit for a while until people started getting up and proceeding to the Pentagon behemoth.

When we reached the Pentagon grounds, comedian Dick Gregory, Green Beret Donald Duncan, and others spoke. After the speeches, though, thousands of people stormed the Pentagon building itself, scuffling with police and soldiers.

"This is more militancy than I bargained for," I said.

"Yeah, getting violent," Lee responded.

"Let's leave," Sharon said, eliciting nods from Lee and me.

A minority had removed the "civil" from civil disobedience, resulting in police blowback, untold injuries, and hundreds of arrests. The three of us narrowly escaped injury and arrest as we fled the scene. On the drive back to Philly, we talked about the confusing tactics of the anti-war movement, but our conversation came to an abrupt halt when the VW sputtered and ran out of gas.

Lifting the front of the hood and feeling the onset of another Lee-and-Karl calamity, I shouted over the freeway noise to Lee as he exited the backseat, "*Déjà vu!* Check the gas tank cap."

"It's tight. Despite your peace decal, I doubt if pro-war folks put anything in your tank."

"I swear the dealer told me there's an emergency lever somewhere 'cuz I asked him how I could manage without a fuel gauge on the dash."

"Yeah, something to access a reserve tank," Lee said as he opened the rear engine cover.

"Hey, I found it, you Bozos," Sharon shouted from inside.

A flip of a lever hidden above the clutch got us to the next gas station.

Not long after the march, authorities arrested Dr. Spock and Yale chaplain William Coffin for delivering sacks of draft cards given to them by war resisters at a rally some time ago.

According to the reading I'd been doing in political sociology, researchers called people like Joan Baez "political altruists." Often society's winners, these altruists care about helping society's losers. Scholars have found that wealth combined with marginality often creates political altruists. This seemed to explain Baez. She enjoyed a privileged childhood and a lucrative music career, but suffered marginalization at times because of her Mexican heritage. Of course, this explanation didn't account for everything. Joan struck me as far more complex—having a taste for luxury, expensive clothing, and fancy cars, yet limiting her concert fees because, as she once said, "Chasing money corrupts people."

Findings about political altruists, my observations of nationalistic uprisings, and my increasing exposure to sociological research—some of it into the struggles of oppressed people—made me question some of what Baez and Sandperl believed.

"I'm not so sure that violence never works when dealing with conflict," I told Sharon one evening.

"That's sacrilege. The Quakers will send you packing," she chuckled.

"I do know for certain, sadly, that nonviolence doesn't always work in conflict situations."

I began to believe that powerless, oppressed people (so-called "first parties" in systems theory) could not be expected to be restrained and saint-like against their oppressors ("second parties"), especially if the second parties engaged in unspeakable brutality (as, for example, Hitler's Third Reich had). Nevertheless, powerful "third parties"—outsiders who respond to or intervene in conflicts between firsts and seconds—*could* be expected to respond using nonviolent, and only nonviolent, means like economic boycotts.

Therefore, I announced to Sharon at dinner one night, "I've decided to focus my research on the use of nonviolent methods of conflict resolution by third parties."

"Luckily, you've explained 'third parties' to me before," she said.

"I'll examine police and other peacekeepers, like the U.N. troops I saw in Cyprus, coming between warring 'first' and 'second' parties."

"Well, this deserves a celebration. How about a glass of wine?"

Curiously, by breaking with Baez and Sandperl's orthodoxy and espousing the use of nonviolence in more limited ways, I became even more committed to the concept.

"I now have a rebuttal to those who claim nonviolence is futile and hopelessly naïve," I said, as I raised the glass Sharon gave me.

One of the sociologists of the day, Talcott Parsons, taught

me—if nothing else—to be eclectic in my theorizing. And so, from a range of thinkers, I created a five-level model or framework for studying two-party violence with increasing numbers of participants as one goes from interpersonal to intergroup to inter-organizational to inter-communal to international violence. My model allowed me to make sense of research regarding violent conflict, from fights between individuals to wars between nations.

Best of all, my model allowed me to give attention to third parties ("peacekeepers") and the means they used to thwart violent acts, whether between spouses, street gangs, political organizations, racial communities, or warring nations. For my doctoral dissertation, I'd focus on specialized family-fight police, gang-control officers, riot-control squads dealing with civil disorders, and UN peacekeeping forces intervening between warring factions.

To keep my heart healthy, I jogged as often as I could around the sprawling Woodlands Cemetery, a block from our apartment building. Sometimes I'd hurdle a few of the shorter tombstones along flat stretches. At other times I'd accelerate to a brief sprint to be able to feel Mother Nature brush my face with air. I loved the rhythm of the pumping action of my arms in synch with the pumping of my legs, something I'd missed during my youth.

Oftimes bystanders in the cemetery's rolling hills would shout, "Who's chasin' you, man?"

Other less charitable souls would scream, "Idiot!"

And others, "It's hot, you fool!"

Without a doubt, Rocky Balboa hadn't yet made it hip to jog in Philadelphia.

I had to give up jogging in late November when the weather got too cold. Soon, though, a fellow grad student introduced me to a sport I had never tried. After treating Sharon and me to Thanksgiving dinner at his family's sprawling Main Line estate, he insisted I shoot clay pigeons. When I fired the shotguns—my first-ever experience with guns—I felt I'd betrayed Baez and Sandperl.

On Christmas Day, my sister Gayle and her husband had Sharon and me over for a wonderful dinner, marred only by the fact that, during a group call home, Mom reported feeling sad with only Dad and Scott around for the holidays.

The next day, Sharon and I traveled to New York to visit the Museum of Modern Art where we enjoyed arguing over the merits of various works. We stayed a few nights with my college buddy Nick Guthrie—back from his Peace Corps stint in the Philippines—and enjoyed visits with my harried, third-year med-school friends at Columbia before catching the train home.

When we woke up the next morning, I asked Sharon, "Let me grocery shop for the week and make dinner tonight? We're staying home, even if it *is* New Year's Eve."

"That'd be great since it'll take me quite some time to find the art supplies I need."

I shopped for the foods I knew Sharon loved the most and bought a nice bottle of champagne and a dozen white roses, breaking the bank in the process. On the way home, I ducked into a small, artsy jewelry shop.

Once back in the apartment, I studied a bit before preparing dinner. I took care to avoid a square foot or so of the kitchen counter top where I'd written a few words earlier in quick-dry washable paint from one of Sharon's paint jars near the sink.

Darkness began to engulf the apartment, so I lit the white candles I'd bought and set on the white table cloth along with silverware and white cloth napkins. When I heard Sharon let herself in at the street entrance, I quickly poured the same color paint over the four words I'd written on the counter earlier. The words disappeared.

I greeted Sharon at the door, saying, "Hope you got what you needed."

"I did." Then scanning the apartment she exclaimed: "My God, you've gone all out, tablecloth, candles—"

"Let's sit and relax with wine," I said as I hung up her coat.

Once on the couch, I started talking about how the planets seemed to have aligned tonight. She looked at me as if I'd become a card carrying member of the Age of Aquarius. Then I said in a rush, "Oh Jeez, I forgot to clean up the paint I just spilled on the counter. It's your water-soluble paint. Could you sponge it into the sink? I've got to check the oven."

She wiped away the new wet paint, and her eyes opened wide as the dried paint message became clear. She read out loud, "Will you ma-marry me?" She looked beautiful as her mouth stayed wide open as the unimaginable, unfathomable words registered in her mind and then in her heart.

But I hadn't asked her to marry me because of her beauty. Or to make an honest woman of her. I had asked her because she was by far the smartest, kindest, most loving woman out there… and she had loved me, for some unknown reason, for years and years despite my delays and doubts. Doubts about her, about me, about lots of things.

I dropped to one knee, pulled out a ring box, and opened it for her to see.

"Oh, Karl. I almost can't see it through my tears."

"I know how much you and your Episcopalian parents value tradition, and I don't care if we're the last couple to marry in this hippie-dippy era of cohabitation. I love you, and want to spend my life with you."

"I love you, too. And, of course, I'll marry you."

We kissed, hugged, and twirled around.

I raised my head and arms toward the ceiling and shouted, "Thank you!" *Thank you for helping me see the light and for helping me overcome my issues and my fear of commitment.*

I slid the ring on Sharon's finger, and while she rotated it, tears still streaming from her eyes—relieved after her long 'journey' with me—I grabbed the dozen roses from their hiding place and presented them to her.

"My God, I don't think I can take any more surprises."

"Well you'd better, 'cuz I've got a bottle of champagne, too, and a romantic day planned for tomorrow."

We drank the champagne cuddled up on the couch, her large radiant blue eyes twinkling as much as the city lights outside our window. After our candlelit dinner, we returned to the couch and spent the night talking about our future together while the rest of Philadelphia ushered in 1968.

The next day, we watched grown men strutting—in elaborate, bright-colored costumes with feathers—in the Mummers Parade down Broad Street in central Philly. We knew that many of the sequined, overweight, white guys with cigarettes in their mouths and beer cans in their hands offended some. A small number of blacks, for example, believe the parade has a racist past because "blackface" used to be worn. Given that embers of racial tension still glowed from the 1964 riot in Philly, this troubled us. Still, historians claimed the parade to be the oldest folk event in the U.S.

After the parade, we strolled hand in hand through the cobblestoned colonial neighborhoods and saw the house where tradition says Betsy Ross sewed America's first flag. When we debated walking home past the Liberty Bell—which we'd seen months before—I said, "Why bother. We can't un-ring the bell."

"You feel you've lost your liberty now that we're hitched?"

"No way." Squeezing her hand, I continued, "I don't know why I said 'un-ring.' Marriage will free us to be more than we could ever be on our own."

Back at home, we called Sharon's parents to tell them the news, and then called Mom and Dad.

"I can't believe it," Mom cried out. "You came to your senses at last, Karl."

"Congratulations! Wonderful news!" Dad said.

"When?" Mom asked, starting to cry.

"This summer. Short engagement." Sharon said, chuckling.

"But long courtship," I added. No one laughed.

"Will your parents have moved to Wisconsin by then, Sharon?" Dad asked.

"Yes, and—"

"Well, have the wedding at our house!" Mom almost shouted. "In our backyard."

"That would be great," Sharon responded. "All our friends and relatives are in California."

Everyone concerned decided July 14 would be a good wedding date. I realized, though, that I'd have to shift into academic high gear in order to complete my qualifying exams and research papers before going to California for the nuptials.

Throughout January, President Lyndon B. Johnson reassured the country that the war in Vietnam proceeded apace. Many even thought victory to be at hand. Also in January, LBJ's administration convicted Mom's hero, Baby Doctor Benjamin Spock, and Yale chaplain William Sloane Coffin of violating the draft laws and corrupting the young.

Suddenly, the Tet Offensive—launched by the North Vietnamese on January 30th— changed everything. Mom wrote:

> *I didn't like TV images of Vietcong rockets slamming into Saigon. Even less did I like seeing enemy troops capturing Saigon's radio station, assaulting the presidential palace, and attacking the U.S. embassy. LBJ lied to us. I agree with Walter Cronkite, who exclaimed as the Tet Offensive unfolded, "What the hell is going on? I thought we were winning this war."*

The Tet Offensive shattered many people's confidence in both the President and his administration. The first month of the Offensive cost the lives of 2,000 American and 4,000 South Vietnamese troops. In addition, countless enemy troops and civilians died.

In mid-March, Mom wrote that she'd decided to support the antiwar candidacies of Eugene McCarthy and Bobby Kennedy because she felt betrayed by LBJ. She wondered if all the antiwar marchers and demonstrators had been right all along.

Sharon's mother, on the other hand, still favored the war and saw the peace symbol as "the footprint of the American chicken." At various times over the years, I tried to argue Mrs. Belton over to the antiwar side. During these marathon sessions, Sharon retreated to watch sports with her dad.

When the Cleft Palate Clinic at Penn reminded me of my upcoming voiceprint appointment to determine my voice quality, Sharon asked, "You value a machine's assessment over a human's?"

"Yes," I said. "I made the appointment back in October when I agonized that I had less confidence in my voice than speakers at the Pentagon rally had in theirs."

"I've always said your voice is fine."

"You're biased."

At the end of my voiceprint session, the tech scanned the printout from the various test sentences I'd read, and after a long silence said, "Your consonants are distinguishable from your vowels, and you have no problems with sibilants and fricatives."

"That's good?" I queried.

"Yup. From all the tests I've run, I can say, 'You're not nasal.' And your delivery and diction score above the average for everyday people."

"Great!" I pumped my arms in the air.

"But don't take my word for it," he said, pointing to several blips on some inked graph paper. "It's here in the printout."

While relieved, I knew I'd always have to fight my perception of having "nasal" speech and cardiac limits. I was no different from a slender person, overweight as a child, who always felt "fat" or a beauty, once a homely wall-flower, always feeling unattractive. We all suffered the psychological equivalent of the "phantom limb" sensations an amputee experiences.

Back at the apartment, I apologized to Sharon for not trusting her assessment of my voice. I even said that a lack of trust—beyond not believing friends, the mirror—may have caused my personal conflict and confusion regarding our relationship.

She hugged me and showered me with an all-knowing smile.

I called Mom on March 13th to wish her a happy fifty-second birthday and told her about the voiceprint results. She said with playfulness, "You are now officially 'normal,' entitled to all the rights and responsibilities thereof!"

In response to a later question about Sharon, I said, "I can't keep my eyes and hands off her. I gaze at her, put my arm around her shoulder, hug her a lot."

"Sounds like love," Mom said. "Just remember to talk to her, too."

Mom later wrote that she'd had the Beltons over for dinner during a visit they'd made to Palo Alto and that she and Sharon's dad had discovered they were born only a few miles apart in Wisconsin. Sharon's mom disclosed she'd been on the lookout for her mother-of-the-bride dress for years. Mom wrote that the Beltons claimed she'd gone beyond the call of duty in her wedding planning since—after all—custom had the bride's family shouldering most of the burden. Mom responded that she enjoyed the planning and that the Belton's move to Wisconsin in January would have made planning a California wedding very difficult.

Sharon wrote Mom on March 20th about some wedding particulars, and Mom responded on the 27th with a note detailing which tasks had been completed and spelling out what the caterer intended to do, including printing "Karl and Sharon" on the napkins. Mom also gave Sharon the dates by which we'd have to order and send the wedding invitations.

On Sunday morning, March 31st, my phone rang.

LIES THAT BLIND

THE SHRILL RING OF my phone cut through a lazy Sunday morning reverie. I picked up the receiver.

"Karl Schonborn?" a stern voice asked.

"Yes."

"Officer Swensen. Just a moment. I'm putting your father on the line."

Silence. An eerie, terrifying silence.

"Son?"

"Dad, what's wrong?"

"I can't believe it. Your mother's gone." Choked-back tears flooded the line. "She died last night, but I just found her."

"Oh, my God. No! No!" I yelled, staggering backwards.

I gasped for air that wouldn't come. The screeching in my ears sounded like metal trolley wheels taking a curve outside our window. I turned to Sharon sitting nearby and said, "Mom's dead." Sharon's porcelain face grew even paler.

"How?" I asked in a quivering voice.

Dad struggled to speak. "She...she hanged herself...with a necktie. We'd been to a party in San Francisco—"

"Hanged herself? Suicide? Not Mom!" I screamed.

Sharon recoiled and then reached for my hand.

"Are you okay, Dad? I can fly out," I said.

Dad said he'd be okay until I arrived and asked me to phone Gayle while he called Scott. I told Dad I loved him. I hung up the phone, drained, speechless, and trembling.

"Oh God, Karl, I'm so, so sorry," Sharon said as we held each other.

"It can't be." I mumbled, "It can't be."

At some point I called Gayle and we both just sobbed. When I offered to book her on my flight to San Francisco, she expressed concern about my upcoming qualifying exams. I said I'd manage somehow.

I hung up, staring into middle space. Reality seemed suspended.

"I never told you, Karl," Sharon said, almost in a whisper, "but a couple of times last summer, when I came to your house, I saw your mom crying, half hidden behind the cars in the carport."

"I had no idea she was that unhappy," I said.

"I'd hug Laura and be with her a bit before we'd both go into the house. You'd be in your room, at your desk. Your dad would be at the living-room desk."

"She must've felt abandoned, everyone else busy."

"Maybe if I'd told someone—"

"You couldn't have known this would happen. Anyway, Mom probably just mixed alcohol with her meds."

"Look," Sharon said. "You'd better make those plane reservations and get packed. You've got a lot to do, hon."

I arranged for Gayle and me to fly at a bereavement discount and got ready to shave. First, though, I used a finger to feel around my now-solid palate and the upper-lip scar that extended upwards to my still-distorted left nostril. I did this to honor Mom, who had shepherded me through all my surgeries.

After shaving, I wiped my face with a towel, pulled on casual clothes, and packed everything, including a suit and dress shirt for the memorial service. When I reached for the only somber-looking tie among my many bright choices, something— maybe a panic attack—prevented me from grabbing it. My outstretched arm just floated motionless in the air.

At last the news had sunk in; my anguish was paralyzing. A

few seconds elapsed, and then I collapsed onto the couch and stared at a wall for several long minutes.

After I pulled myself together, Sharon sat down beside me. I appreciated her closeness and liked that she waited a moment before putting her arm around me.

"You don't need a tie," she said. "You always look dressy in shirts, even collarless ones." She squeezed me tight.

Her warmth helped melt the icy terror in my heart and soul. I got up to finish my travel preparations.

Gayle and I talked non-stop, tearing up now and then, as we navigated Philly's air terminal, boarded our plane, and completed the first leg of our flight west.

During our layover in Denver, we watched President Johnson on an airport TV. He stunned us and everyone else watching when he announced he'd had a change of heart about the war and had ordered a halt to the bombing of North Vietnam! Even more astounding for a dyed-in-the-wool politician, LBJ said he'd also decided not to run for a second term as president. He needed to concentrate on negotiating a peace treaty.

Looking around the terminal, I saw that everyone nearby appeared dazed like us, but for very different reasons. Oddly, it gave me comfort to have others around me confused and in shock.

The plane landed in San Francisco in heavy rain, which fit our mood. Dad and Scott met us at the airport gate, and we all sat down in a quiet area to wait for the rain to let up.

"Dad, tell us what happened," Gayle said. "Start at the beginning."

"Your mother arranged a pre-birthday party for me with friends in the City yesterday."

"I crossed the bridge from Berkeley and attended for a coupla hours, too," Scott interjected.

"Laura had been depressed of late, but she seemed happy at

the party. We both had a lot to drink." He looked sheepish. "I drove us home anyway. We arrived after ten, and I went to bed while she lingered in the hall bathroom."

"The one you guys just remodeled?" I asked.

"Yes. When I got up around seven-thirty this morning, I found her hanging..." His voice broke. "In the shower." He put his head down and sobbed.

When he recovered his composure, he said, "I think mixing alcohol with her meds—"

"Put her in a fog?" I ventured.

"Exactly. Somehow she spiraled downward Saturday night—"

"And felt compelled to end her life." Scott interjected.

"Yes. Alone and in absolute silence," Dad said, starting to sob, but stopping himself.

"Did she leave a note?" Gayle asked.

"No. I looked for one this morning and again before leaving for the airport."

Dad gave us more details. He either needed to get them out, or he suspected we would ask sooner or later. He told us about the cop who'd responded before the coroner arrived: "I couldn't believe he had his gun out when I opened the door to let him in."

"Guess they can't be too careful," Scott said.

"After the coroner removed Laura's body, the officer took me down to the station and asked me lots of questions, some of 'em over and over."

"Why?" Gayle cried out, eyes ablaze. "You're no murderer! You didn't kill her!"

"Cops treat spouses as prime suspects," I explained.

"Officer Swensen said I'd remain a suspect until he sees the coroner's report."

"Why do they even need an autopsy?" Gayle moaned.

"The officer said they treat suicide as a violent crime, where autopsies are mandatory," Dad said. "It'll take several weeks to get the results."

When we arrived home, I noticed a bowl, a box of powdered sugar, and a container of vanilla extract sitting on the counter of Mom's tidy kitchen. Dad said Mom had planned to frost the cake she'd baked to honor his 52nd birthday today.

"It's not a happy time, Dad…but Happy Birthday, anyway," I said, putting my arm around him.

"Thanks, son."

During the next few days, the four of us spent a lot of time telling visitors and ourselves how Mom had filled our lives with incredible love, warmth, and beauty for so many years. And that is what Reverend Dan Lion said at her crowded memorial service at the Unitarian Church on Friday, but not before the assassination of Martin Luther King, Jr. traumatized us—and the entire nation. Rioting in cities across the country didn't help matters. Whole city blocks in D.C—some near where I'd lived as an intern—went up in flames. My world seemed to be unraveling.

After sitting down in a front row seat before the start of Mom's service, I stared at my lap and noticed a fuzzy thread coming loose. My suit pants were unraveling, too.

I glanced at the cover of the program that read: "Celebrating the Life of Laura Schonborn." I didn't feel like celebrating anything. I just sat there, tieless. Though Professor Rieff may have seen it as disrespectful, I couldn't bring myself to wear a tie to Mom's service.

Reverend Lion took the pulpit and spoke of Mom's many wonderful qualities. And then he said, "Of late, though, she suffered a great deal."

Without elaborating, he went on to quote passages from Frost and Emerson, as well as Eastern poets Gibran and Tagore. Reverend Lion concluded, "Since Laura loved to weave, poet C.

Day-Lewis's words strike me as appropriate here. They go something like:

> *She has lived out life's pattern.*
> *And the master-weaver has called it good.*
> *He has put away the loom.*

Because Reverend Lion didn't mention Mom's favorite poems and songs, or include reminiscences from loved ones, the service seemed impersonal to me, like a Catholic funeral mass. No one had asked any of us in the family to write a eulogy.

I had to get back to my studies and exam prep, so I said a sad farewell to my sibs the next morning. As Dad hugged me goodbye at the airport, I asked him to send me a copy of the autopsy report, since I might be able to help with medical terms. I studied on the plane, but also read and ruminated over a *Time* magazine article about Joan Baez's recent marriage to an anti-war activist who'd grown up in Fresno. The rough landing in Philly foreshadowed the rough weeks that lay ahead.

I loved being back in Sharon's arms, but did not relish communicating the mixed messages I'd heard about Mom.

"Reverend Lion and a few family friends believe depression, essentially mental illness, killed Mom," I said.

"And you? Sharon asked.

"I don't think Mom intended to kill herself. Rather, she mixed alcohol with her meds…and this caused her to impulsively hang herself."

"What about your dad?"

"He straddles the fence. He believes depression *plus* alcohol and meds killed her."

By studying for my exams, I kept my grief at bay and my mind from speculating further about the *why* of Mom's suicide. Still, as I studied one of the subfields in sociology, Deviance, I could not help myself wondering if the theories applied to Mom in any way. I looked at the dustcover of one of my deviant-behavior books, which showed the unraveling of a piece of fabric representing "society."

Inside, sociologist Emile Durkheim asserted that "anomic" type suicide results from the lack of direction, restraints, or measuring sticks stemming from dramatic social upheaval. I wondered, briefly, if social fabric tears from the breakdown of the family, religion, and consensus over Vietnam had contributed in any way to the tear we'd just sustained in our own family fabric.

Qualifying exams spanned several grueling days. It wasn't pretty, but I passed, allowing me to continue toward my doctorate. I spent many days finishing the various papers I'd started at different points during the year. And just when I thought I could relax, Professor Paul Mott confronted me.

"I've got a huge lecture class that I'm sure would love to hear about your work," he said.

"Not my theoretical model of third-party intervention?" I countered.

"I've actually heard Professor Evan rave about your model—"

"Okay, how about applications of the model, namely police management of violence?"

"Perfect. A very timely topic! Thanks." He patted me on the back.

"Well, thank you."

As I prepared for the lecture over the next week, I reminded myself that my voiceprint had turned out normal. Still, my heart pounded wildly as I walked to the lectern.

I almost opened the lecture saying, "Be ready for me to die of stage fright or heart failure in front of all five hundred of you."

Instead, I smiled from ear to ear and started my lecture, knowing I had left the old me behind.

The students loved the lecture, and I enjoyed giving it. *Maybe*

I could be a professor, I thought. This would answer Lee Sims' mom's frequent query, "How're you gonna support yourself while you're saving the world?"

Once school obligations ended for me, Sharon asked me to find out more about Mom's mental state and the circumstances surrounding her suicide. Sharon told me, in all honesty, she might hesitate marrying into my family if I carried genes for depression and mental illness because she thought she carried them from her family already. I agreed to ask more questions for her sake, for mine, and for ours together.

I called Dad and probed, "What's your feeling about Mom's mental state over the years...and its link to her suicide?"

After thinking it over, he replied, "I think she was depressed for years. Yes, serious depression killed Mom."

"Why do you think it killed her?"

"Well, Dr. Steinman treated Mom as if she had depression. Genetic-induced, rather than life-induced, depression."

We talked some more, and then I asked, "What about the autopsy report? Sharon and I still need more details."

"I forgot to send it. Sorry. I'll try to."

When I hung up, I folded my arms across my chest and stared at the floor—mad at Dad for failing to send the autopsy report... and mad at Mom for killing herself. Mom's suicide shattered the "normal-ness" I'd finally begun to feel at age twenty-four. I resented her, too, for forcing me to deal with her death on top of my papers, exams, and wedding—now in jeopardy.

I also resented that I could no longer just study violence in *other* people's lives. My aloof clinical stance, and maybe my sense of superiority vis-à-vis them, had slipped away. To study violence, to see it in the news—even to see the effects of world wars in other countries—none of it had really touched my life until now. Even childhood bullies had seemed tame because I always thought I could outrun or outsmart them. But violence had truly struck home, and I could not run from it. I had lost a degree of innocence.

I paced the room for a while, bothered that Sharon thought depression genes—in addition to my cleft genes and my heart-defect genes—might be the third strike against me as a mate. I'd lost my mother. I didn't want to lose my fiancée or, to be more precise, the love I'd found, pushed away, lost for a time, then pursued anew and won.

Since I had no new information to report to Sharon about Mom's mental state, I worried our upcoming trip to California for the summer would be a one-way trip for her. She and I answered an ad looking for someone to deliver a car to the West.

We set out in early June. We'd driven but a few hundred miles when we heard a news flash that artist Andy Warhol had been shot.

"Jesus Christ," Sharon cried out.

"Shot by a troubled feminist writer who acted in one of his films," the newscaster said. "Police report that the assailant said Warhol had Quote too much control of my life Unquote."

As art aficionados, Sharon and I hung on every news report, hoping Warhol would survive. He pulled through, but the incident took a permanent toll on his art and his life.

Three days later, as we sped past fields of Iowa corn under a dark moon, we heard that Bobby Kennedy had been shot three times in the kitchen of an L.A. hotel.

"The country's gone fucking insane!" I screamed out the window.

For the next twenty-four hours, we again listened to news updates on the radio. A different outcome this time: Bobby succumbed to his wounds. Stunned, we went through the motions of driving and talking for a while. Like my own mother's death, the violence seemed unreal, and yet I knew it surrounded me. A whirlwind had taken over the nation.

We arrived in Palo Alto on Sunday under a murderously dark night sky, and in short order settled into my old room at the end of the hall. Sharon went to bed right away and, after she had fallen asleep, I asked Dad if I could look at the autopsy report.

"It's at the office, but I can tell you what it says," he replied.

"I'd really rather see it—the medical jargon, you know."

"You don't trust me?"

"Well, ahh…Just bring it home tomorrow. Please. I need the details…mainly for Sharon's sake."

Was Dad hiding something? Should I be suspicious? I'd been caught so unawares by Mom, maybe I didn't know Dad that well either.

The following day—to be better prepared to interpret the autopsy—I researched mixing alcohol and psychiatric meds at the Stanford medical school library where I still had access. I also researched the signs of strangulation versus hanging, and read up on postmortem lividity (color) and rigor mortis (stiffness) and how they help determine the time of death.

That evening I asked Dad for the report as soon as he arrived home.

"You know, Karl, I couldn't find it," he said, avoiding eye contact.

"C'mon, Dad. You're playing games, damn it!" I said and stomped out of the living room. Tomorrow I would go to the Santa Clara County coroner's office for my own copy.

The next morning I raced to the dingy morgue, got the report, and went outside to escape the dank odor of death. What I read made my heart almost leap from my chest; my hands shook so hard, I could hear the report papers rustle.

What shocked me wasn't the gruesome part, saying Mom had sustained a fracture of her larynx in a way consistent with hanging, not choking. (Strangulation has a distinct "signature.") What shocked me was another part of the report. I drove home and agonized all day about confronting Dad. After all, he *was* my father and my hero; a man whose approval I'd sought all my life.

As soon as he came home from work and Sharon was out of earshot, I blurted out, "You lied to us."

"What're you talking about?"

Glaring at him, I said "Mom killed herself on your birthday!"

"How do you know that?"

"I've got the autopsy report here," I said, waving it in the air. "It says she died at six-thirty in the morning on March 31, on your birthday. Not the night before."

His shoulders sagged. After a long silence, he said, "I know."

"Then why did you keep it from us?"

"I thought she'd died the night before—until I saw the autopsy report." Almost whispering, he added, "I—I just couldn't bear to have you kids—or our friends—know she killed herself on my birthday. I bent the truth. I'm sorry." His eyes filled.

Another long silence.

I wanted to say, "I understand. It's okay," but I seethed inside. Instead, I said, "The coroner found no drugs or alcohol in her system."

"I'm sure she drank that evening, took her meds—"

"Did you in fact *see* her drink, take her meds?"

"No."

"So much for an accidental mixing. She killed herself on purpose. Alcohol's irrelevant, anyway. Even if she had mixed alcohol and her meds, she would have digested them by early morning...before deciding to hang herself."

Dad looked down, clasping and unclasping his hands. "I know."

"What bothers me most is that she died at six-thirty a.m., and you didn't hear her!" I threw the report at Dad.

"Watch yourself, son. I know you're upset, but do you know what you're implying?"

I cringed, hating to have to say the next words. "Yes. I'm suggesting you didn't stop her."

"How can you say that? Anyway, six-thirty a.m. is just a guess on the coroner's part."

"No, it's not. He found exactly four hours of postmortem lividity and rigor mortis when he autopsied her at ten-thirty a.m., meaning she died at six-thirty a.m. Tissues and tables of lividity do not lie."

"I woke up around seven-thirty. I'd slept soundly." Dad said.

"You wake up at six a.m. all week long, so you can catch the early train."

"What? What do you want from me?"

"The truth! You should've been stirring at six or six-thirty. There were abrasions on Mom's right knee—there must've been a thump when her knee hit the shower-tub wall—"

"I didn't hear a thing!" Dad protested.

"The bathroom door was ajar. You didn't hear her scream, or gasp, or something?"

"She ended her life to be free of her demons. She looked peaceful when I found her."

"I doubt that. I bet she looked contorted or frantic. It's a horrible way to die!" I shouted. "I bet you heard something, but felt ambivalent. Maybe I'd feel that way, too. Tired of her being whacked out on Thorazine all the time. Tired of her menopausal complaints—fatigue, cramps, hot flashes—"

"I wish I'd heard her," Dad said, looking away.

Not satisfied, I blurted out, "I still think she cried out for help, and you ignored her or maybe didn't act fast enough."

"How dare you!" he shouted. He turned and left the room.

An hour later, Dad left the house saying he had prior plans for dinner out that night. When Sharon returned home, I told her about the autopsy and my talk with Dad. She stood there, speechless.

After much discussion and a quiet-but-unsettling dinner, Sharon said, "Before we mail the invitations, I'd still like to know more about your mom's mental state."

I told her I'd try to find out more. Still, I could not quite process what I already knew. As I lay down to sleep, the autopsy findings triggered nightmarish thoughts about Mom's final moments.

I called Gayle and Scott and told them what I'd learned. The autopsy findings shocked them, as did the fact that Mom had killed herself on Dad's birthday. Even more, it bothered them that Dad might have failed to respond to a possible cry for help, and that Dad had withheld information from us. Scott declared he'd "lied," while Gayle said he'd "spun" the story, concluding, "Mom's death posed the biggest PR challenge Dad ever faced."

The next day, to ease the tension between us, I asked Dad to walk with me along a path near the San Francisco Bay. We talked about his job and my research. Then, after a long silence—and in an uncharacteristic effort to guilt-trip him because of my accumulated frustrations—I said, "Mom must've been very angry with you to kill herself on your birthday."

"She didn't like me bringing HUD work home. But, the contractor and mortgage broker scandals have kept us super busy on top of everything else."

"You think she committed suicide because of a hard-working husband?"

"She had her demons."

"Maybe so." Then, swallowing hard, I said, "Aunt Irene thinks you were having an affair."

"What?" Dad shouted, stopping in his tracks. "That's ludicrous! Just ludicrous. Irene always disapproved of our move to California. She thought life in the fast lane would kill us."

"Maybe it did. Maybe it killed Mom."

"How so?"

"Well, the fast pace, your long work hours, so many of your couple friends splitting up: the Zajacs, Fergusons, other Unitarians—"

"Your point?"

"Sooo, have you had an affair? All your traveling—"

"No." His eyes pierced mine. "No! I know I can't prove it, but you'll just have to believe me, son....I loved your mother."

I flashed on memories of Dad flirting with women, of Mom with Erik Gaspar and Jed Palmer. "Well, maybe you and Mom acted out Roger Vadim's *Dangerous Liaisons*, trying to make each other jealous."

"That's preposterous!"

"Aunt Irene even thinks you wanted out of the marriage."

"I didn't want out of the marriage. In fact—" He caught himself.

"In fact...what?"

"Your mom wanted out. She was the one pushing to separate."

I was dumbstruck. For a moment neither of us spoke. Then Dad said, "She wanted to start a trial separation the day after my birthday. Since she preferred radio and TV news, she cancelled the newspaper as of that day, thinking I'd no longer read it on the train to work. She thought I'd be living in the City."

"So did you get an apartment in the City?"

"No, but I did move into your bedroom."

"Whoa!" I shouted. "You were *sleeping* in my room, on the other side of the wall while Mom was *dying* in the bathroom? And the noise—"

"I didn't hear a thing. I know it sounds implausible. Maybe the clothes in the closet absorbed the noise. Anyway, I was tired and trying to sleep in that Saturday."

We walked a bit in silence, the Baylands' grasses waving in a slight breeze.

"I...uh...hate to ask this," I said, "but was Mom wearing her wedding rings when you found her?"

"I didn't notice. Why?"

"Cops check to see if married suicide victims remove their rings before they kill themselves. Helps establish motive."

"Come to think of it, the coroner gave me an envelope with Laura's rings in it."

"Maybe she didn't want a divorce after all," I said, staring at the Bay.

"She said she wanted to live on her own," Dad said. "Maybe the *Feminine Mystique*, that book her psychiatrist pushed, got to her. I don't know. Dr. Steinman never involved me in Laura's treatment."

Disgusted, I said, "Dr. Steinman's not my favorite shrink."

"Maybe she took her life because she got cold feet the day before the separation," Dad said. "She realized she'd be alone, unable to cope or support herself."

"I don't buy that," I said. "She'd been alone plenty this last year. And in prior years, too, what with all your traveling, your time in boot camp, your early months in D.C. And she'd worked part-time jobs of late and could always rent rooms to Stanford students for money. Plus alimony?"

"She knew she'd have to do all the paperwork to kick me out—because I didn't want to leave."

"Why would Mom try to kick you out if you hadn't had an affair?"

"Depression? Things didn't come easy to her anymore. Stuff overwhelmed her. I guess she feared the future."

"Something misfired when she had her breakdown," I said. "Were you having an affair then?"

"No! Of course not!" He clenched his fists. "And Laura's and my life together really isn't any of your business!"

"Yes, it is, Dad. She was my mother," I said, looking at him steadily, "and you're my father. And Sharon's worried about the kind of family she's marrying into."

THE TIE THAT BINDS

THE NEXT DAY, GAYLE arrived from Philadelphia with her husband. They had rented a place close to Stanford since they both had summer obligations on campus. Scott had just driven down from Berkeley to live at home for the summer. To update them both, I proposed we meet for coffee at the Varsity Theatre courtyard.

Sharon joined us, and we found some privacy under a tile-covered arcade along the side of the always-crowded courtyard café. I'd already told Sharon some of what I'd learned on my walk with Dad.

"Did you guys ever see Mom flirt or act inappropriately with a man?" I asked.

"No!" said Gayle. "Mom and Dad were straight arrows."

Scott raised an eyebrow. "Why do you ask?" he said and continued checking out the courtyard's Spanish architecture.

"Because I can't figure out why last summer I found Mom sitting close to Erik Gaspar on our living room sofa—almost in the dark—while Dad was away."

"My God," Gayle exclaimed, "The 'Freedom Fighter' from our church?! He's married!"

"Now that I think about it," Scott said, "I saw one of Dad's long-time buddies at the house once when Dad wasn't home. And Jed Palmer, too."

"I must've seen Jed the same day you did," I said.

"You don't think Mom?" Gayle sputtered.

"Did Dad know about all these visits?" asked Scott.

"Don't know. Her behavior's sure confusing," I admitted.

"Maybe she just wanted some male attention," Sharon said, "but she couldn't keep friendships with men from escalating."

"She did seem to flirt with my clarinet teacher, Don Jurgen, after lessons, but that was a decade ago," Gayle said.

We all stared at each other—feeling awkward and uncomfortable—as we thought through the implications of this new information.

"Maybe Aunt Irene got things backward," I said.

"What do you mean?" Gayle asked.

"On the plane home after the memorial service, Aunt Irene told several people she thought Dad was having an affair and wanted out of the marriage."

Gayle and Scott recoiled, wide-eyed, and said, "No!" at the same time.

"I asked Dad, and he denied both accusations."

"What else was he gonna say?" Scott said.

"Perhaps Mom thought he'd had affairs, and thought what's good for the goose is good for the gander," Gayle speculated.

"Dad denied he and Mom played 'jealousy' games,'" I said.

"That would be so bourgeois," Scott said.

"And *that's* so Berkeley," Gayle retorted. (She'd shared with me her concern that U.C. Berkeley had boosted Scott's cynicism and alienation.)

"But, here's what really shocks me," I said. "Dad divulged that he and Mom were planning to separate."

"No way!" Gayle said, slamming the table, almost spilling our coffees. "Our parents separate? They never even fought."

"Leaving aside all these latest allegations of infidelity, they seemed to have had the perfect marriage," Sharon said.

"Until Karl went away to college. Then Mom had her break," Scott said.

"When were they gonna split?" Gayle asked.

"The day after Dad's birthday," I replied.

"Jeez! So Mom killed herself just before the split," Gayle exclaimed.

"What proof is there they planned to separate?" Scott challenged.

I explained Mom's canceling of the paper and Dad's moving from my bedroom back to the master bedroom 'because we kids would be home for the memorial service.' "But the real kicker is that Dad said the separation was Mom's idea."

"Jesus Christ!" Gayle exclaimed, her eyes wide open.

"Dad says he didn't want it and hadn't looked for another place to live."

We were silent, each with our own thoughts.

"I'm afraid, honey," I said, turning to Sharon, "the Schonborns don't look so great all of a sudden."

"Believe me, the Beltons don't win any prizes, either."

All of us needed a breather, so we paused to fetch coffee refills.

After we returned to the table, Scott said, "The *Feminine Mystique* may have put the separation idea into Mom's head. She told me Dr. Steinman encouraged her to read Friedan. Pushed her to stand up to Dad."

"Then why did Steinman medicate her so much?" Gayle asked.

"Yeah, why *did* Steinman prescribe Thorazine anyway?" I demanded.

"It's for schizophrenics, maybe manic-depressives in a pinch," Sharon said, having learned from her mom's shrink.

"A well-known psychiatrist named Peter Breggin claims Thorazine creates passivity and blocks emotion," I said. "Like putting a patient in an emotional strait-jacket."

"Then Thorazine would only have weakened Mom's resolve, sapped her strength to confront Dad," Gayle surmised.

"At least Steinman didn't subject Mom to a lobotomy or electric shock," Scott said with a wan smile.

"Steinman seems to have turned Mom into a psychiatric invalid," I added, "just as Dr. Robertson turned me into a cardiac invalid when I was a teenager."

"Did anyone check Steinman out in 1962 when Mom had her break?" Scott asked.

"No, but I did at the library yesterday," I said. "Judging from the dates on his resume, Mom had to have been one of his first patients."

"That could be a plus," said Scott, "but odds-on a minus, I'd say."

"He grew up and got his entire education in New York City," I said.

"So, what did he know of the challenges suburban housewives face?" Sharon wondered.

"New to his practice. New to the area. Just great," Gayle stated.

"So he starts pushing Thorazine right away?" Scott exclaimed.

"To be fair," Sharon noted, "there aren't many drugs available for mental illness. And, like the Stones' song says, pills are 'Mother's Little Helpers.'"

"In 1962, I think Steinman confused Mom's grieving—really 'longing'—with serious depression," I said. "They're not the same thing. Grieving is life-induced and may've triggered Mom's break. Serious depression? Who knows? It may be life-induced, genetic-induced, or a combination."

"How could Steinman confuse grief with depression?" asked Gayle.

"He just did," Scott said.

"But he's been closer to Mom than we have," Gayle said.

"Speak for yourself," Scott countered. "I lived at home with Mom for three years after her break, and on and off since. You know, Mom got back into skiing at age fifty. Not something depressed people do."

"But Mom thought she didn't measure up," Gayle asserted.

"How do you know that? From Aunt Irene?" I asked.

"Maybe so," Gayle admitted, sheepishly. "I guess I never heard it from Mom herself."

"Aunt Irene claims Dad always criticized Mom, lowered her self-esteem," I said.

"Look," Scott said, "Mom camped with the Unitarians and traveled to L.A. twice in the last six months. Doesn't sound like depression to me."

"L.A.?" said Gayle. "Easy—to say 'goodbye' to her old friend Ruth Rowley."

"But I asked Ruth about that at Mom's service," I countered. "She denied Mom said 'Goodbye,' shared dark secrets, or was suicidal."

Folding her arms across her chest, Gayle said, "You guys make good points, but I still think she had serious depression."

Sharon chimed in, "Did Laura exhibit any changes in her appetite, appearance, interest in sex—as depressives often do?"

"Appetite?" I answered. "The coroner described her as 'well nourished.' Appearance? Stylish to the end. Sex? Well, Thorazine tends to shut a person down."

"Yes, but she still enjoyed sex," said Gayle. "She complained once that she and Dad only had it when he wanted it. Maybe his busy schedule determined their sex life. If so, it suggests a power disparity between them."

"Bingo!" said Scott, brightening up. "Disparity's more key than depression. Maybe the power differential affected their relationship. Mom strikes me as no more depressed than millions of bourgeois women with busy husbands!"

"Go on, Scott," Sharon encouraged.

"Most important, Dad and Steinman benefit from labeling Mom 'seriously depressed;' Dad escapes blame and Steinman covers his ass by intimating she's got problems too deep-seated to treat."

"It's obvious, Scott, you've read Marxian theories of patriarchy," I said. "I buy into some of them."

"Glad to hear it, Comrade," Scott said, winking. "Check out Jessie Bernard, a sociology prof at Penn State who writes about patriarchy."

"Okay, okay," said Gayle. "I'll revise my 'serious genetic depression' explanation. Maybe Mom had a mix of life-based problems, like 'empty nest blues' and stress from trying to meet too-high standards." Gayle looked at her watch. "Oops, I've got to get going."

As we left the courtyard, Gayle said she hoped anyone overhearing our conversation would forgive us for being so detached about something as emotional as suicide. The irony Gayle expressed wasn't lost on me since I'd often thought of the detachment Mom must have experienced in her final moments. Of course, we four had an excuse for *our* detachment—being young, naive to the ways of the world, and in profound shock over Mom's death. I still sought reasons, though, for why Mom— if she was like so many who attempt suicide—detached from her emotions just before taking her life.

That night as we lay in bed, Sharon said we had to mail the wedding invitations the next day, at the latest. She said she'd learned almost enough about Mom's situation to make a decision about our getting married.

When she saw me tense up, she said, "Your fact-finding and Gayle and Scott's input have been great."

I relaxed a bit.

"Depression's a traveling companion of people who commit suicide," she continued. "But in your mom's case, stress, anxiety, and maybe menopausal hormonal swings traveled with her, too. Other companions?"

"Well, not brain abnormalities for sure. The coroner found none in his cross-sections of Mom's brain."

"What about blaming herself for your clefts?"

"If she did in the early years, she knew she'd gone the extra mile getting me to surgeons, therapists, specialists—and had long since made up for anything she might have done to have caused the clefts."

Sharon touched the box with the printed invitations sitting on the nightstand and looked into my eyes. "Then let's send these out.

"You mean it?" I asked. "Are you *sure*?"

"Yes."

"Is it 'normal' to have a celebration so soon after someone's death?"

"I've seen 'normal,'" Sharon said, "and I'm not impressed."

I reached for Sharon and gave her the biggest hug I could.

The next morning I found Dad alone in the kitchen making coffee.

"Dad, we're going through with the wedding after all."

"That's great! I know Sharon had understandable second thoughts."

"Still okay with having it here? Guests checking out the bathroom and all?"

"Wouldn't have it any other way. Nor would your mother." He paused and looked away. Turning back, he continued, "Anyhow, it's time to move forward."

"Well, I-I'd still like to clarify one thing about the past." I dreaded asking him any more questions; it seemed like pulling down the statue of a former hero. "I love and respect you, Dad, but I'm worried that you may have abandoned Mom at some point—emotionally if not physically."

"Huh?"

"Someone who loves deeply despairs deeply when love is lost. Just as in 1962, when Mom's dad died and she lost his love, she may have felt—"

"The loss of mine?"

"Yes. She may've thought you'd become married to your work. Or thought you'd become married 'emotionally' to someone else."

"I told you I've had no affairs."

"Maybe she sensed you yearned for one."

"Jesus, Karl!"

"Maybe she felt she *had* to kick you out, felt you'd never leave on your own because you wanted to fool around but still keep the stability of a marriage."

"For Christ's sake!"

"Did she confront you on the drive home from Saturday's party?"

"It was a quiet ride."

"Something must've happened that changed everything. Otherwise, why would she have baked a cake before the party and left a bowl and frosting ingredients out to decorate it the next day? It doesn't make sense. "

"You think I don't know that?"

"You're sure it was a quiet ride home?"

"We weren't mute, if that's what you mean."

"I bet she asked you if you were gonna keep your end of the separation bargain and move out after your birthday. I bet you said 'No.'"

"That's my business. It's personal."

"If you refused to move out, Mom doubtless stopped talking during the rest of the ride, seething inside. Once home, she probably felt stuck. She'd finally expressed her feelings, skating out on thin ice. When she demanded you move out, you refused."

"You don't know what you're talking about."

"Then tell me what happened."

He looked down at his hands, looked up at me, but said nothing.

I had no choice but to continue. "Maybe she was in such pain, hurt so much, she couldn't see her options. She didn't see a way out."

Dad rubbed the back of his neck. "You've got her punishing me for sins I didn't commit."

"Maybe she just wanted to get your attention, have you come running, cut the noose, give her the praise and love she needed."

Dad began to tear up. "I may've asked too much, given too little encouragement. I've always been a perfectionist, and maybe she believed she could never meet my expectations—making sure car repairs, bathroom remodels, a lot of things were done right."

He leaned against the kitchen wall, signaling tiredness or agreement or both. "And maybe I did yearn for excitement. Did yearn for someone new. Didn't date enough before marrying. Didn't see the world. Not sins...but shortcomings."

I had arranged for Scott and Gayle to meet Sharon and me the next day at Stanford's student center after Gayle's summer class got out. Beforehand, Sharon and I checked out the view from the fourteenth-floor observation deck of Hoover Tower, next to the center. We couldn't believe how much development had occurred over the last few years due to the energy of Stanford engineering prof, Frederick Terman, the "Father of Silicon Valley." We saw new buildings everywhere—IBM, Xerox, Syntex, Hewlett-Packard, and others that would one day become just as well known.

At the center, Gayle and Scott rose to greet us. "Congrats on deciding to proceed with the wedding!" Gayle said as she embraced us both in a big hug.

Scott congratulated us, too, and Sharon thanked the two of them.

"I hope you're both still willing to be members of the wedding party?" I asked.

"Absolutely," Scott replied, shaking my hand after hugging Sharon.

"Sure thing," Gayle said. "But we're not here to talk about the wedding."

"Yes," Scott said, "Let's try to get closure on the mystery that was our mother."

I updated everyone about my last talk with Dad. My supposition regarding the ride home from the party intrigued them. The fact that Dad neither accepted nor denied it gave it more credence, as did his words of contrition and body language. After some discussion, we all seemed to agree that Mom's suicide had not been planned, but was the result of something disturbing that had happened that evening. Something that had changed things irrevocably and irreparably.

A waitress brought the light snacks we'd ordered. Turning toward Scott, Gayle said, "I've been thinking about your Marxist-feminist analysis of Mom. I don't agree with it."

"How so?" he replied.

"Mom's issues didn't come from Dad or a patriarchy, but from low self-esteem stemming from childhood trauma or emotional abuse."

Scott fired back. "Low self-esteem is a byproduct of our capitalist society that insists on creating winners and losers."

"That may be so," Gayle replied, "but I'm talking *really* early influences. Yesterday, I phoned some Stenerson relatives other than Aunt Irene to see if Mom experienced trauma growing up. One of Mom's brothers said she might've been traumatized watching her parents treat her sibs harshly for being rebellious. That alone might've caused Mom's shyness, her lack of assertiveness."

"And?" I said.

"Mom might've experienced Grandma as not only harsh, but controlling and perfectionistic."

"I agree with you," I said, "at least regarding Grandma's perfectionism. Her cataloging, cross-filing, and caring for her stamp collection were amazing."

"Some of her traits probably made her a good office manager at Grandpa's insurance agency and later at their church," Scott said.

"And then Mom up and marries Dad who has some of the same traits," I said.

"Add to all this Grandpa's ambition, which may've caused him to ignore Mom while he built his business," Gayle continued.

"A money-hungry, neglectful father? Didn't I just say Mom's low self-esteem was a byproduct of capitalism?" Scott said, beaming with certainty.

"Grandpa certainly had ambition," I said. "Cousin Clyde once told me Grandpa charged extra premiums for garages already covered in homeowners' policies."

"Sheesh," said Sharon.

"And Clyde also said when Grandpa became a stockbroker, he charged him and his other grandkids the same commission he did for adult clients."

"That reminds me," Gayle said. "Clyde's mom, Aunt Jenny, thinks Grandma may not have wanted a third child—her husband, Uncle Jim—or a fourth, our mom. Aunt Jenny guesses Grandma sensed she couldn't manage a lot of kids, given she grew up as an only child."

"Mom's childhood traumas might have come to the fore during her nervous breakdown," I said. "And so, too, old feelings of shame over giving birth to a cleft kid. Lately, new feelings of shame over a problematic marriage may've compounded matters."

"All this in someone with high expectations for herself," Sharon said. "Her *own* perfectionism might have increased her feelings of being unworthy."

"All very interesting," said Scott, "but my money's still on patriarchy and capitalism."

"You're misguided!" said Gayle. "The patriarchy bit's okay, but the Marxism—"

"You guys could argue forever," Sharon interrupted. "Karl's been thinking about Laura's final moments, what she may have experienced."

Turning away from Scott to face me, Gayle said, "Tell us, Karl."

"Some of it's grim, based on autopsy findings," I warned. "You all okay with that?"

Everyone nodded.

"Okay, here's what I think may have happened."

After removing her makeup and brushing her teeth, Mom left the hall bathroom for the master bedroom and crawled into bed alone. She slept fitfully because of her still-strong anger at Jack for his refusal to move out of the house. She woke up before 6 a.m., still agitated and got up to try to walk it off. She soon found herself in the family room looking at her beloved floor loom, but with no desire to weave. She felt stuck. Had Jack sabotaged her life, just as workers had once thrown their shoes into industrial looms? Could she no longer weave a satisfying life for herself?

She left the family room and passed the floor-to-ceiling living room windows showcasing trees in the backyard lit by fading moonlight. Even though these windows made Eichler homes chilly, her heart and face burned with defiance. *I'll show Jack. Punish him.* Then, strangely, the opposite notion filled her, *No wonder Jack and my father went from protecting, to controlling, to abandoning me—I'm unworthy. Nobody could love me. Stuck again!*

And then came the idea of suicide. Had her friend Mary's hanging planted the idea years ago—like the contagion effect in other kinds of violence? Or was this the first time Mom had thought of "the unthinkable," of killing herself? By now she was back in the master bedroom, Jack still sleeping in the adjacent room.

She picked up the birthday tie she had just purchased to give to Jack and walked to the newly-remodeled bathroom. Courage or cowardice? Something had cut her off from all feeling as she tied the necktie around the upper rail of the shower door.

I paused to be sure everyone wanted me to go on. Their eyes said "continue," regardless of whatever their hearts may have been saying.

Free of alcohol and meds, Mom methodically knotted the other end of the tie around her neck. *He'll listen to me now.* After bending her legs, intense neck pain may have caused her to reverse her decision. Maybe she struggled to stand, banging her knee against the tub in the process. Maybe she banged the tub on purpose for Jack to hear. Or maybe her knee hit the tub minutes later as a final reflex of her dying body.

No one heard. Jack didn't come.

Excruciating pain shot through her neck and head, but before she could scream or struggle further, a flood of carbon dioxide to her brain cut off her ability to do either. With luck, the carbon dioxide kept her from experiencing suffocating breathlessness. And after five minutes, her consciousness would have shut down—and along with it, any hope of being saved—beginning a final twenty-minute descent into eternal blackness.

As I ended my narrative, a vise-grip sensation in my head spread from temple to temple, squeezing tears from my eyes. I reached for Sharon's hand and held it tight. Everybody's face glistened with tears.

After a long pause, Scott said, "You mean her neck didn't snap, causing her to die in an instant?"

"That only happens in a long-drop execution," I said. "She would have choked, then suffocated bit by bit."

"God, Karl," Gayle said. "I wonder if she knew how painful it would be."

A profound sadness hung in the air. We quickly found excuses to break up. After hugs all around, Sharon and I walked away in silence, hand-in-hand.

I called college roommates Ned Hooper and 'Stark' Starkweather, both back East at the time, to see if they could be groomsmen in the wedding along with Scott and Lee Sims. Stark regretted he couldn't make it, but Ned said he could if I promised to set him up with one of the bridesmaids.

Sharon and I continued the wedding and reception arrangements that Mom had started. Sharon ordered a dress, and her mom got her long-awaited mother-of-the-bride outfit. I arranged to rent a traditional morning coat, striped pants, and a tie. I regarded the tie as a way to move forward.

Sharon and I asked Reverend Lion to perform the ceremony in our backyard. In our prenuptial counseling session, Reverend Lion stated, "You both need to give equal weight to facts *and* feelings in married life."

"During fights in particular, I s'pose," I said.

"Yes," Reverend Lion replied. And as he walked us to the parking lot, he emphasized, "Make time to do things together that you both enjoy. And *listen* to each other."

Despite the tension between Dad and me, I made a point of reaching out to him, knowing—after all his revelations—that Mom's death had brought him as much mind-numbing pain as any of us had experienced. Mom's suicide ended her pain, but left him plenty: he had had to answer innumerable questions raised by the police as well by relatives and friends. In addition, his birthday would never be the same.

After Mom's cremation, Dad said, "There is nothing I can do, but I cannot do nothing." So, after some thought, he arranged the planting of a Japanese maple tree in the courtyard of the Palo Alto Unitarian Church. Under an overcast sky one afternoon, we spread Mom's ashes around the tree and said a few words. Tears welled up in my eyes as Scott said, "We never got to say 'goodbye' to you, Mom. Now we can come and say 'hello' and 'goodbye' whenever we want."

As Dad and I—wiping our eyes—trailed behind Gayle and Scott on the way to our cars, I said, "I'm sorry I've pressured you so much of late about Mom."

"Believe it or not, I've appreciated it, as well as your medical and psychological expertise."

"Thanks, Dad."

"I've been too hard on you and the rest of the family over the years," Dad said in almost a whisper. Stopping, he looked me full in the face. "By the way, I forgot to congratulate you on your lecture at Penn. You should be proud of yourself."

"I am. Thanks to you...and thanks to Mom." I put my arm around his shoulders.

"I love you, Dad."

"I love you, too, Son."

A few weeks later, driving full tilt along Sand Hill Road past the offices of Silicon Valley venture capitalists, Sharon and I laughed and smiled a lot...at long last.

I turned onto La Honda Road to get to the Skywood part of Woodside, and we soon emerged above the clouds, the layer of light fog that had spread beneath us covered the foothills we'd just traversed. We drove farther up the coastal range to reach Lee Sims' parents' new house and our rehearsal dinner.

At one point during the dinner on the Sims' deck—replete with spectacular views—those present raised loving toasts to Sharon and me. Mrs. Sims toasted the fact that my hoped-for professorship would keep us from starving. Her son, Lee, ended his toast with almost-predictable corniness, "All my love to Karl and Sharon. May they not be barren!"

Mrs. Sims brought out bright, solid-color shawls for the women as a slight chill settled in after dinner. Sharon's red shawl set off her white dress and large blue eyes; she looked more beautiful than ever. As we all talked into the night, our grand view of Palo Alto, Silicon Valley, and the Bay slipped into darkness punctuated by shimmering lights.

The next day, Ned checked me over just before the afternoon ceremony. He asked, "Are you sure you can handle a tie? It's not too soon?"

"Yes. This short ascot tie is fine. Not sure I could manage a long tie, though."

"Here, let me adjust it," Ned insisted as he pushed an errant bit of tie under my gray vest.

"Thanks." I stepped back. "It's odd. I feel Mom's love. I feel like she's here. I feel whole…no not whole. I feel normal. All of my life, I've been chasing normal."

"Haven't we all? Hey, I gotta go protect your get-away car," Ned said as he left the bedroom staging area.

I glanced at myself in the mirror. *Not bad looking*, I thought.

Checking my pocket to be sure I still had Sharon's wedding ring, I walked out to meet my bride.

ACKNOWLEDGMENTS

JUST AS IT TAKES the interrelating of family, friends, and intimates to create a real life story, it sometimes takes many of the same people to retell it decades later. I acknowledge the twin gifts of many of these people—the gift of being part of my story in the first place and the gift of helping me with forgotten details when I got around to telling it. Besides my sibs, I'm indebted especially to my aunt, Jean Plith, and to my parents' good friends, the late Dan and Eva Lion.

I would also like to acknowledge more recent friends who played important roles in the development of this book. Some provided encouragement; others, advice. Included among these: high school classmates Jean Herz Felger, Ann Frye Giglioli, Pam Kiraly West, and Charlie Haid, as well as long-time friends Karen Fredrick and Pam and Allan Fried.

Colleagues and acquaintances who write for a living supported me and advised me, too, but often with the now common world-weariness of writers: Jacqueline Doyle, Elizabeth Fisher, Sheldon Greene, Lynn Hanna, Sara McAulay, and Carl Tighe. Charitable English friends, Debbie Jackson and Mark Perry, and others of the Belfield Ave Book Club in Manchester, England—along with Madeleine Rose from nearby Withington—reminded me early on that reading and writing still matter in many places.

The early initial readers of *Cleft Heart* know no equal. Despite wading through very rough drafts, the following managed to offer invaluable feedback: Julio Alfaro, Mary-Catherine Haug, Kelly Radimer, Nancy Rivara, Jeane Samuelsen, Sheila Warbasse, and in-laws Vicki Horn and Andrea Lowther. Long-time friend Kathleen Gardiner Dillwood—bless her heart—read not one, but two entire rough drafts.

The readers of later drafts often told me to "murder my darlings" because favorite phrases or passages of mine failed to pass muster. I'm indebted to longstanding colleague Shirley Foster Hartley, college classmates Dennis Mack and Warren Rothman, Schonborn-side relatives (Toni Hansen, Judy Silver, Penny Juve, Doug/Phil Meddaugh, Dona/Larry Plith) and Stenerson-side relations (Jane/Clyde Stenerson) who all offered vital critiques. Bruce Cribley, Bruce Fleming, Kathleen Graeven and Ann Tipton, M.D. brought their respective medical and psychotherapeutic insights to bear on the manuscript.

Elisa Morris from the publishing world put her faith in my story and for that I'm grateful beyond words. Sally Hollemon and Sandra Woffington worked their editing magic on key drafts, sharing their incredible storytelling skills along the way. To them I'm eternally grateful.

If I gave short shrift to some one or some event in my story or messed up in another way, it is totally my doing and not the fault of any of the aforementioned.

My wife—and my children John and Lindsay—all read parts of the manuscript and helped in countless ways. They also put up with me during the writing of this book. For all that and so much more, I love them dearly.

DISCUSSION QUESTIONS & TOPICS

Spoiler alert: Don't ruin your reading experience; finish the book before looking below. Be aware, too, some answers to questions are provided in parentheses.

ESPECIALLY FOR READING GROUPS

1. Of the many themes explored in this book—birth defects, discrimination, bullying, war, nonviolence, suicide, relationships, career choice—which resonated most with you?

2. Has bullying changed since the fifties and sixties? Has the motivation behind bullying changed: that is, were the motives behind Karl's bullies different from today's motives? What can children, adults and schools do to stop bullying?

3. Do you believe in the survival of the fittest? If so, do doctors and others play god by cheating fate in developed countries and are anti-bully campaigns unnecessary?

4. Which of the protagonist's antagonists strikes you as the most hurtful? Do you believe that while sticks and stones can break your bones, words will never hurt you?

5. What drawbacks to being "normal" does Karl discover? (One answer: If he lost his sympathy for non-normals by being part of the majority, he *could* perpetuate we-they perceptions.)

6. How is Karl typical of a sixties counterculture young man? (His interest in travel, nonviolence, war resistance, making art, etc.)

7. How is Sharon *atypical* of a sixties counterculture young woman? (Belonging to a sorority, wanting to be engaged by twenty-one, resisting cohabitation due to parental/religious disapproval, etc.) What do you think "getting married" symbolized to Sharon?

8. Do you subscribe to the notion that we're put here for a purpose? Was Laura's purpose fulfilled when Sharon became engaged to Karl? Did Laura pass a caregiver "torch" to Sharon in a real or symbolic way? If so, when?

9. Which of the love stories in the book—Laura-Karl, Sharon-Karl, Blair-Karl, Ellen-Karl—intertwine the most? How does the "love" in the various love stories differ?

10. Describe Karl's relationship with each of the following: Carolyn, Sharon, Red, Blair, and Ellen. Does each relationship—including the brief experience with the girl in Morocco—reflect where Karl is in terms of sorting out his identity and coming of age?

11. Why does Karl fall so hard for Ellen? How is his involvement with her similar to, or different from, Sharon's with Christos?

12. How do you explain Laura's death? (You might start by using a combo of N.A.S.H terms—Natural causes/genes, Accident, Suicide, Homicide.) Is your explanation different from Karl's?

13. Do you think either Jack or Laura cheated on the other? Why? If they both did, were they unfaithful for different reasons?

14. How do you feel about Aunt Irene's statement to the effect that California exemplifies life in the "fast lane" and that life in that lane can kill you?

15. Does the protagonist remind you of someone in your life? In what way are they similar and dissimilar?

16. How does Karl feel about religion: for example, do you think he struggles to maintain traditional faith despite being part of a progressive church?

ESPECIALLY FOR STUDENTS
Essay topics:

1. When the author says he feels "at home" in Sharon's arms, does this mean Sharon is a substitute for his mother? Why or why not? (See questions 8 through 10 above for ideas.) Explain whether home was a source of comfort for you.

2. Elaborate on some of the moral issues explored in the book. (Fidelity to others in relationships, the importance of genes in mate selection, the need to protest certain wars, etc.)

3. Do characters in the book see a range of options in their choices? Who is in the Fate camp and who is in the Self-determination camp? If you put Laura in the Fate camp, at what point does her self-destruction become inevitable? Does this make her a tragic heroine?

4. In what ways do the main characters change by the end of *Cleft Heart*? Explain how these changes are triggered by a. choices they make, b. events external to themselves, c. insight or recognition of something about themselves, or d. a combo of these.

5. What are some of the mistakes made by Karl and others we root for? Do they make them because of habit, yearning, desperation, or something else?

6. How does the author portray "abnormality," "perfection-ism," and "depression" in *Cleft Heart*? Have you ever worried about such things?

Questions about the book's structure:

1. What do you consider to be the climax of the book—Laura's death, Jack's confession, or something else? Explain why.

2. In what ways does the author foreshadow his teen health problem? (Skin color at birth, symptoms while playing, etc.) Is this, or *any*, foreshadowing effective in storytelling?

3. Enumerate the conflicts, challenges, or obstacles the main characters face in *Cleft Heart*.

4. What do the main characters want and why: i.e., what are their goals and their motivations?

5. What events or twists move the story in a new direction? (Karl collapses in Mexico, Laura suffers a breakdown, etc.)

6. Why is swimmer Steve Clark important in the book? (Clark is a literary foil, a character who contrasts with the protago-nist to highlight particular qualities.)

7. What role does World War II play in the book?

8. Are Karl's problems mostly external or internal? (Hint: Is Dumbo's problem his big ears or how he feels about his ears?)

9. Is *Cleft Heart* more a "man vs. nature" or "man vs. man" sto-ry? Explain your reasoning.

**If you've enjoyed this book, please check out
Wayman Publishing's other publications!**

Waymanpublishing.com

ABOUT THE AUTHOR

KARL SCHONBORN EARNED HIS various degrees from Ivy League institutions and became a professor specializing in the study of social and psychological aspects of violence. He is the author of four other books. He and his wife have two grown children and live in the San Francisco Bay Area.

For further discussion of issues in this book and for photos from the *Cleft Heart* story, visit the author at:

www.karlschonborn.com

CPSIA information can be obtained at www.ICGtesting.com
Printed in the USA
LVOW12s2126231114

415250LV00001B/40/P